MODERN BANKING: CHALLENGES AND TRENDS

Modern Banking: Challenges and Trends

Editor:

Rahmaoui Naima

ArclerPress

www.arclerpress.com

Modern Banking: Challenges and Trends
Editor: Rahmaoui Naima

708 3rd Avenue, 6th Floor
New York
NY 10017
United States of America
www.arclerpress.com

ISBN: 978-1-68094-492-1

Library of Congress Control Number: 2016951353

About the Editor

Rahmaoui Naima

Naima obtained her academic Master degree from economics university in 2012,her interests financial corporations,and marketing ,she's currently working as a financial manager.

Contents

List of Contributors

Vlad Miranda-Petronella
"Dimitrie Cantemir" Christian University Bucharest Faculty of Economic Sciences of Cluj-Napoca, 56. Teodor Mihaly Street Cluj Napoca, 400591

Asst.Prof.T.A.More
Department of Electronics and Telecommunication Engineering, PREC, Loni Savitribai Phule Pune University, Maharashtra, India

Sarwade Sukanya
Department of Electronics and Telecommunication Engineering, PREC, Loni Savitribai Phule Pune University, Maharashtra, India

Hajare Nikita
Department of Electronics and Telecommunication Engineering, PREC, Loni Savitribai Phule Pune University, Maharashtra, India

Bhakre Ashok
Department of Electronics and Telecommunication Engineering, PREC, Loni Savitribai Phule Pune University, Maharashtra, India

A. Salma, C. Sarada Devi
Student (B.E[ECE], University College of Engineering Arni, India)

V. Saranya
Student (B.E[ECE], University College of Engineering Arni, India)

Bharath E
Dept. of Commerce, NDRK First Grade College, University of Mysore, Hassan

Dhananjaya K M
Dept. of Commerce, NDRK First Grade College, University of Mysore, Hassan

Anoop C.N
Dept. of Electronics, Post Graduate Centre, Hemagangothri, University of Mysore, Hassan

Raghavendra B V
The institute of Company Secretaries of India, Mysore Chapter, Mysore

Ismail M. Romi
Assistant Professor, College of Administrative Sciences and Informatics, Palestine Polytechnic University, Palestine

Jeffrey E Jarrett
University of Rhode Island, Management Science and Finance, 7 Lippit Road/ 333 Ballentine, Kingston, USA

Ruby Shukla
Chandigarh Business School, Landran, Mohali, Punjab, India

Pankaj Shukla
RIMT, Mandi Gobindgarh, Punjab, India

Arian Eshraghi
Sharif University of Technology, Tehran, Iran

Manoranjan D
Faculty of Management Sciences, Siksha O Anusandhan University, Bhubaneswar, India

Snigdha S
Faculty of Management Sciences, Siksha O Anusandhan University, Bhubaneswar, India

Bhusan PB
Faculty of Management Sciences, Siksha O Anusandhan University, Bhubaneswar, India

Amola Bhatt
Nirma University Institute of Management, Ahmedabad, Gujarat, India

Shahir Bhatt
Nirma University Institute of Management, Ahmedabad, Gujarat, India

Fadare OA
Department of Accountancy, Universiti Utara Malaysia, Malaysia

Ibrahim MB
Department of Accountancy, Zenith Bank PLC, 19 Abdulkadir Road, Bauchi State, Nigeria

Edogbanya A
Department of Accountancy, Kogi State University, Anyigba, Nigeria

Bharti M
Prestige Institute of Management and Research, Indore, India

Khasawneh MHA
Princess Sumaya University for Technology (PSUT), Amman, Jordan

Chai Lee Goi
Curtin University of Technology, Malaysia

Ahmed EM
Faculty of Business, Multimedia University, 75450, Melaka, Malaysia

Phin GS
Faculty of Business, Multimedia University, 75450, Melaka, Malaysia

E. Abbasi
Department of Business Management, Alzahra University, Tehran, Iran.

H. Ranjbar
Master Students of Business Management- Financial, Kermanshah Science and Research Branch, Islamic Azad University, Kermanshah, Iran

S. Ranjbar
Master Students of Business Management- Financial, Kermanshah Science and Research Branch, Islamic Azad University, Kermanshah, Iran

M. Shabanpour
Master Students of Business Management- Financial, Kermanshah Science and Research Branch, Islamic Azad University, Kermanshah, Iran

S. Alipour
Master Students of Business Management- Financial, Kermanshah Science and Research Branch, Islamic Azad University, Kermanshah, Iran

Preface

Banking occupies one of the most important positions in the modern economic world. It is necessary for trade and industry. Hence it is one of the great agencies of commerce. Modern banking services presence is very helpful to the economic activity and industrial progress of the country. The banking industry is on a major technological up gradation drive after having successfully introduced international standards in their operating norms. It is commonly perceived that technology is important to enhance the quality of customer service and to make it customer friendly. Banking industry is fast growing with the use of technology in the form of ATMs, on-line banking, Telephone banking, Mobile banking etc., plastic card is one of the banking products that cater to the needs of retail segment has seen its number grow in geometric progression in recent years. Today, the concept of core banking has made 'Any Where and any time' banking a reality. Along with technology, banking services have also evolved and the delivery of various banking products are carried out through the medium of high technology at a fraction of the cost to the customer. This book focus on the challenges facing the adoption of the modern banking services, and it's devided to 16 chapters. The chapters from 1 to 5 review the most important modern banking services like automated teller machine (ATM),smart cards, smart banking lockers..ect. the chapters 6,7,8,9,and 10 descuss the challenges and factors affecting the adoption of modern banking services. Chapters 11 and 12 evaluate the adoption of modern banking services through a Survey on Perceived Risk of Adopting Internet Banking,and the Impact of Dimensions of Mobile Banking on User Satisfaction. Some case studies of adopting modern banking in several coutries were reviewed in chapters 13,14,15,16. I hope this book is a good source for researchers in the modern banking industry.

Editor

Rahmaoui Naima

INTRODUCTION

A commercial bank is a financial institution that provides various financial service, such as accepting deposits and issuing loans. Commercial bank customers can take advantage of a range of investment products that commercial banks offer like savings accounts and certificates of deposit.

The term "Banking Technology" refers to the use of sophisticated information and communication technologies together with computer science to enable banks to offer better services to its customers in a secure, reliable and affordable manner and sustain competitive advantage over other banks. Banking Technology also subsumes the activity of using advanced computer algorithms in unraveling the patterns of customer behavior by sifting through customer details such as demographic, psychographic and transactional data. This activity also known data mining, helps banks achieve their business objectives by solving various marketing problems such as customer segmentation, customer scoring, target marketing, market-basket analysis, cross-sell, up-sell, customer retention by modeling churn etc. Successful use of data mining helps banks achieve significant increase in profits and thereby retain sustainable advantage over their competitors. From theoretical perspective, Banking Technology is not a single, stand-alone discipline, but a confluence of several disparate fields such as finance (subsuming risk management), information technology, communication technology, computer science and marketing science.

Banking Industry

The banking industry is an enormous sector of business and finance that has existed in human civilization in some form for thousands of years. In the modern world, the banking industry plays a large part in financial dealings, as it is a major and popular means for investing, borrowing, and storing money. Banks exist all over the world, and are usually heavily regulated by world governments in order to prevent corruption and protect the money of the general public.

Though there is some evidence of a banking industry in ancient Greece and throughout other early civilizations, the Middle East and Asia are believed to have played an important part of the development of a banking industry. The word "check" derives from an old Arabic word for a promise of payment on delivery, and historical records show some evidence of an international banking trade between Islamic nations and China as early as the 9th century.

Many historians trace the foundations of modern banking to 14th century Italy, where wealthy Italian families established banks for the lending and investing of money on trade and commerce. Banks sprang up throughout Europe during the following centuries, concentrating in the great ports of the old world where commerce was a part of daily life. With the shift from precious metal currency to fiat money systems, the banking industry was less limited by finite resources and could expand ever further. The development of computer technology also playing a critical part in creating a global industry, since users were no longer limited by the need to physically visit a bank to manage transactions.

The banking industry provides clients with a variety of services and options. The most basic function of a bank is to provide customers with a safe, guaranteed record of their accumulated money, usually done through a checking account that can be easily accessed for withdrawals and deposits. Banks also provide savings accounts, which are also easily accessed but provide a slightly higher interest rate for funds. For many people, involvement with the banking industry is limited to these two basic accounts, but this is only a bare minimum of what the industry offers.

Banks play a major part in the investing and loaning of money. Most banks can use the funds deposited in accounts to loan out money or make investments; this practice allows a constant flow of lending and borrowing that keeps money circulating throughout the economy. Loans that many banks offer include commercial loans, property loans, vehicle loans, and lines of credit. Investment services offered by many banks include retirement, certificate of deposit (CD), and money market accounts.

Investment Banking Industry Development

Investment banking is a type of banking industry that focuses on aiding companies in securing the capital needed to underwrite different projects, including managing the issuance of securities. Investment banks also assist with the details surrounding acquisitions and mergers, and even aiding clients in the selection of foreign exchange and other types of investment opportunities. When it comes to investment banking industry development, making the best possible use of industry analytics that shed light on the course of the economy is essential. In addition, the development of opportunities in emerging markets, and even considering of trends associated with different investment markets, will aid in allowing the industry to continue expanding.

One key element of investment banking industry development is the ability to accurately assess what is happening in different investment markets and relate those events to future market movements. This is crucial if the industry is to provide competent recommendations to clients about how to manage certain types of projects or investments and have a reasonable expectation of success. In order to effectively evaluate what is happening in those marketplaces and come up with solid projections, it is important for industry analysts to make use of every available analysis tool. Doing so increases the accuracy of the evaluations and makes it easier to use the data to develop business deals that benefit everyone involved.

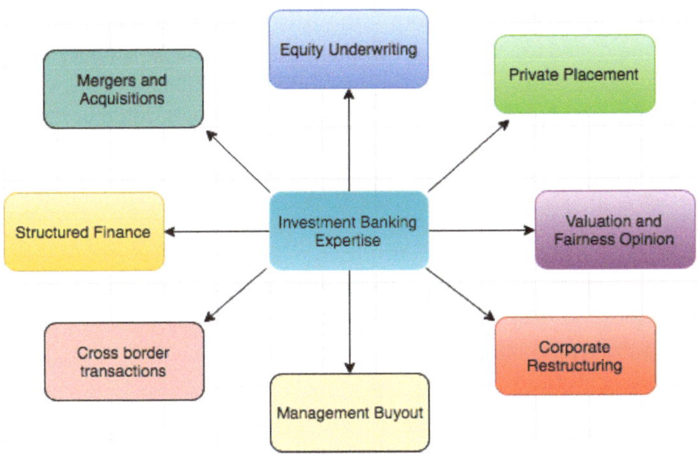

Another important tip with investment banking industry development is using analysis techniques to track what is happening with deals already in place. By determining if certain types of investments are continuing to perform as anticipated, investment bankers can translate that data into useful information regarding the type of investments to continue pursuing. If there is an obvious downward trend with certain types of investments within specific markets, those may go from being considered relatively safe to somewhat unstable. When this is the case, the industry as a whole may begin to lean more toward other types of investment activities.

Being on the lookout for new types of opportunities is also part of investment banking industry development that is productive. Along with investments in emerging technologies, this type of forward-looking approach can also include monitoring emerging markets and identifying opportunities in those nations. This can allow investment banking as a whole to tap into markets while the competition is still somewhat low and generate a great deal of return before everyone else discovers the opportunities. The end result of this type of investment banking industry development is that certain investment banks are firmly established in those markets and are in a better position to compete with other investors who may come along at a later date.

Limited Service Bank

A limited service bank is a type of banking location that offers only a portion of the total financial services provided by the main operation or larger branches of the banking corporation. Banks of this type are sometimes located in or near residential areas and provide a roster of the more common banking services to serve clients, while still offering a wider range of services at branches that are considered full-service. A slightly different type of limited service bank is a banking corporation that offers only a select range of financial services at any of its branches.

As the term relates to the establishment of smaller and more specialized branches, a limited service bank is usually a branch that provides basic services such as the ability to make deposits and withdrawals from established bank accounts. In some cases, this limited branch may provide drive-up services only, or be limited to strictly walk-in traffic. With this application, services such as the ability to apply for a loan or establish new accounts cannot be managed at the limited service bank, but can be conducted at a full service branch that is located elsewhere in the city.

When limited service bank is used to identify the scope of services provided by a banking corporation, the term usually indicates that the corporation will only offer certain services to its clientele. For example, if a bank does offer checking and savings accounts along with loan services, but does not offer credit card services or investment services to its clients, it may be classed as a limited service bank. In some cases, this type of banking enterprise may partner with other firms that offer those additional services, allowing customers to access them with relative ease, courtesy of the affiliate agreement that exists between the financial entities. When this sort of arrangement is in place, customers can often receive discounts on those additional services, owing to their established relationship with the limited service bank.

Being classified as a limited service bank does not mean the institution is lacking in quality or reputation. It is not unusual for certain types of banks to specialize in certain types of financial services as a means of providing highly competent support for customers who are especially interested in those particular services. As with any type of banking institution, consumers should evaluate both the range of services provided and the general reputation of the institution before choosing to establish accounts.

Types of Banking Industry

Banks employ many people in a number of different positions. Most banking industry jobs are in the commercial banking sector, and include positions such as bank tellers, loan officers, customer service representatives, branch managers, and debt collection associates. Education requirements and salary depend on the position that is held.

One of the most widely held banking industry jobs is that of bank teller. This position requires daily interaction with bank customers. A teller handles deposit and withdrawal requests and may also assist customers with purchasing traveler's checks or money orders. As banking services increase, many bank tellers have also been given the responsibility of selling services such as enhanced checking accounts to bank customers.

Loan officers assist customers in applying for loans. A person holding this position helps a customer choose the best loan — such as a mortgage loan, business loan, or line of credit — for his or her needs and then processes all the paperwork that is involved in the loan application process. A loan officer analyzes the information provided and then recommends either approving or denying the loan based on the customer's creditworthiness.

Customer service representatives help bank customers open or close accounts and also assist in answering account questions or fielding customer complaints. People holding these banking industry jobs may work directly with customers in a bank branch, or they may speak with customers over the phone or via e-mail. The nature of this position makes it necessary for customer service representatives to be very familiar with all of the services and accounts that a bank offers.

Branch managers are responsible for all aspects of a bank branch. Supervisors of different departments answer to the branch manager, and the manager implements policy to increase productivity and branch profits. The manager also resolves any customer complaints that cannot be fixed by a customer service representative. A person in this position may work with high profile customers who have large amounts of money in the bank's system.

Banks offer personal, small business, and mortgage loans as well as home equity loans and lines of credit. When a customer who has received a loan defaults on the required payments, a debt collection associate will contact him. If the customer is unable to pay the total amount due, the debt collection associate may work with the customer to set up a repayment plan. People holding these banking industry jobs recover vast amounts of money for banks each year.

Investment Banking Services

An investment bank helps businesses issue securities, or stocks. There are a number of investment banking services in the marketplace that work with various types of businesses. To choose the best investment banking services, you should look at the experience of the firm, its contacts in the investment world, the level of service that firm will provide and whether the firm is sensitive to the needs of the business. It also is important to choose an investment bank that you can trust.

A good investment bank will use its experience to negotiate the best deal possible for its clients. Each investment situation is unique, so you should find an investment bank that has experience in dealing with businesses of a similar size and in a similar industry to the business for which you are choosing investment banking services. The contacts that the investment bank has will have a huge impact on the services that it can provide. The investment bank should have extensive contact with investors, both foreign and domestic, to ensure that the business gets the most competitive deal possible.

Many firms like to offer investment banking services only to large companies. The larger the company, the more personalized attention it will receive from highly experienced senior level. So when choosing investment banking services, make sure to look at whether this level of service will be provided. Also, make sure that the investment bank has the needs of its clients as its top priority. An investment bank that is only our for itself might make decisions that are not in the best interest of its clients.

By looking at these basic criteria, you should get a good sense of whether an investment bank will be able to meet your needs. Choosing the proper investment banking services can help a business grow and reach its goals. Making a poor decision, however, can be costly.

Online Investment Banking

The Internet has made most banking activities possible without needing to visit a brick-and-mortar bank. One such activity is online investment banking. This is when companies offer shares, and investors buy and sell them, via the Internet. There are traditional brick-and-mortar banks as well as completely virtual banks that offer online investment banking services.

Companies are now able to put shares up for auction online. When a company offers public shares for the first time, these are known as Initial Public Offerings (IPOs). By selling IPOs online, and having all related banking services carried out electronically, banks have the option of reducing their transaction costs. This means online investment banking can sometimes be a less expensive option.

Online investment banking might also favor more equitable and market-directed trading. Investment brokerages sometimes engage in spinning. This is when they try to court the interest of executives of large companies by offering them desirable IPOs, possibly at the expense of smaller would-be investors. This is arguably less common in online investment banking wherein the ranking of bids for particular stocks are carried out automatically, and the highest bidders should therefore win the stocks. That said, the web is certainly no guarantee against unfair or exploitative behavior, so precautions should be taken.

One should be very selective in choosing where to do his or her online banking. A good approach is to list the services and costs one is seeking and then measure various online banks or brokers against these criteria. It is also advisable to thoroughly investigate their reputations. For companies offering IPOs through online investment banking, it is probably best to stick with well-known banks, as they are more likely to be trustworthy, ethical businesses.

While there are many benefits to online investment banking, there can be certain drawbacks as well. People may find they miss personal face-to-face customer service. It is much easier for most people to develop a warm working relationship with a living person than with a computer screen. Also, technical difficulties can occur. These can either be on the part of the online banking system itself or user-related.

The expression “time is money” is particularly relevant when applied to making investments. One advantage to online banking could be an increased facility of after-market, outside-office-hours trading, but a person who frequently struggles with computers might find technical delays too cumbersome. For a web-savvy investor, however, the benefits to online investment banking most likely will outweigh the challenges.

Middle-Market Investment Banking

Middle-market investment banking refers to the process by which specialized investment firms advise and help raise capital for companies considered middle market. Although various firms use different parameters, a company is generally considered to be middle market if it brings in yearly revenue between $25 million US Dollars (USD) and $1 billion USD. These companies are generally privately-owned and may need the capital to survive tough financial times or to undertake a new business initiative. By using middle-market investment banking, these companies can help locate the capital to achieve their ultimate business goals.

Investment banking is a crucial service used by many companies. The various investment banks can provide a vast array of services to their clients that go beyond the securing of investment capital. These firms have the experience in the business world that allows them to analyze the business models of their client companies and suggest ways for these companies to succeed in the long-term. When this process occurs with the companies that fall somewhere between market-dominating blue-chip companies and small companies just starting out, it is known as middle-market investment banking.

Companies that are considered middle market may have different reasons for needing the services of an investment bank to help them acquire the funding they desire. Many middle-market companies are ones that have seen better times but are currently struggling, and investment capital can serve as a lifeline for such companies. On the other hand, some middle-market companies may be on the upswing, and an infusion of funding can be the impetus for ascension to bigger and better things. In either case, middle-market investment banking may be the perfect solution.

Funding acquired through the process of middle-market investment banking can come in various forms. A privately-owned company may reach out to private-equity investors, who donate the capital in return for a stake in the company's ownership. The extreme version of this arrangement occurs when investors essentially buy out the company in question.

Using middle-market investment banking can also be a way for privately-owned companies to go public. Middle-market companies often require the funding that comes from an initial public offering on the stock market, and an investment bank can be the conduit to help this occur. No matter the situation, an investment bank has the ability to analyze the specific situation and make suggestions based on what is right for the company. The investment bank also has the connections, through its business experience, to connect a company seeking funding with the investors willing to provide it.

1
CHAPTER

E-BANKING- MODERN BANKING SERVICES

Vlad Miranda-Petronella

Keywords: e-Banking, Mobile Banking, Home Banking, risk, comparative analysis

Internet Banking, Mobile Banking or Home Banking are modern banking instruments, intended to the banks' customers, natural or legal juristic persons, for the payment of bills, accomplishment of transfers, money transfer from an account to an another and so on.[[7]].

The Internet-banking can be used from any computer connected to Internet, no matter where it is. Practically, in the most of cases, the user of this service doesn't need to have his own computer, an I-Cafe being useful for him. There are the same operations as for E-banking: transmission of payment orders, transfers, exchange, view of the accounts' situation etc. Banks started to jump over the primary stage of E-banking, directly to Internet Banking.

The E-banking services subsist from more than 20 years, and in Romania, beside ING Barings and ABN Amro, they are the founders of this kind of services. The operations that can accomplish by E-banking are starting from the view of companies' account balances, arriving to payments, transfers and exchange, creating term deposits etc.

The Electronic-banking or E-banking is the first of these banking services that really economize time, because it allows to the user to accomplish from behind the computer many operations in the bank account, without being necessary to go to the bank, to wait at the office, to complete forms, to sign it, to stamp it, to allow it to the clerk, all these needing many time.

Citation: Vlad Miranda-Petronella, e-Banking- Modern Banking services, https://doaj.org/article/3ea0daf25ed546b0857410d2d6245f78.

To exemplify, we will refer to the order ticket, that is a payment instrument and credit title, under private signature, by which a person, named under-writer or issuer, in quality of debtor, must pay to a person named beneficiary, in quality of creditor, a sum of money, in a certain term or at presentation. The obligation of the under-writer (the issuer) of a ticket at order is identical with that of the acceptant draw of a bill, because it must absolutely pay at term the sum inscribed on the title, so the order ticket must contain the following obligatory mentions:

a) The name of order ticket. The absence of the name of order ticket attracts the nullity of the title;

b) The unconditional promise to pay a determined sum (sum that must be mentioned in ciphers and letters). The issuer (the under-writer) must absolutely pay a sum of money. Any conditions, limitations or anti-performances that add to the promises to pay the order ticket attract the nullity of the title;

c) The name of the person for which or at the order of which the payment must be accomplished (the beneficiary). The banks only accept order tickets where the name of the person for which or at the order of which the payment must be accomplished- the beneficiary of the order ticket- is indicated very clear.

d) The date of issuance. The date of issuance must be unique, possible and certain. The order tickets will wear clear mentions respecting the day, the month and the year of the issuance, to admit:
    - the estimation of the date of payment on a certain period after the issuance;
    - the finding of the legal capability of subscribers at the moment of signing on the title;
    - the determination of the subscribers' rights for the bill action against the bill obligators (protest, regress etc.)

e) The signature of the issuer (under-writer), and, for legal juristic persons, the stamp. The comparison between the necessary time for the manually complement and the time necessary for the electronic complement is not necessary, because, in fact, there is many time economised: time with the complement, time to go to the bank, time to waiting at the pay office and time necessary to the office operator.

The services offered by E-banking are the following:

- payment orders in lei;
- scheduled payment in lei;
- global payment orders used for the employees salaries;
- intra-banking transfers between the own accounts of card and/or current;
- intern or extern currency payments;
- exchanges;
- the visualisation in any moment of the account balances opened
- information about different appreciations

- possibility to visualise and to print the statements
- definition of the beneficiary of the payments, directly by the client.

The banking transfers, the payment orders, the banking changes and the operations' historical consultation can be applied directly from the mobile phone. Demirbank has introduced, for the first time in Romania, the service Mobile-banking. The bank doesn't collect any tax for this service, and the client need only a mobile phone with WAP (Wireless Application Protocol) and a subscription for this service. To use Mobile-banking, a client of the bank must sign a contract with the bank. He receives a "user-name" and a password, and after this he can use his mobile phone for baking operations. There is only one constraint- the money from the account can be transferred over a predefined list of companies. In the case in which the mobile phone is lost and, hypothetically, the person who found it would know the "user name" and the password, he could transfer the money only over a company from the predefined list.

A successfully system is that system that evolve, that adapts the faster to the needs of every customer, so the customer must analyse the hard and the poor points at the banks' offers and to choose what corresponds to his demands.

In this sense, we took over some information from four banks, to create a comparative analyse of the opportunities.

THE TRANSILVANIA BANK[6]

Transilvania Bank, conscious of the dangers that result from the informatics identity robberies, firmly engage to assure the dates' privacy of it's customers and of their transactions. At the same time with the bank's efforts for the dates' security, because of the risk development of the illegal attacks, online or otherwise, and of the sophisticated methods, it is necessary that the customers be conscious of the potentially menaces, that he can identify a malevolent action and to apply the adequate protection measures. To keep the privacy of the personal information and of the security of the on-line activity, the bank demands to the customers to NOT communicate any information regarding the personal identity, the accounts, the card number, the expiry date, the code PIN or other banking produces and services detained. If the method used is the e-mail, than an electronic message is send to the customers, pretending being sent by a lawful source (in this case, the bank), message which demands some confidential information, which can be introduced using a link over a site indicated in the message text. This link directs the customers over a false site that reproduces very well the original page of the bank or of the e-Banking product used. By introducing the personal and confidential data and validating it, the attackers take possession of these information and they can use it to scroll operations in the account of the identity attacked by them. The fishing-attack can be realised also by the phone: a person pretends that he calls from the bank and, by inventing technical problems (for example in the payment system), he demands confidential data as: the PIN code, the account number, the password. Transilvania Bank will never admit e-mail messages that contain links over different sites where you must introduce information about the personal identity, the accounts, the card number, the date of expiry, the PIN code or other banking products and services that you use.

Transilvania Bank engages it-self to assure the higher security standard in its own systems, but you, as final user, you are playing a very important role in the assurance of the information security sent by internet.

THE COMMERCIAL ROMANIAN BANK

The service Home banking MultiCash BCR admits the realization of banking operations in lei and currency, convenient and in totally security, directly at the customer's seat, by an application that will be installed on the customer's PC. The Internet service Banking e-BCR/e-BCR+ offers the opportunity to effect convenient and in maximal security of the banking operations in lei and currency, from any computer connected at the Internet. [7] The customer signs the Convention for authorized legal and physical persons, regarding the accomplishment of banking operations by MultiCash and e-BCR/e-BCR+; he must dispose of a minimal technical endowment, consisting in: a computer compatible IBM, Pentium II, modem/connection at the Internet and operation system WINDOWS 2000, XP, ME etc.[6].

The operations that can be effected by the service MultiCash/e-BCR/e-BCR+ [6]:

- payments from the accounts/undercounts in lei and currency, in intra and inter-banking system;
- sale/buy of currency;
- visualization of the statements for the own accounts (inclusive Maxicont) and for under- accounts (in lei and currency);
- constitution of deposits at term in lei and in currency;
- consultation of the informative report of the Treasury Direction, which contains information about:
- appreciation, interest rates of deposits at term, the quotations of the deposits Certified with discount, the quotations of the Stock Exchange;
- the import/export of payment Orders/ statements in/from other applications;
- liquidation of deposit before the term;
- buy/buyback of deposit certificates with discount ACTIV BCR.

Customer's advantages [6]:

- the program installation (only for Multicash), the training for the customer and the technical assistance are free;
- permanently electronic link with the bank with intention to transfer the payment orders and to obtain financial-banking information;
- rapid and secure transfer of the sums in currency for and from Romania;
- security and privacy of the transactions effected;
- operations control from distance by using the electronic and/or dispensed signatures or the facility of
- subscription, using the function Sign;

- control over the rights of access and operation of users of the company and/or the facility to decide over the
- users' rights of operations, inclusive sum limits on day/operation

The collection and the payment operations in intra and inter-banking system are commissioned according to the price list in force. [6]

The level of commissions can modify making allowance of the bank policy, and the modifications are posted at the BCR centres.

UNI CREDIT ŢIRIAC BANK [7]

Uni Credit Ţiriac Bank started an age group for the use of the services Online Banking and Business Net, that address to the physical persons, respectively to little and middle companies. For contracts concluded until 31 March 2009, the banks offer gratuity in using the appliance "digipass" for six months. After these six months, the customer can choose the take-back of the access appliance at the accounts of the issuer branch office and the closure of the account for Online Banking, or he can choose to use it on, paying the guarantee. "

In 2008, the number of transactions realised by internet banking by the bank customers physical persons and little and middle companies doubled relative at 2007. It is certain that the banking operations at distance are more and more appreciated and they will probably continue to develop, considering also the costs advantages. The company new-launched is one of the measures that regard the amelioration of services quality, in this case by offering to the customers who want to manage their banking accounts from distance the most advantageous access at internet banking", has declared Zoltan Major, vice president Uni Credit Ţiriac Bank, responsible of Retail Division. The bank perceives commissions 50% lower for the operations realised by internet, comparative with those from pay box.

ING HOME'BANK

Description:

- ING Home'Bank is your own bank, to which you can dial at any hour and from anywhere in the word;
- ING Home'Bank- you can effect banking operations 24 hours from 24, 7 days from 7, wherever you are in the word, as long as you have access at a computer connected at the Internet;
- you have total security by: the most advances date encryption algorithm and by the certificate VeriSign SSL, for the website identity and authenticity verification.

BENEFITS [6]

- With ING Home'Bank, you can verify the balances of all your accounts opened at ING, debit accounts or credit accounts, as well as the deposits and the assurances afferents to credits;

- your on-line bank from ING allows you to effect payments and transfers in lei and currency over the accounts opened at ING Bank or at other banks from Romania and in foreign countries;
- you use and reimburse the credit lines; - you pay the utilities bills;
- you effect exchanges, without commission;
- you verify the transactions effected during the last six months

On the BCR site, at a simple search, you can find information about the benefits of this kind of transactions and how you can realise them, what do you need for such a transaction. Unfortunately, there are too few information about security, or even at all, and this is the reason for which it is questionable the election of this bank services. The third offer of UniCredit Ţiriac Bank in an offer in process, but we can't find anything about the benefits and the security of these services. We also find articles about robberies from this bank by the fishing method, but this cannot convince us to choose this bank as new customers who care about their money. From these banks, the most preferable is Transilvania Bank, because it specifies the security measures for the financial cash of customers, the operations that can be effected and protection measures for the customers. On the BCR site, at a simple search, you can find information about the benefits of this kind of transactions and how you can realise them, what do you need for such a transaction. Unfortunately, there are too few information about security, or even at all, and this is the reason for which it is questionable the election of this bank services.

The third offer of UniCredit Ţiriac Bank in an offer in process, but we can't find anything about the benefits and the security of these services. We also find articles about robberies from this bank by the fishing method, but this cannot convince us to choose this bank as new customers who care about their money.

CONCLUSIONS

By making a comparative analysis, on concrete situations, over the four banks taken in our study, we can note that the problems opened by e-banking, are:

- the risk of fraudulent attacks;
- comfort in using the application;
- the customers' option behind the multitude of e-banking applications and the criterions that lie at the bedrock of the choose of one application;
- the commissions and the taxes that banks perceive for these applications;
- the diversity of the operations offered by the application;
- the rapidity in the information transfer from the payer over the bank;
- the transfer rapidity between the banks;
- the rapidity to actualize the information after having finished the transfers;
- correction possibility in the case of the introduction of some incorrect information or some possible mistakes;

- the compatibility with financial- bookkeeping systems, those that belong to the banks and also those that belong to the companies;
- the way in which this kind of operations answer or fold on the customers' needs

Consequently, we consider the these problems resolution supposes first of all a marketing study on the banking market and a comparative analysis of the banking offers, so that the decision for one version can be the best and folds on the beneficiary demands. Starting by the e-banking definition, given by the ORDER no. 389 from 27 June 2007, as a payment instrument with access at distance, represents the computational solution that allows to the holder to have access at distance at the capitals from his account, purposing to obtain information about his account situation and the situation of the effected operations, of the payment and of the capitals transfers over a beneficiary, by a computational application, of a authentication method and of a communicational average, the e-banking is absolutely necessary in the integration conditions. The analysis of the computational commerce indicates us an ascending evolution from the view point of the clients, but also from the view point of market transactions until October 2009, date after which, because of the economical crisis, the situation will change: the value volume on the first trimester of 2009 diminish in comparison with the same period of the year 2008, but the transactions number in the same period grows up. We consider the these problems resolution supposes first of all a marketing study on the banking market and a comparative analysis of the banking offers, so that the decision for one version can be the best and folds on the beneficiary demands.

REFERENCES

1. Stoica Maricica, Management bancar, Ed. Economica, Bucuresti, 1999
2. Turcu Ion, Operatiuni si contracte bancare. Tratat de drept bancar, Ed. Lumina Lex, Bucuresti, 2004.
3. http://www.ebanker.ro/Produse.aspx
4. http://www.bancatransilvania.ro/printeaza.php?id=426
5. http://www.infobancare.ro/internet-banking/BCR/Home_Banking_MultiCash_BCR. html#detalii
6. https://www.sparkasse.at/PFA/Servicii_electronice/Multicash/eBCR+/sPortal.portal; jsessionid=LGTPJr9Nr7x7nQVbjW5dHzzvLGhpy1fllnsjDwncl TnJ3Sr2 T8NL!2003172691?_nfpb=true&_windowLabel=LABEL_ MENU&_urlType=action&LABEL_MENU_sh=6737810a802 407f4a54e7b9f3122 65e &LABEL _MENU_zz=31481.853136499492&LABEL_MENU_ pc=1&cci=09002ee2803 9426b&desk=bcr_ro_0785&&navigationLink=TRUE &menu_navigationId=02181191493609119000194&menu_chronicleId=09002ee2803942b7&navigationId=02181191493609119000194[13
7. http://www.atitudinea.ro/articole/bancar/unicredit+tiriac+bank+ofera+acces+gratuit+timp+de+6+luni+la+serviciile+de+administrare+a+conturilor+prin+internet
8. http://www.ing.ro/ing/ing/Home-Bank.html
9. https://www.bcr.ro/bcrro

10. http://www.bancatransilvania.ro/
11. http://www.inm-lex.ro/fisiere/pag_33/det_48/256.pdf
12. http://www.euroavocatura.ro/legislatie/200/Legea_nr__58_1934,_asupra_cambiei_si_ biletuluila_ordin__Actualizata_2008
13. http://www.bnro.ro/500.htm?aspxerrorpath=/apage.aspx
14. http://www.ing.ro/ing/ing.html
15. http://www.ingromania.ro/wps/portal
16. http://www.banking.ro/

2
CHAPTER

SMART BANK LOCKER ACCESS SYSTEM USING IRIS ,FINGERPRINTS,FACE RECOGNIZATION ALONG WITH PASSWORD AUTHENTICATION AND BILLING SYSTEM

Asst.Prof.T.A.More, Sarwade Sukanya

Keywords: ARM 7, MATLAB, Camera, DC Motor

INTRODUCTION

Every person has precious accessories such as gold, jewellery or in terms of cash. To prevent it from any mishandling. We keep it in a locker system of bank concern with it likewise in old way system of a bank there was a private key system which is associated with the concern user and every time he or she has headache to carry key with him or has keep burden of key lost or key duplication problem. So to overcome above major drawbacks the recent system of biometrics is introduced. It is very advance as compared to any traditional system. This system comes with the features of which included not only face detection but also fingerprint detection technique, iris detection technique, along with password authentication For banking which provides genuine access to the customers who will overcome the problem associated with unauthorized access. As above mention proposed system includes face detection technique which gives us effective and fast access .Secondly fingerprint detection technique gives easy access to system which contains specified finger pattern of that person. Also password verification is provided in system using dot mat format in MATLAB tool.

Finally technique provides more secure approach to the system by scanning mechanism. By combination of all these above secured technique gives us better advancement in banking security systems.

Citation: Asst.Prof.T.A,Sarwade Sukanya,Smart Bank Locker Access System Using Iris, Fingerprints, Face Recognization Along With Password Authentication And Billing SystemInternational Journal of Engineering Research and Applications, 2015;5(3)96-101, ISSN : 2248-9622.

BLOCK DIAGRAM OF PROPOSED SYSTEM

In this proposed system we are using ARM microcontroller LPC 2148 as it is a 64 bit microcontroller along with four security technologies i.e. face reorganization, fingerprint reorganization, password, and iris reorganization in series combination.

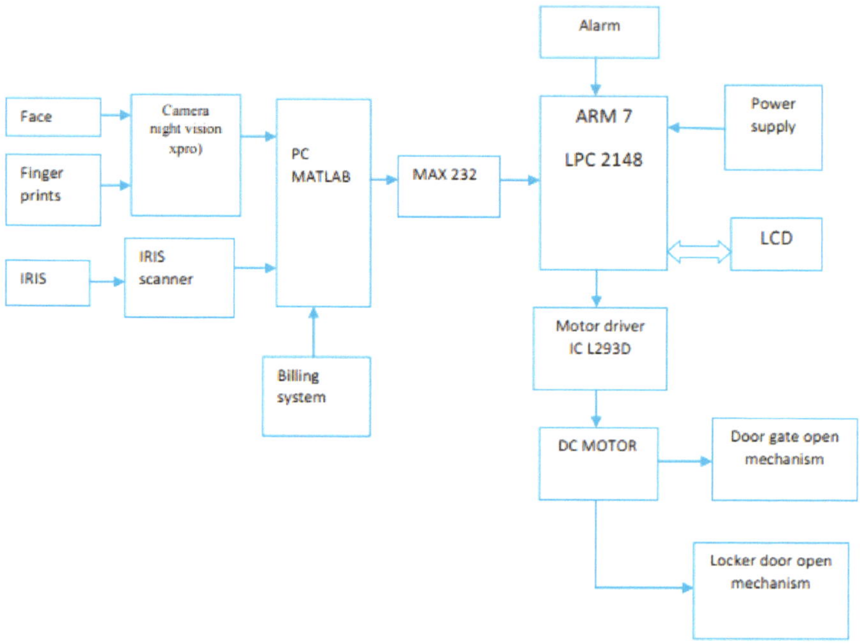

Figure 2.1: Block Diagram of Proposed System

Initially bank customer go through face reorganization when the customer enters into the bank locker system, he has to recognize his face through captured face image using camera i.e. night vision xpro. For face reorganization we are using the principle component analysis algorithm in MATLAB is used for face reorganization technique [8]. For image recognition and compression PCA is most successful techniques that have been used. PCA can perform various operation prediction, redundancy removal, feature extraction, data compression etc. Because PCA is a classical technique which can do something in the linear domain, applications having linear models are suitable, such as signal processing, image processing, system and control theory, communications, etc. The main idea of using PCA for face recognition is to express the large1-D vector of pixels constructed from 2-D facial image into the compact principal components of thefeature space. This can be called Eigen space projection. Eigen space is calculated by identifying the eigenvectors of the covariance matrix derived from a set of facial images (vectors). All this process is done in matlab software & captured image is compared with database stored in the PC and if it is match with the stored database then first gate of locker will be open automatically. For the locker gate we use Motor driven IC L293D which is driven by LPC 2148 which has sufficient output current of 600mA to drive the DC motor and then bank customer will go for the next technology i.e. Fingerprint. [8].

A fingerprint is made of a series of ridges and furrows on the surface of the finger. The uniqueness of a fingerprint can be determined by the pattern of ridges and furrows as well as the minutiae points [3].Minutiae points are local ridge characteristics that occur at either a ridge bifurcation or a ridge ending. Fingerprint matching techniques can be placed into two categories: minutiae based and correlation based. Minutiae-based techniques first find minutiae points and then map their relative placement on the finger. [7]In Matlab for fingerprint recognition we use Gabor filter.For Fingerprint recognition is considered using a combination of Fast Fourier Transform (FFT) and Gabor Filters to enhancement the image. An input fingerprint is first matched at a coarse level to one of the pre-specified types and then, at a finer level, it is compared to the subset of the database containing that type of fingerprints only [7]. If captured image is compared with stored database in PC and if captured image is authorized then bank customer will go for next step i.e. Password.

Password module is a secret word or string of characters used for authentication to prove identity or gain access to a resources and it is programmed in matlab software. That string is in the form of dot mat (.mat) format. If string is valid then next process is Iris reorganization.

The iris pattern is unique to each person and to each eye, and is essentially stable during an entire lifespan. These reasons make iris recognition a robust technique for personal identification. The first automatic iris recognition system was developed by Daugman. He applied Gabor filters to the iris image for extracting phase features, known as the Iris Code. Use 2D wavelet transform at various resolution levels of concentric circles on the iris image. They characterize the texture of the iris with a zero-crossing representation. Employ a bank of spatial filters, with kernels that are suitable for iris recognition to represent the local texture features of the iris [6].If the given iris matches with stored database in pc then the person is authorized otherwise it is unauthorized. After this whole process door is open and bank customer enters into the locker system. An alarm circuit is to interface to ARM7 for security access when an unauthorized access is done alarm will ring to give intimation. If authentic, then only using the gate control the door will be open [1].

III.SYSTEM FLOW STEP-I

Face Reorganization using PCA algorithm

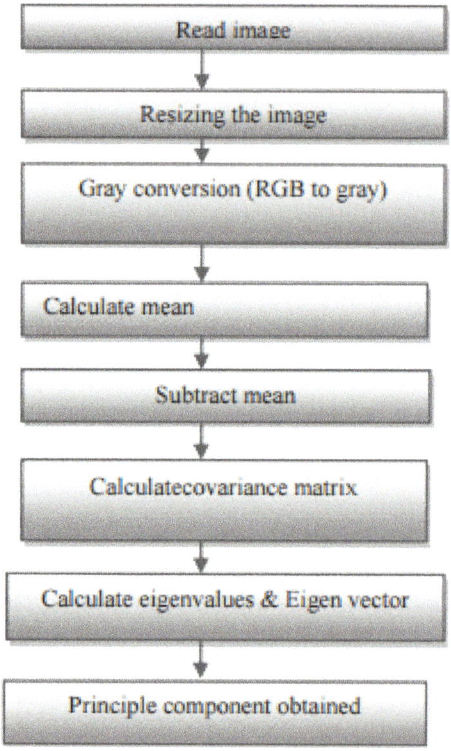

Figure 3.1: System flow for Face Reorganization.

For face reorganization we use principle component analysis algorithm. Initially we are acquiring data through camera night vision xpro. Read image operation is performed in which image is shown on screen. After resizing operation of image is done in which we are predefined setting the format of image for e.g. (200*200) size of image and whatever image is shown on screen earlier is converted into column and row format of matrix then RGB to gray conversion is done. The basic purpose is to make image in gray color because RGB format image contains each pixel of three values i.e. from 0-255 each for Red, green and blue color. If RGB to gray conversion is there then time is reduced used for each pixel of RGB color and for gray color each pixel contains only one value i.e.0-255. So we use RGB to gray conversion. After gray conversion unnecessary part of image is removed so that concatenation of faces should be done then create tensor image then calculate the mean of captured image then subtract the mean image from the tensor image vector. Find covariance matrix for captured image & then calculate Eigen values & Eigen vectors. Finally we got principle component of image.

STEP-II FINGER PRINTS AND IRIS REORGANIZATION USING GABOR FILTER

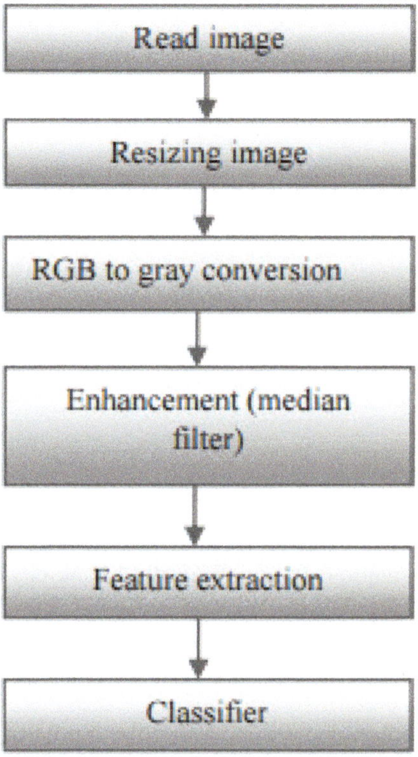

Figure 3.2: System flow for Fingerprints & IRIS reorganization.

For both fingerprint and iris reorganization system we use Gabor filter. Initially we are acquiring data through camera night vision xpro. Read image operation is performed in which image is shown on screen. After that resizing operation of image is done in which we are predefined setting the format of image for e.g. (200*200) size of image and whatever image is shown on screen earlier is converted into column and row format of matrix then RGB to gray conversion is done. The basic purpose is to make image in gray color because RGB format image contains each pixel of three values i.e. from 0-255 each for Red, green and blue color. If RGB to gray conversion is there then time is reduced used for each pixel of RGB color and for gray color each pixel contains only one value i.e.0-255. So we use RGB to gray conversion.

Next step is Enhancement process in which we have used median filter is a nonlinear method used to remove noise from images. It is widely used as it is very effective at removing noise which preserving edges. The median filter works by moving through image pixel by pixel, replacing each value with median value of neighboring pixel then the next step is feature extraction.

STEP-III Password Authentication

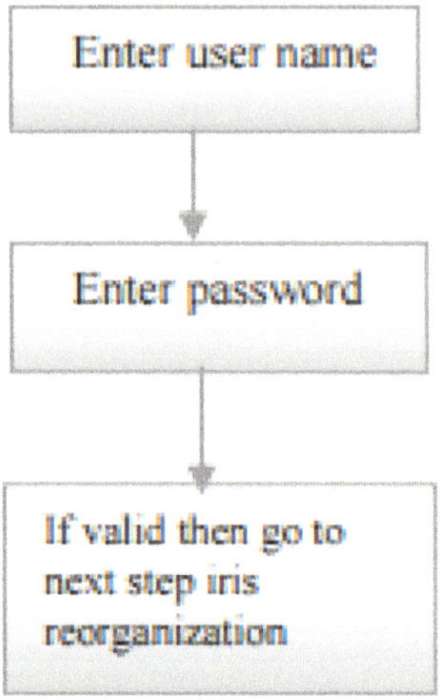

Figure3.3: System flow for Password Authentication.

After the fingerprint reorganization, if bank customer is authorized then move towards password authentication. In that, first of all bank customer have to enter their username and then enter the password using keyboard and if that password is valid then go for next step i.e. iris reorganization. If that entered password is invalid then it indicates unknown user

RESULT ANALYSIS

We created database for customers as per our requirement.

1. Output of STEP-I (PCA) algorithm for Authorized Person

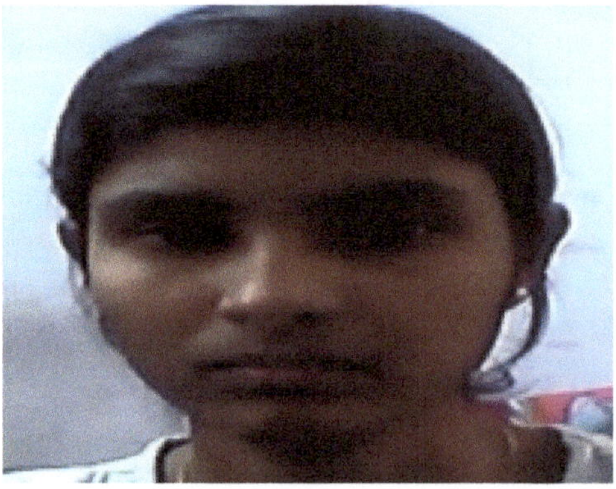

Figure 4.1: Image capture by camera i.e. input image.

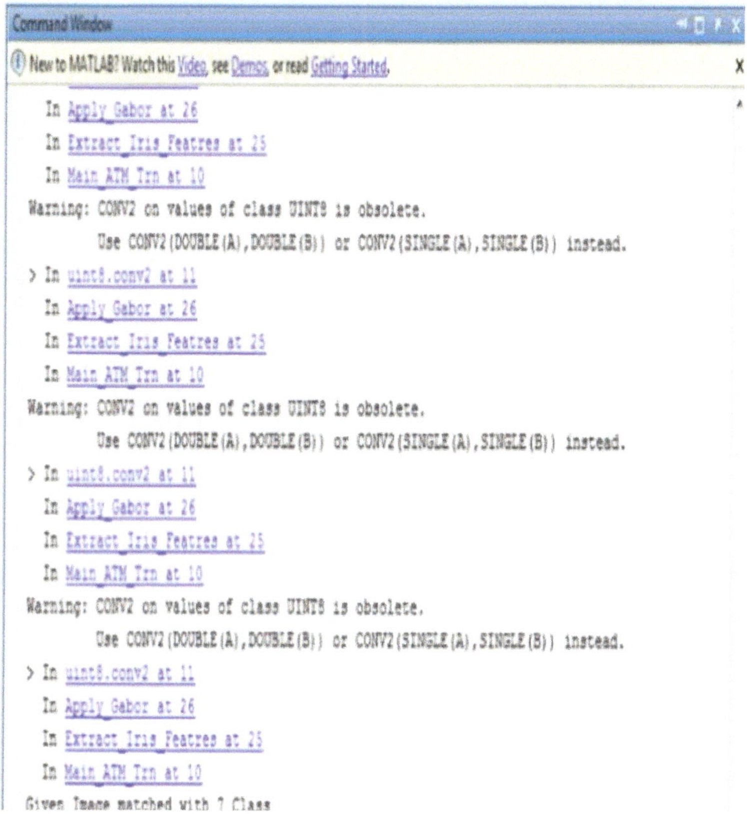

Figure 4.2: Execution of PCA algorithm

Figure 4.3: Output image after the execution of PCA algorithm.

2. Output of STEP-II (Gabor Filter) for finger prints

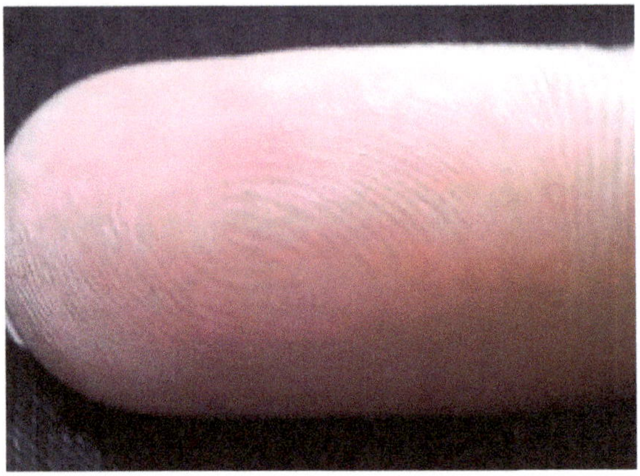

Figure 4.4: Input image of fingerprint captured by camera.

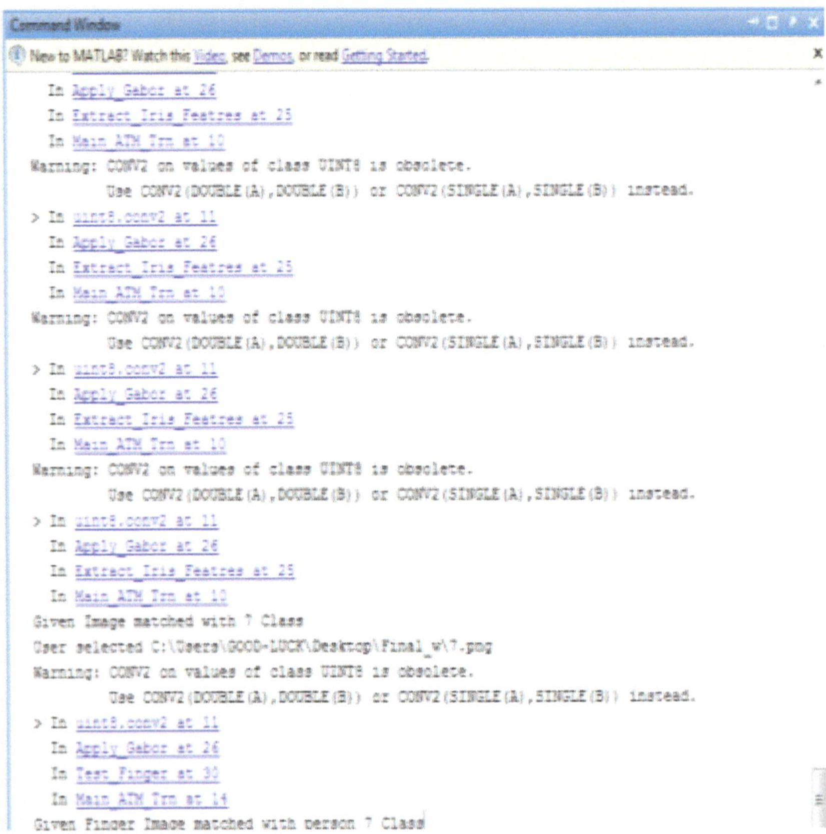

Figure 4.5: Execution of Gabor filter for Fingerprints.

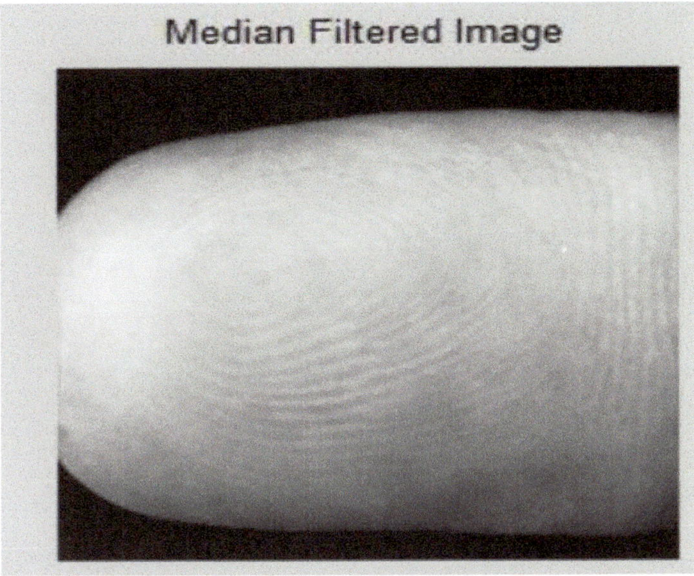

Figure4.6: Output image after the procedure of Gabor filter.

3. Output of STEP-III Password Authentication

```
Command Window
New to MATLAB? Watch this Video, see Demos, or read Getting Started.
Warning: CONV2 on values of class UINT8 is obsolete.
         Use CONV2(DOUBLE(A),DOUBLE(B)) or CONV2(SINGLE(A),SINGLE(B)) instead.
> In uint8.conv2 at 11
  In Apply_Gabor at 26
  In Extract_Iris_Featres at 25
  In Main_ATM_Trn at 10
Given Image matched with 7 Class
User selected F:\Final_w\7.png
Warning: CONV2 on values of class UINT8 is obsolete.
         Use CONV2(DOUBLE(A),DOUBLE(B)) or CONV2(SINGLE(A),SINGLE(B)) instead.
> In uint8.conv2 at 11
  In Apply_Gabor at 26
  In Test_Finger at 30
  In Main_ATM_Trn at 14
Given Finger Image matched with person 7 Class
Enter the Username'Sukanya'
Enter the Password'1234abcd'
```

Figure 4.7: Execution for Password Authentication.

3. Output of STEP-IV (Gabor) algorithm for IRIS

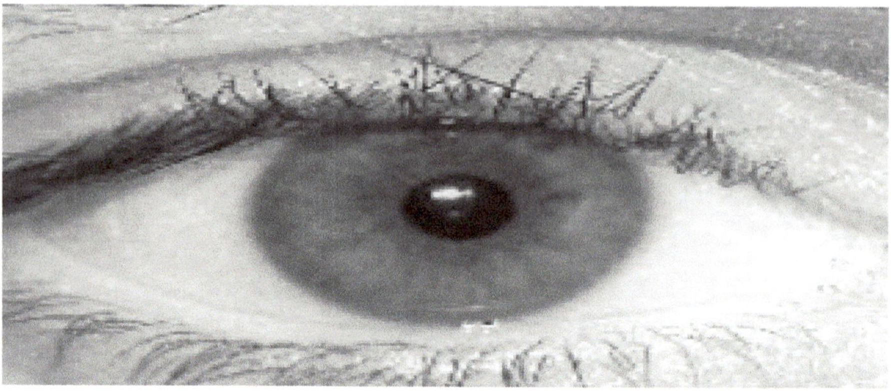

Figure 4.8: Input image of IRIS captured by camera.

Figure 4.9: Execution of Gabor filter for IRIS.

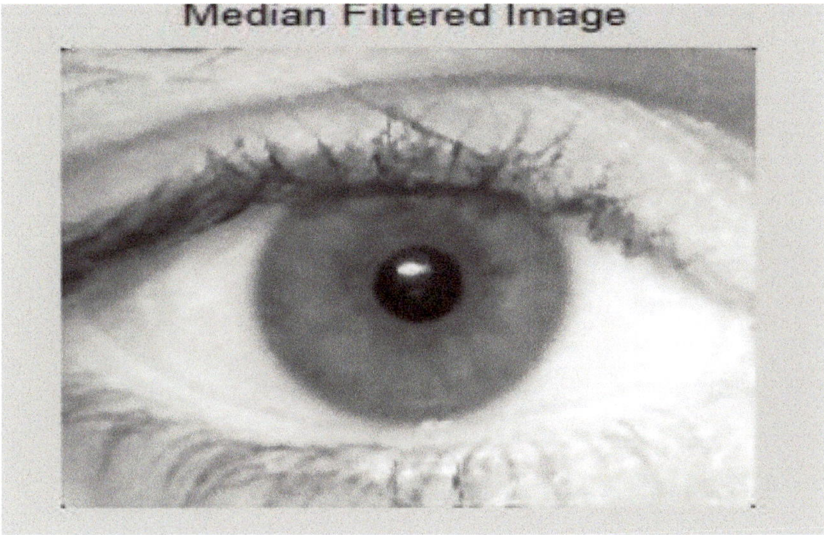

Figure 4.10: Output image after the procedure of Gabor filter.

Billing System Step-V

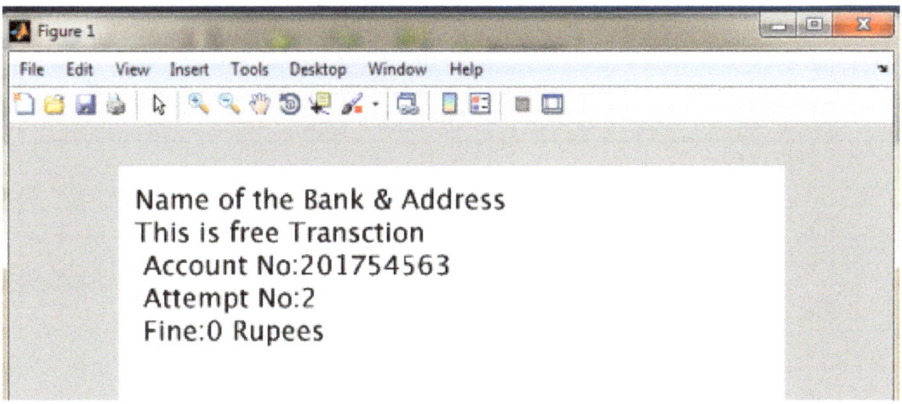

Fig.4.11: Execution of billing system for free transaction

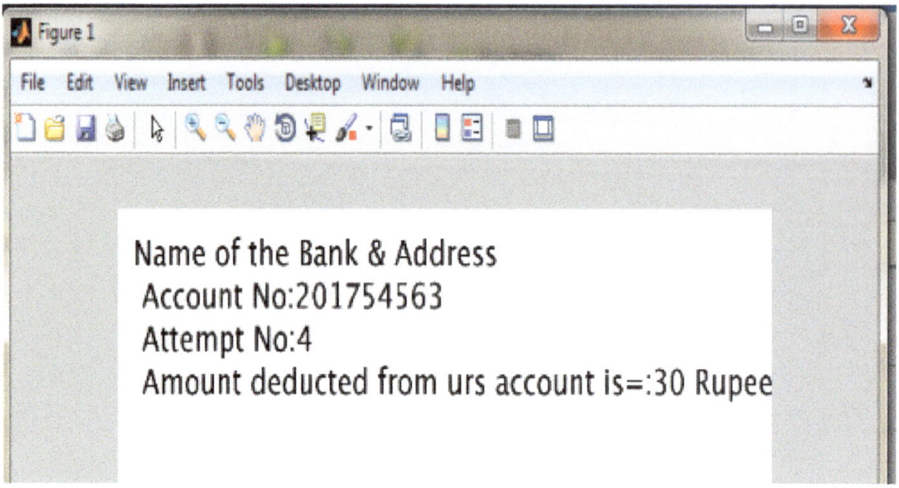

Figure 4.12: Execution of billing system for Paid transaction.

Table 4.1: Total Execution time.

	Time Consumed (in msec)
STEP-I	336.258
STEP-II	645.114
STEP-III	330.984
STEP-IV	669.102
STEP-V	67.404
Total time	2051.184

MERITS& DEMERITS

Merits

1. It is fully automatic security system.
2. Frauds in banking can be reduced to great extent.
3. Manual mistakes in the field get reduces.
4. Ensures total genuine access of the locker.
5. Highly advanced microprocessor controlled locking system.

Demerits

1. Processing time is somehow high

FUTURE SCOPE

In proposed system we have obtained the Locker security in terms Sequential fashion of biometric parameters .in Future to make more secure system we can go for the fusion of the biometric parameters.

REFERENCES

1. www.google.com//seminar report on locker access system using iris & fingerprints.// smart bank locker access system_final_report.pdf.
2. Josef Bigun, Julian Fierrez, HartwigFronthaler, Klaus Kollreider, Javier Ortega-Garcia Fingerprint Recognition Fernando Alonso-Fernandez and (in alphabetical order)
3. Andrew W. Senior and Ruud M. Bolle IBM T.J.Watson face recognition and its applications Research Center, P.O. Box 704, Yorktown Heights, NY 10598, USA. {aws, bolle}@us.ibm.com
4. MichaelBoyd,DragosCarmaciu,FrancisGian naros,ThomasPayne,William Snell. MSc Computing Science Group Project Iris Recognition
5. Chetna R. Koli, Nikita S. Kheratkar, Pooja S. Ganganalli, T. G. Shirsat International Journal of Advanced Research in Computer Engineering & Technology (IJARCET) Volume Bank Locker System Using Iris.
6. Shirke Swati D. Prof.Gupta Deepak MECOMPUTER-I Assistant Prof. ME COMPUTER CAYMT's Siddhant COE, CAYMT's Siddhant COE Sudumbare, Pune Sudumbare,Pune IRIS RECOGNITION USING GABOR.
7. D.ShekarGoud (1) IshaqMd (2) PJ.Saritha (3) 1P.G. Student (Embedded Systems), ELEN, Patancheru, India. 2P.G. Student (Embedded Systems), ELEN, Patancheru, India.3Associate Professor, ECE Department, ELEN, Patancheru, India. A Secured Approach for Authentication System using Fingerprint and Iris.
8. Face Recognition using Principle Component Analysis Kyungnam Kim Department of Computer Science University of Maryland, College Park MD 20742, USA
9. V. Shiv Naga Prasad University of Maryland shivnaga@cs.umd.edu Justin Domke University of Maryland domke@cs.umd.edu Gabor Filter Visualization
10. 1.Varun Gupta Dept. of Instrumentation & Control Engg. National Institute of Technology Jalandhar, Jalandhar, India varun gupta793@indiatimes.com,2. Gavendra Singh Dept. of Instrumentation & Control Engg. National Institute of Technology Jalandhar, Jalandhar, Indiajadaungs@gmail.com ,3. Ramveer Singh Dept. of Computer Science &Engg. Babu Banarasi Das Institute of Technology Ghaziabad, India sahil70itian@gmail.com, 4. Rajvir Singh Dept. of Instrumentation & Control Engg. National Institute of Technology

Jalandhar, Jalandhar, India dhanoarajvir@gmail.com5. Harsimran Singh Dept. of Instrumentation & Control Engg. National Institute of Technology Jalandhar, Jalandhar, India harsimrans329@gmail.com An Introduction to Principal Component Analysis and Its Importance in Biomedical Signal Processing.

3

CHAPTER

SMART CARD FOR BANKING WITH HIGHLY ENHANCED SECURITY SYSTEM

A. Salma, C. Sarada Devi, V. Saranya

Keywords: Automatic Teller Machines [ATM], biometrics, fingerprint, Global System for Mobile Communication [GSM, Personal Identification Number

INTRODUCTION

An automated teller machine (ATM) or cash machine is an electronic device that allows a bank's customers to make cash withdrawals and check their account balances without the need or human teller. In most modern ATMs, the customer identifies him or herself by inserting a plastic card with magnetic strip or plastic Smart card with a chip that contains his or her account number [2]. The customer then verifies his or her identity by entering a pass code (i.e.) personal Identification number (PIN) of four digits. The use of the password or PIN schemes was introduced in the early days of multi-user (timesharing) machines and its use has continued into today's highly networked and distributed systems [2]. The system does not further identify the user if the password or PIN is incorrectly entered because the password or PIN is meant to be known only to the authorized user. This allows anybody related or unrelated to the user who knows the user's password or PIN to make illegal access or withdrawal. Moreover there is a limitation in transaction for the other bank customers in using the ATM of some other bank crossing the limit they have to pay transaction fee.

Personal identification based on biometrics has been receiving extensive attention in public security and information security domains [3]. The biometrics identification uses physiological characteristics of humans and distinguishes one from another. These

Citation: A Salma,C Sarada Devi,V Saranya,2014, Smart card for banking with highly enhanced security system, international journal of electronics and communication engineering, ISSN: 2348 – 8549.

characteristics are face, facial thermo grams, fingerprint, iris, retina, hand geometry etc. The Identification and authentication is a process for verifying a user identity. Identification is concerned with how the user provides his or her unique identity to the system [3]. The identity must be unique so that the system can distinguish one user from another. Authentication, on the other hand, is the process of associating an individual with his/her unique identity, which is the manner he/she establishes the validity of his/her claimed identity.

Authentication consists of three methods:

- Something you are (e.g., biological characteristics)
- Something you possess (e.g., a token or a card)
- Something you know (e.g., password or PIN)

The use of biological characteristics such as fingerprint has always been a better identification method rather PIN. The easiest biological characteristic to capture and process is fingerprint [5]. Among all the biometric techniques, fingerprint based identification is the oldest method which has been successfully used in numerous application. In this paper we propose a radically new set of banking transaction protocols with new architectural design [4]. We believe that the implementation of this model will make banking transactions more user friendly, more inexpensive and more secure.

FINGERPRINTS

Fingerprints basically consist of ridges (raised skin) and furrows (lowered skin) that twist to form a distinct pattern as shown in Fig 1. When an inked imprint of a finger is made, the impression created is of the ridges while the furrows are the un-inked areas between the ridges.

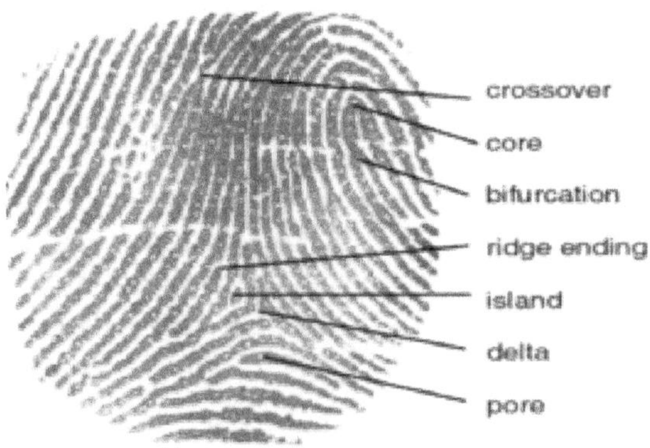

Figure 2.1: Fingerprint image.

Although the manner in which the ridges flow is distinctive, other characteristics of the fingerprint called 'minutiae' are what is most unique to the Individual [1].

FINGER PRINT AUTHENTICATION

Here the methodology of the project involves the use of a fingerprint biometric device incorporated to an existing ATM screen with the aid of an existing pin code system. The software development kit (SDK) helps to model the various stages of the authentication (fingerprint and pin) on the ATM screen [3]. The integration of the two technologies requires the incorporation of a card and fingerprint reader to the ATM and the interaction of the biometric system with the ATMs and the authorizing system.

The card and fingerprint reader are installed on the ATM which has been already designed using C programming language; it also has the capability to operate on a network while the ATM server is up [1].

The ability to identify a customer based on fingerprint is incorporated in the ATM by changing the software and programming on the software development kit (SDK). User screens are created to guide the client through the process of entering the fingerprint and receiving notification of fingerprint acceptance or denial [1].

The Biometric system is implemented with a C programming language. Here it is designed with a C language to initialize client program, identification, fingerprint and normal transactions. The C language is written to initialize an existing pin code system which operates on the biometric system. The program is fully designed into the system through software changes on the software development kit. The application solicits the capture of the user's fingerprint and PIN number; the biometric system activates the sensor; the sensor captures the fingerprint, encrypts it and sends it to the biometric system [1]. The biometric system de-encrypts and processes the fingerprint, using the PIN, compares the captured fingerprint to the stored templates for the database user, and notifies the application of the results of the validation process and hence, provides appropriate transaction authorization or denial.

EXISTING SYSTEM

In existing ATM system all ATM machines are connected to their respective bank servers and all bank servers are connected to a single interface i.e. National Finance Switch (NFS) [3]. When user swipes his ATM card at respective bank's ATM machine, then that ATM machine directly links to its bank server for validation of ATM card. If the ATM card is belonging to the same bank then transaction proceeds else connects to the respective bank's server via NFS for further transaction.

Disadvantages

- User has to carry more than one ATM card for more number of bank accounts and also user has to remember password for each ATM card.
- User has to pay extra charges when transactions are done from different bank's ATM other than ATM card after fee transactions over.
- Do not have finger print recognition and theft detection in ATM.

PROPOSED SYSTEM

Universal ATM implementation requires minor change in present banking network. The routing algorithm and protocol needs to be changed [4]. The idea behind this universal ATM card is that the customers can use a single ATM card to operate different bank accounts instead of having individual card for each bank account and maintaining their pin's, carrying the cards safely which is a tedious process at present scenario. The technology behind the product of the service is that adding all the user bank accounts to a universal ATM card. In this the user swipes his/her smart card in the ATM machine, then it request for authentication in the server side [4]. After the user is authenticated with his fingerprint, then it displays the list of all banks that the user is having account. Now the user can select the bank from which he/she is willing to perform transaction. After selecting the bank the request is sent to the corresponding bank through a network and links it with the banks server for accessing the database of the user or customer so that the transaction is processed. In case of theft, if the ATM machine is broken or damaged, the door of ATM center is locked automatically and buzzer is activated to alert the security.

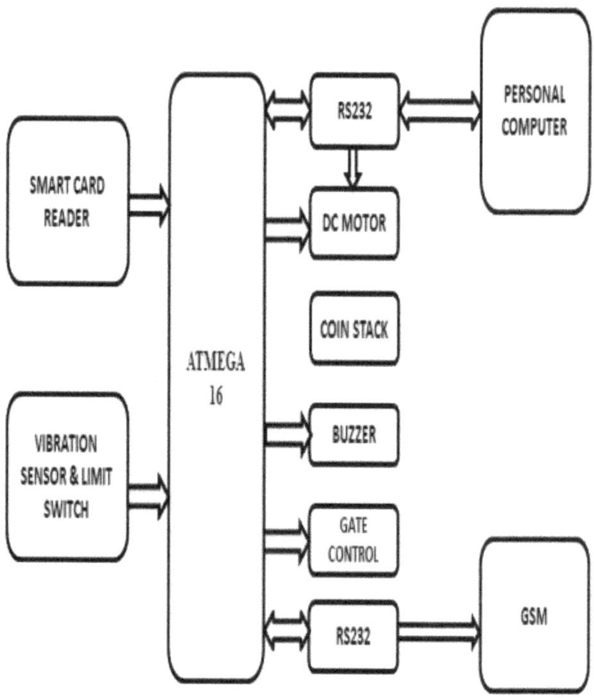

Figure 4.1: Block Diagram

ATMEGA16 is used in this project. If the user swipes the smart card with the help of Smartcard reader it will read the Radio frequency of that smartcard and send to the microcontroller. The microcontroller and the personal computer will connect through RS232. Then the personal computer will ask for fingerprint authentication. It will access the user fingerprint and then it will ask the user to give pin password. If both the fingerprint and pin password matched with the database which is already stored in a microcontroller of that particular database, then it will shows some list of banks where the account holder has account. With the help of vending machine using solenoid relay the user can withdraw the cash. If a thief tries to break the ATM the vibration sensor which senses some voltage due to vibration and it will make an alert using the buzzer. The limit switch will have two modes normally closed and normally opened. Actually it will be in normally opened condition which is connected with the vending machine. If a thief tries to break the ATM machine it will become normally closed and make the buzzer to alert.

Figure 4.2: Prototype model.

Figure 4.3: Display of multiple Account details.

With the help of GSM module which is connected to RS232 it will send information to nearby police station and the door of an ATM machine will be automatically closed with the help of DC motor. Figure 4.2 shows the prototype model of smart card for banking with highly enhanced security system, which we have implemented. Fig 4.3 shows multiple account details of the user. GSM module is also added to this system to send instant password to the user number after user swipes his ATM card.

GSM

Global System for Mobile Communication (GSM) is the most popular standard for mobile phones in the world. This has also meant that data communication was built into the system using the 3rd Generation Partnership Project (3GPP). GSM also pioneered a low-cost alternative to voice calls, the Short message service. GSM is a digital mobile telephone system that is widely used in Europe and other parts of the world. GSM uses a variation of Time Division Multiple Access (TDMA) and GSM is the most widely used of the three digital wireless telephone technologies (TDMA, GSM, and CDMA). GSM digitizers and compresses data then sends it down a channel with two other streams of user data, each in its own time slot. It operates at either 900 MHz or 1,800 MHz frequency band. GSM is the default wireless telephone standard in Europe. GSM has over one billion users worldwide and is available in 190 countries.

Technical Details

GSM is a cellular network, which means that Mobile phones connect to it by searching for cells in the immediate vicinity. GSM networks operate in four different frequency ranges. Most GSM networks operate in the 900 MHz or 1800MHz bands. Some countries in the Americans (including Canada and the United States) use the 850 MHz and 1900 MHz bands because the 900 and 1800 MHz frequency bands were already allocated. The rarer 400 and 450 MHz frequency bands are assigned in some countries, notably Scandinavia, where these frequencies were previously used for firstgeneration systems.

The Future of GSM together with other technologies is part of an evolution of wireless mobile telecommunication that includes High-Speed CircuitSwitched Data (DSCSD), General Packet Radio System (GPRS), Enhanced Data rate for GSM Evolution (EDGE), and Universal Mobile Telecommunications Service (UMTS).

FUTURE ENHANCEMENT

Since more than one bank accounts are being added, the existing PIN security and finger print authentication is not sufficient enough, so we can also embed a biometric scan like face recognition and vein authentication in the smart card i.e. multicomponent card. So that the user holds the card such that the face and vein rests on the biometric scan reader while he/she swipes the card and the image is authenticated at the real time. No one other than the user can use the card.

CONCLUSION

Thus the user can manage his/her multiple accounts in various banks with the help of this single smart card which provides easy access and reduces the complexity of managing more than one ATM card and their respective passwords. In this project Fingerprint provides a more viable method of identifying users' sufficient security level for the ATM system. The use of human characteristics in this prototype development tackles a lot of security implementation issues in identification and authentication of ATM. The Implementation of ATM security by using fingerprint recognition and GSM MODEM took advantages of the stability and reliability of fingerprint characteristics. Additional, the system also contains the original verifying methods which are inputting owner's password and which is send by the controller. The security features were enhanced largely for the stability and reliability of owner recognition. The whole system is built on the technology of embedded system which makes the system more safe, reliable and easy to implement. Hence, the vulnerabilities of the ATM fraud will be reduced in future.

Advantages

The advantages of proposed system

- More user friendly than present system.
- Reduces transaction cost.
- Make banking system more inclusive.
- User can perform transactions for all his bank
- Accounts using single ATM card.
- Enhanced security system.
- Sending theft information to the nearby
- Police station.

REFERENCES

1. H. Lasisi and A.A. Ajisafe, "Development of stripe biometric based fingerprint Authentications Systems in automated teller", IEEE 2nd International Conference on Advances in Computation Tools for Engineering Applications, 2012.
2. Gokul.R, Godwin Rose Samuel.W, Arul.M, Sankari.C, "Multi Account Embedded ATM Card" International Journal of Scientific & Engineering Research, April-2013
3. Harshal M. Bajad1Sandeep E. Deshmukh2Pradnya R. Chaugule3Mayur S. Tambade4, " Universal ATM Card System ", International Journal of Engineering Research & Technology (IJERT), October – 2012.
4. Ronald Petrlic University of Paderborn, "Integrity Protection for Automated Teller Machines", International Joint Conference of IEEE 2011.
5. Ugochukwu Onwudebelu, Olumide Longe, Sanjo Fasola, Ndidi C. Obi and Olumuyiwa B. Alaba , "Real Time SMS-Based Hashing Scheme for Securing Financial Transactions on ATM Systems", 3rd IEEE International Conference on Adaptive Science and Technology (ICAST 2011).

4
CHAPTER

AUTOMATED TELLER MACHINE (ATM)

Bharath E, Dhananjaya K M, Anoop C.N, Raghavendra B V

INTRODUCTION

The revolution of technology has influenced almost every faces of life; among them is the banking sector it has changed the phase of banking. The introduction of electronic banking has drastically changed the ways, banks were operating. As technology is now considered as the main contribution for the organizations' success and as their core competencies. So the banks, be it domestic or foreign are investing more on providing on the customers with the new technologies through e banking. PC banking, mobile banking, ATM, electronic funds transfer, account to account transfer, paying bills online, online statements and credit cards etc. are the services provided by banks. Also the feature which is commonly unique to internet banking includes importing data into personal accounting software. Some online Banking platforms support account aggregation to allow the customers to monitor all of their accounts in one place whether they are with their main bank or with other institutions. Banking through internet is considered as a complimentary delivery channel for the services rather than a substitute for the brick and mortar banking branches. Here we have considered the ATM as the son of technology helping bankers and its impacts on banking. A survey is made on this by considering all class of people.

ATM

Now our relationship with money can be fluid and convenient with the automated teller machine (ATM) that allows user to access 24 hours a day 7 days a week. An automated teller machine is also known as automated banking machine or cash point or cash

Citation: Bharath E,Dhananjaya K M,Anoop C N, Raghavendra B N,2016,Automated teller machine (ATM), international journal of management and business studies, http://www.ijmbs.com.

machine. This is a computerized telecommunication device that provides the clinets of a financial institution with access to financial transaction in a public space without the need for a cashier, a human clerk or a bank teller. It enables the users to funds in our savings, money market status, check other accounts. Each bank has its own ATM's but certain features are common to all, an account, an access card and an ATM. A standard cash machine looks like a panel inset into a wall. The panel usually contains a screen on which the ATM displays messages, a key board, slots for access card insertion and withdrawal and deposits. ATM are designed to be practical, easy and they are user friendly.

1. CPU (to control the user interface and transaction devices)
2. Magnetic and/or Chip card reader (to identify the customer)
3. PIN Pad (similar in layout to a Touch tone or Calculator keypad), often manufactured as part of a secure enclosure.
4. Secure cryptoprocessor, generally within a secure enclosure.
5. Display (used by the customer for performing the transaction)
6. Function key buttons (usually close to the display) or a Touch screen (used to select the various aspects of the transaction)
7. Record Printer (to provide the customer with a record of their transaction)
8. Vault (to store the parts of the machinery requiring restricted access)
9. Housing (for aesthetics and to attach signage to)

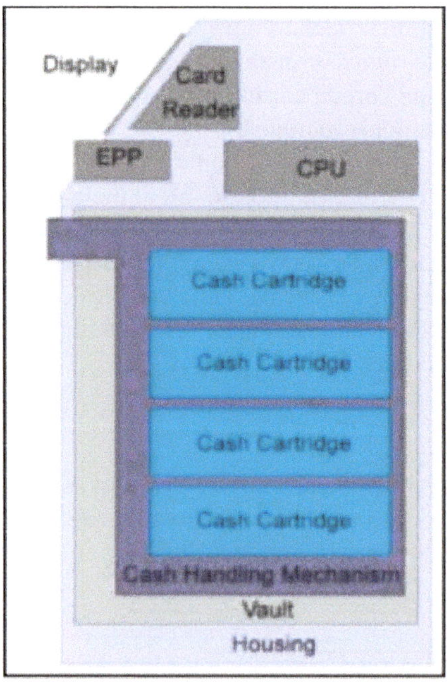

Figure 1: Block Diagram of ATM.

ATM Features

1. Cash withdrawal.
2. Purchase mobile phone recharge vouchers
3. Deposit cash and cheques (at selected ATMs)
4. Obtain a summary of balances for all your accounts
5. View and print a mini-statement (last 10 transactions)
6. Transfer money between linked accounts

ATM (Debit) Card Structure

Figure. 2: An Example of the Front of a Typical Debit Card.

1. Issuing bank logo
2. EMV chip
3. Hologram
4. Card number
5. Card brand logo
6. Expiration date
7. Cardholder's name

Figure 3: An Example of the Reverse Side of a Typical Debit Card.

- Magnetic stripe
- Signature strip
- Card Security Code

There are currently three ways that debit card transactions are processed: online debit (also known as PIN debit), offline debit (also known as signature debit) and the Electronic Purse Card System. One physical card can include the functions of all three types, so that it can be used in a number of different circumstances.

The usage of ATM's has drastically increased that can be clearly viewed by the Table 1. Which is showing the number of ATM existence after corresponding financial year.

Table 1: Number of ATM's After Financial Year

Year	No. ATM's
2005-06	21110
2006-07	25247
2007-08	34542
2008-09	43651
2009-10	56178
2010-11	75178

ATM Security

The application of cryptography (hidden or secret) to electronic funds transfer systems has shown that attacks may occur in different sub-systems. In other words, the protection of Electronic funds transfer terminals from attack by unauthorized outsiders is realized. Terminal's protection from authorized insiders is an impossible task. In order to go beyond these problems, the combined implementation of physical security, procedural protection and cryptography should be applied.

SURVEY

We have done a survey on ATM questions containing about its uses advantages, opinons, belief on it and advancements as they expect. We met about 500 people of all class irrespective of gender. People took this survey positively.

Questionire

1. Do you use ATM?
2. Are you ATM Friendly?
3. Why you are ATM Friendly?

4. Do you visit regularlly?
5. How do you feel using ATM?
6. What are the services you like in ATM?
7. Why you like those services?
8. Is ATM made your bank work easy?
9. In Future What do you expect from ATM?
10. Are you comfort with present system of ATM?
11. Are you enjoy the present services of ATM?
12. What is your opnnion regarding Introduction of ATM?
13. Is it Secure?
14. Is it Easy?
15. What is your feedback Regarding the ATM?

Conclusion of Survey

The survey report is based on answers of about 500 people is concluded so that people have accepted the technology which has enabled them to reduce their work by ATM's some statistics are stated below.

Statistics of Survey

From the it is clear that 98.4% people use the ATM's, 83.2% people agreed that ATM's have reduced their work, 74.6% is comfort with present service and 6.8% says they still not comfort. 87.4% people says ATM transactions are secured but 4.4% people say it is still insecure. 97.8% people say it is easy to use ATM's.

Table 2: Statistics of Survey

Question No.	Yes	No	Neither yes nor no
1	492	8	--
8	416	--	84
10	373	34	93
13	437	22	41
14	489	5	6

Enhancement of Services of ATM's

People have suggested to enhancement of features ATM's:

1. Establishment of ATM centers in rural areas.

2. ATM card issued must be able to access all the accounts of all the banks the person consists.
3. Mobile ATM's.

CONCLUSION

In this paper we have clearly seen that enhancement of banking and users of bank due to popularity of the ATM's as seen by the numbers of ATM's. 98.4% people use ATM's and people still expecting the enhancement of services of ATM's. By this we can clearly understand the impact of the technology on popularity of banking.

ACKNOWLEDGEMENT

The authors are thankful to Ms. Deepa C N, Lecturer, Department of Commerce, NDRK College, Sri. Koogegowda, HOD, Department of Commerce, NDRK college, Prof. K. Shama Bhat, Principal, NDRK College, who enhanced our knowledge throughout this work and also thankful to all the people who co-operated in our survey especially Arjun B S, Managing Director, Arjun Associates, Hosdurga, gave very useful advancements required for ATM stated point 2 and 3 in section 2.4.

REFERENCES

1. B.S.Raman,"Banking theory and practice", United publishers, manglore, 2nd edition, 2009.
2. Prof. K Ramamurthy Rao, Prof. K Sharada,"Banking theory and practice", Mysore book house, 1st edition,2011.
3. Mohammad Khurram Manzoor, Hassan H. Sumra, Momina Abbas,"The Impact of E-Banking on the Profitability of Banks A Study of Pakistani Banks", Journal of Public Administration and Governance, 2011, Vol. 1, No. 1
4. [Online] Available: http://www.en.wikipedia.org/wiki/atm
5. [Online] Available: http://www.en.wikipedia.org/wiki/ Debit_card

5
CHAPTER

MAPPING E-BANKING MODELS TO NEW TECHNOLOGIES

Ismail M. Romi

Keywords: E-Banking, Banking models, E-Banking technologies, E-Banking success, Banking functionalities

INTRODUCTION

Financial institutions are facing significant pressure to make their operations and processes more efficient and effective. Meanwhile, banks play a crucial role among these institutions, therefore; banks are required to provide solutions, and to cope with the variable changes in the economy, technology, and business and financial laws. Traditional banking models are no longer sustainable, and unable to meet the changing needs of customers [1]. Where, the shift towards e-banking produces many challenges. KPMG [2] report those challenges in four main areas, mainly, regulations and regulators, economic environment, changing customers, and the march of technology. Where, those challenges implies that banking sector have to operate in a dynamic environment in which information systems plays a vital role. Therefore, modern banking has tendency of dynamic evolution, adapting its business to valuable changes occurring in the global marketplace. Milan et al. [3] suggests that banks require new philosophy, new strategies, new structures, and new banking models based on new technologies can provide sustainability to banking system. To achieve that; banks are required to map its business models and strategies with the latest technologies, in order to compete well in the marketplace, and satisfy its customers. Meanwhile, empirical results about this type of mapping are inconsistent; because prior researches didn't take

Citation: Ismail M Romi (2015) Mapping E-banking Models to New Technologies. J Internet Bank Commer 20:112.

all aspects of e-banking as a whole, but focuses on some aspects of e-banking such as models, or technology, or management, and so forth. Therefore, the main objective of this study is to provide further insight into e-banking, the latest technologies, and then find out e-banking requirements that enable banks to cope the dynamic evolutions in its environments.

BACKGROUND AND LITERATURE REVIEW

E-banking

The review by Oyewole et al. [4] to the study of Egland et al. [5] suggested that; e-banking or internet banking is the employment of a remote delivery channel in performing banking services. Angelakopoulos and Mihiotis [6] indicate that; e banking covers a wide spectrum of banking transactions, which the customer can perform electronically without the need to visit a brick-and-mortar branch. According to this broad definition a lot of services and technologies constitute what is known as e-banking. Rusu and Shen [7] added that; the Internet has been used to support many traditional banking services, such as managing an account and transferring funds among different accounts. It also enables some new services, such as electronic bill payments and online investment. Where; Devi [8] suggested that the ranges of services provided by the e-banking are: internet banking, electronic transfer fund (ETF), electronic clearing services (ECS), telebanking, mobile banking, electronic data interchange (EDI), automated teller machine (ATM) and so on. Milan et al. [3] added that a new banks model were emerged, this type of banks is called virtual banks; which have a business model that provides online services with a lower operating costs.

The reported statistics in the past few years show that the online banking grows up rapidly. Statista [9] shows that 423.5 million people accessed online banking sites in 2012 from internet audience, i.e. 28.7% of the internet audience worldwide accessed online banking. Where, 45% in internet audience accessed online banking in North America, 37.8% from Europe, 25.1% from Latin America, 22% from Asia, and 8.8% from the Middle Ease and Africa. In 2013, Pew Research Center reported that 51% of U.S. adults, or 61% of internet users accessed online banking, meanwhile, in Europe the percentage reaches 43%. Eurostate [10] statistics show that 45% of the European internet users accessed the online banking. Factbrowser [11] shows that online users willing to conduct online banking are 46% from Asia Pacific, 45% from Africa and the Middle East, and 36% from Latin America.

The interest with e-banking came from the tremendous amount of benefits from the services covered when using such systems. Salehi and Alipour [12] classified those benefits from several viewpoints, bank's point of view, customers' point of view, economical benefits, and society perspective. From the banks' view point; the benefits are: better branding and better responsiveness to the market, enjoying a better brand image, and offering a perfect opportunity for maximizing profits. From the customers' point of view, the benefits are: increased comfort and timesaving, quick and continuous access to information, better cash management, and providing faster, easier and more reliable services. Meanwhile, the economic benefits are lower operational costs of banks, potentially lower margins, and expand reach through selfservice. From society perspective e-banking business makes access to finance from banks attractive. E-Finance offers the following attractive benefits for society: ease of use, lower costs of financing, convenience, timesaving's, and operational efficiency.

E-banking business models

Romi [13] reviewed the definition of business model in the literature, and find out that a business model is architecture of a business for creating value that incorporates the business strategy and its alignment with information technology that produces value to stakeholders. Table 1 shows the definitions provided by Laudon and Traver [14] to the components of a business model. Milan et al. [3], determined a set of factors that affect the development of e-banking; which are developing information systems using Internet and Web technologies that is suitable for financial transactions, conducting financial transactions digitally, developing business models depending on knowledge and new technologies, enabling financial business systems to operate globally, implementing ISO standards which concerned with safety and information protection.

Table 1: Business Model Components [14]

Business Model Components	**Question to ask**
Value proposition	Why should the customer buy from the firm?
Revenue model	How will the firm earn money?
Market Opportunity	What marketspace does the firm intend to serve and what is its size?
Competitive Environment	Who else occupies the firm's intended marketspace?
Competitive Advantage	What special advantages does the firm bring to the marketspace?
Market Strategy	How does the firm plan to promote its products or services to attract its target audience?
Organizational Development	What types of organizational structures within the firm are necessary to carry out the business plan?
Management Team	What kind of backgrounds should the firm's leaders have?

KPMG [2] argues that banks needs new business models that enables banks to reduce costs, cope with complex value chain, standardized data requirements, and delivers distinctive customer service. KPGM [2] shows that some banks start to implement the horizontally-integrated model; which uses business process that cross functional areas in the bank to provide common services, rather than products, thus the model operates by dividing the value chain into a particular parts across the whole product.

Table 2: Key Components of Accenture Models [1]

Model	Definition	Key Components
1. Intelligent Multichannel Bank	Engaging with customers on their financial needs effectively. • Integrated multichannel architecture, powered by analytics. • Advanced digital advisory. • Need-based offerings optimized by channels.	• Advanced multichannel integration focusing on digital channels and an integrated architecture. • Pervasive analytics based on effective customer data collection, micro-segmentation and predictive modeling to determine the most effective basket of products. • Real-time interactions management that can increase conversion rates from inbound and outbound contacts. • Advanced advisory services leveraging digital channels and personal analytics. • Product offerings and related pricing schemes based on micro-segments and optimized by channel.
2. Socially Engaging Bank	Interacting with customer to increase customer intimacy. • Customer engagement.	• Social media monitoring to identify opportunities to engage customers, mitigate risks and promptly react to issues • Social digital marketing building on clustering to enable the bank to

	• Leverage influencers. • Co-creation based on increased customer intimacy.	better defines the best content for individual customer profiles and attracts them. • Social CRM enriching customer data with social media data, thus facilitating more effective propositions.
3. Financial/Non-Financial Digital Ecosystem Bank	An ecosystem selling financial and non-financial services, leveraging in particular the power of mobile technology. • Bank with an extended proposition (financial and non-financial). • M-payment services	• Mobile payments based on Near Field Communication (NFC) or mobile wallet, that enhances bank competitiveness in the payment arena and helps retain existing customers • Enriched propositions through mobile commerce focused on financial and non-financial offerings, mobile marketing, m-loyalty and m-analytics • Alliances and partnerships with non-banking operators and creation of related content.
4. The "do the basics right" Bank	• Optimized branch network and contact center. • Enhanced digital channels. • Need-based offerings and consistent sales behaviors.	• Branch network optimization (number and size of branches), reviewing network architecture (i.e. hub and spoke model) • Basic multichannel integration, alignment of channels and integrated governance processes for real-time banking • Proactive and reactive

	• Basic multichannel integration.	management interaction based on customer needs • Operational customer segmentation driven by a needs-based offering structure • Sales force effectiveness powered by consistent sales behaviors and tools • Simple and clear communication with customers • Performance management (new customer-oriented metrics) and tailored compensation schemes.

Accenture [1] suggest three business models for banking and called them the next generation banking models. Those models are intelligent multichannel model, socially engaging model, and financial/ non-financial digital ecosystem model. Where banks have to consider these models when defining their own models. Accenture provides the definitions and key components Table 2 to each of the suggested models, besides the definition and components of the traditional banking which they called it the "do the basics right" bank model-model 4 in Table 2. Accenture [1] adds that; the selection from the specified models depends on bank potential capabilities, and suggests the capabilities matrix to measure bank capabilities.

E-banking technological features

E-banking and e-commerce formulated as the use of Internet, the Web, and other features to conduct transactions electronically. Therefore, the required features for e-commerce can be settled to e-banking. Researchers [14,15] found out the features of e-commerce technology. Those features include ubiquity; which refers to the availability everywhere, and at any time, global reach; which refers to the ability of e-banking technology to permit transactions to cross cultural and national boundaries, universal standards; which refers to the technical standards of the Internet, richness is the complexity and content of a message, interactivity; which refers to conducting online dialogues with the consumer, information Density; which refers to the total amount and quality of information available to all consumers, and stakeholders, personalization/and Customization; this component refers to allowing personalized messages to be delivered to consumers., and social technology; which refers to using content generation, distribution, and supporting social networks [14,15].

To achieve those requirements, Laudon and Traver [14] suggests that implementing e-banking requires the banking transactions to be conducted everywhere, at all times, and cross cultural national boundaries taking into consideration global banking and internet standards. In addition to the ability of technology to handle with customer dialogues and messages; which may include all types of presentations, video, audio, and so forth. Laudon and Traver [14] adds that; the used technology must have the ability to handle with huge amount of data in all time including peak time using scalability, and handle with the changes of the delivered message based on a user's preferences.

KPMG [2] provides a clear image of the cross-cultural banking. Where, any proposed model must take into consideration the decentralized and fragmented structure, cutting cost, and using complex IT architecture. Therefore, IT architecture must be capable to operate in a dynamic environment, taking into consideration to operate using service oriented architecture (SOA) principles, standardization and subdivide value chain activities, reporting requirements [2].

E-banking success factors

E-banking can be classified as an information system; which consists of computer hardware, software, databases, procedures, and users. Researchers classified information systems success factors, and hence, e-banking success factors as a set of dimensions and aspects that produce the net benefits of information system. Those dimensions include the e-banking system quality, the quality of the produced information, and the quality of the services provided by e-banking, e-banking use, user satisfaction, and net benefits produced from using e-banking [16-20]. Romi [21], tests (Figure 1) the impact of information systems quality, the quality of the produced information, the quality of the services provided by the information systems on the stakeholders requirements, mainly; information system use, information systems user satisfaction and net benefits in the financial institutions, and find out that system quality, and service quality explains 78.2% of the variance in system use, the service quality, and information quality explains 77.2% of the variance in user satisfaction, and the system use, and user satisfaction explains 54.9% of the variance in the net benefits. Therefore, the model (Figure 1) provides a good explanation of information systems success,and thus e-banking success. These results implies that e-banking success depends on many factors, mainly, systems quality, service quality, and information quality. Table 3 provides the definition of Delone and Mclean [17] to these factors, and the constructs of each factor, which are tested by Romi [13].

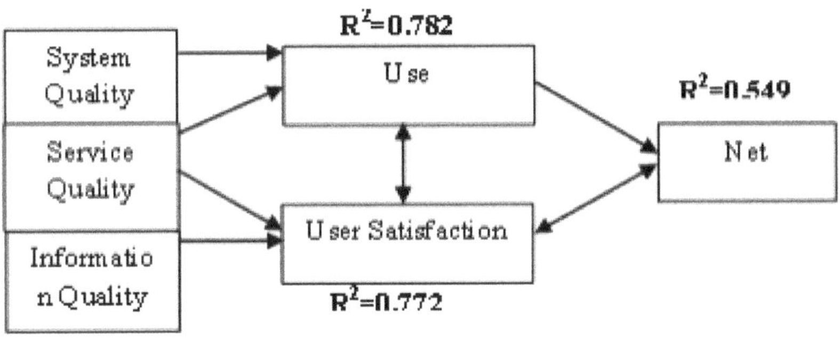

Figure 1: Information Systems Success Model [13].

Table 3: E-Banking Success Factors [13,17]

Success Factor	Definition	Factors Constructs
System Quality	Defined as a set of constructs related to information system that determines the quality of the systems.	System reliability, easy to learn, ease of use, user preemptive, flexibility, and integration with another systems,
Information Quality	The degree to which information presents the required benefits.	Availability, timeliness, relevancy, accuracy, appropriateness, completeness, concise representation, interpretability.
Service Quality	A set of characteristics related to services submitted by information systems to customers.	Services reliability, assurance, empathy, and security.

E-banking requirements and features

The literature provides answers to some questions that are essential to use the best technology in banking operation "e-banking". Meanwhile there are many challenges that have to be considered while implementing this type of banking. Those challenges are reported by KPMG [2], which includes the efforts by regulators to produce a new regulations to avoid new banking crises (regulations and regulators), economic environment; where banks are required to operate in the reduced economy growth and any other expected economic situation, changing customers behavior towards banks; where they are more warily and less trust to banks, and the changing technology; where banks are required to upgrade their information systems to cope with the complicated and rapid changes in technology. Addressing those challenges requires an insight analysis to all aspects of banking processes and operations, as well as the banking environment. Where, the literature provides an analysis to some aspects to e-banking requirements. Accenture [1] suggested three models (Table 2) that can be implemented in banking operations depending on bank capabilities. Where, the key components of the predefined models provide the functionalities of banks. Meanwhile, the study of Rusu and Shen [7], and Devi [8] provides banking functions that are required by customers, such as managing accounts, electronic bill payments, online investment, internet banking, electronic transfer fund (ETF), electronic clearing services (ECS), telebanking, mobile banking, electronic data interchange (EDI), automated teller machine (ATM) and so on. Meanwhile, e-commerce technological features; are determined by Laudon and Traver [14] and Shafiyah et al. [15]; which include global reach, ubiquity, richness, interactivity, personalization/ and customization, information density, universal standards, and social technology. Depending on the success factors provided by Delone and Mclean [17], and tested by Romi [13] in the financial institutions, E-banking success factors include three main constructs (Table 3), mainly; e-banking system quality, the quality of the produced information, the quality of the services provided by e-banking. The provided analysis shows that; even if banks achieve all given requirements, the challenges still need more investigation and analysis. This is consistent with the results of Milan et al [3], which argues that; banks require new philosophy, new strategies, new structures, and new banking models based on new technologies can provide sustainability to banking system.

Mapping E-Banking to New Technologies

Figure 2 presents a proposed model for e-banking. Where the model is composed of five main domains, mainly; bank functional and non-functional requirements, customer functional and non-functional requirements, bank technological capabilities, customers technological capabilities, and suppliers technological capabilities.

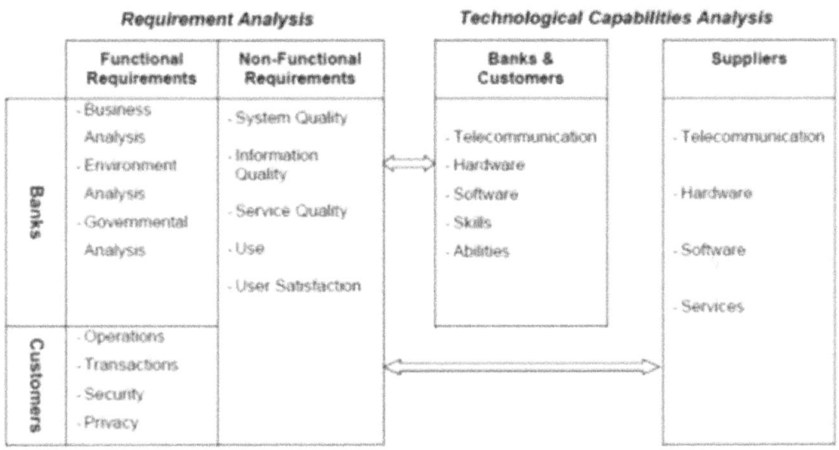

Figure 2: E-Banking Model.

The e-banking model based on five key domains

Banks requirements: Determining banks requirements requires an insight analysis to business, environment, and regulations.

a. Business analysis

This phase includes analyzing banks scope, vision, mission, strategy, policies, procedures, programs, daily operations, synergies, core competences, and all aspects of banks daily work. To achieve the best in this step, analysts have to take into consideration the suggested banking models in the literature [1,2].

b. Environmental analysis

Analyzing the stakeholders, who have direct or indirect impact on banking, in order to determine alliances, economical situations, and so forth.

c. Governmental analysis

This phase includes analyzing governmental and international laws and standards related to financial operations.

Customer requirements: Identifying the target customers (individual, business corporations, and governmental) who will use e-banking, and their characteristics. Then determining customer's goals in the form of functional and non-functional requirements.

a. Functional requirements

This type of requirements, incorporate all required operations and transactions that the customer needs from banks.

b. Non-functional requirements

Non-functional requirements, affect customer satisfaction. Therefore, an analysis to these requirements must be conducted. In general, common non-functional requirements can be considered that have a direct or indirect impact on customers acceptance to e-banking. The information systems success model (Figure 1) presents the main dimension of the user acceptance to an information system, and hence, to e-banking, which includes; system quality, information quality, service quality, use, and user satisfaction.

Banks technological resources and capabilities: Information technology (IT) can be defined as all sources of technology, which is used to create, store, disseminate, exchange, and use information, which includes hardware, software, and telecommunications. Meanwhile, IT capabilities include the skills and abilities of IT-workforce, which includes technical skills, management skills, and relationship skills [22]. In this phase, an analysis must be conducted to all technological resource available at banks, and then analyzing the available capabilities.

Customers technological resource and capabilities: The information technology resources available to customers; which includes hardware, software, and telecommunications. The customer capabilities include the skills and abilities of customer to use e banking. In this phase, a survey, and analysis must be performed to intended customers, and then analyzing the available capabilities of customers.

Information technology supplies: An Information technology supply is the market, where, banks can collect IT requirements and services. This phase includes analyzing the available hardware, software, and telecommunications in the market.

Requirements Bidirectional Fit to Technological Capabilities

To develop an e-banking system that matches between banks and customer's capabilities that matches the latest technologies, two type of bidirectional fit take place. First, the requirements bidirectional fit to supplier's technological capabilities. Second; the requirements bidirectional fit to banks and customers Capabilities.

Requirements bidirectional fit to suppliers technological capabilities

Achieving this type of bidirectional fit requires developers to analyze the latest technologies in the market, and then analyze banks and customers requirements as if they use this latest technology. This is an essential step that enables banks to keep up to date with technology. In case the current requirements are less than latest technology capabilities, developers can take into consideration the current requirements, and leave the remaining requirements for future work as a plan.

Requirements bidirectional fit to banks and customers capabilities

Prior researches find out that the successful system is the one that accepted by customers. Therefore, developers have to match between bank and customers functional and non-functional requirements from one side, and match between banks and customers capabilities from the other side. After that, a match must be conducted between the requirements and actual capabilities.

CONCLUSION AND RECOMMENDATIONS

This study reviews the literature that is concerned with e-banking requirements, and then conducted an analysis to the available requirements. This can be summarized in:

a. E-banking requirements, which can be determined from the banking models, mainly; intelligent multichannel bank, socially engaging bank, financial/non-financial digital ecosystem bank, and the do the basics right" bank.

b. Customer requirements, which includes managing accounts, electronic bill payments, online investment, internet banking, electronic transfer fund (ETF), electronic clearing services (ECS), telebanking, mobile banking, electronic data interchange (EDI), automated teller machine (ATM) and so on.

c. E-banking features to be considered during the implementation of e-banking, which include global reach, ubiquity, richness, interactivity, personalization/and customization, information density, universal standards, and social technology.

d. E-banking success factors, which includes e-banking system quality, the quality of the produced information, the quality of the services provided by e-banking.

e. The results show that prior researches focused on some aspects of e-banking; some of these researches works on banking requirements, others' works on technology, meanwhile; the rest works on customer requirements.

f. The current study, proposed a model for e-banking, which is composed of five main domains, mainly; bank functional and non-functional requirements, customer functional and non-functional requirements, bank technological capabilities, customers technological capabilities, and suppliers technological capabilities. And then, matches e-banking systems to latest technologies. Where, two types of bidirectional fit take place; first, the requirements bidirectional fit to supplier's technological capabilities, and second, the requirements bidirectional fit to banks and customers Capabilities.

REFERENCES

1. Accenture (2012) Banking 2016: Accelerating growth and optimizing costs in distribution and marketing.
2. KPMG (2012) Optimizing banking operating models- from strategy to implementation.
3. Milan DN, Jelena V, Sava S (2011) Electronic banking models.International journal of economics and law 1: 24-37.
4. Oyewole O, Abbe M, El-muade, Gambo J, Arikpo, Abam I (2013) E-banking and Bank Performance: Evidence from Nigeria.International Journal of Scientific Engineering and Technology 2: 766-771.
5. Egland KL, Furst K, Nolle DE, Robertson DD (1998) Banking over the Internet. Quarterly Journal 17.
6. Angelakopoulos G, Mihiotis A (2011) E-banking: challenges and opportunities in the Greek banking sector. Electronic Commerce Research 11: 297-319.
7. Rusu RF, Shen K (2012)An empirical study on E-Banking acceptance in the United Arab Emirates (UAE).Journal of Electronic Banking Systems2012: 1-9.
8. Devi PA (2010) Customers' Perception of E-Banking: Factor Analysis. The IUP Journal of Management Research 6: 1-14.
9. Statista (2015) Global online banking penetration in April 2012, by region.
10. Eurostat (2015) Individuals using the internet for internet banking.
11. Factbrowser (2015) Online Banking Facts and Statistics.
12. Salehi M, Alipour M (2010) E-Banking in Emerging Economy: Empirical Evidence of Iran. International Journal of Economics & Finance 2: 201-209.
13. Romi IM (2013) Testing Delone and Mclean's Model in Financial. American Academic & Scholarly Research Journal 5: 121-129.
14. Laudon KC, Traver CG (2014) E-commerce 2014: business, technology, society (10thedn.).
15. Shafiyah N, Alsaqour R., Shaker H, AlsaqourUddin O (2013) Review on Electronic Commerce. Middle-East Journal of Scientific Research 18: 1357-1365.
16. Delone WH, Mclean ER (2003) The Delone and Mclean Model of Information Systems Success: a Ten- Year Update. Journal of Information Systems 19: 9-30.
17. Delone WH, McLean ER (1992) Information systems success: The quest for the dependent variable. Information Systems Research 3: 60-95.
18. DeLone WH, McLean ER, Petter S (2008) Measuring information systems

success: models, dimensions, measures, and interrelationships. European Journal of Information Systems 17: 236-263.

19. Seddon PB (1994) A partial Test Development of Delone and Mclean's Model of IS Success. ICIS 1994 Proceedings. Paper 2.The international Conference of Information Systems, Vanconver.
20. Seddon PB (1997)A Re-specification and Extension of the Delone and Mclean's Model of IS Success. Information Systems Research 18: 240-253.
21. Romi IM (2012) Mobile Commerce Success Factors for the Various Business Models. Proceedings of 2ndComputer Science On-line Conference in 2012, Open Publish Proceedings series, Czech Republic.
22. Ravarini, Aurelio (2010) Information technology capability within small-medium enterprises PhD thesis,School of Computer and Security Science, Edith Cowan University, Australia .

6
CHAPTER

INTERNET BANKING

Jeffrey E Jarrett

INTRODUCTION

In his book (The New Economics) Deming [1] quoted from an advertisement of a group of consults in management that "Computerized quality information systems provide the vital link between high technology and effective decision making". Although he spoke about quality management and continuous improvement , he characterized most effective decision making in business and other areas as heavily dependent on the growth of technology and its use rather than simply "mergers and acquisitions" as the source of profitability in the new world emerging from great strides in technology. As we observe internet banking and financial services grew tremendously in participation assets and volume in the twenty-first century with the growth of the use of portable electronic devices (mobile phone and others) to access the internet. Along the great growth of internet participation came also a huge amount of services provided by suppliers to allow easy transfer of financial assets one party to another both domestically and to a global participator. Along with the participation of suppliers and customers came with participators without scruples who contributed fraud, conflict and theft to the process. This, of course, created to very fast growing commercial ventures; internet crime and security. For a discussion of the great increase in internet banking and commerce in developed and lesser developed nations [2-5]. Also Mai Hitt and Chen [6] discussed the motivations of customers in some regions with high density to generate more interest in internet banking than customers in low density regions. Of more interest, they concluded that customers tend to increase their internet banking activity and e-commerce activity as they perform more transactions through internet services.

Citation: Jeffrey E Jarrett, 2015, On Internet Banking .Journal of Internet Banking and Commerce 20:101.

Security along the supply chain of the transfer of financial and similar assets is one of the great growth industries of the twenty-first century. The industry not only has banking and the financial services industry as its customers but all activities that use data from banks and other financial institutions. Today, that is almost every commercial, governmental, military and all services provided to the supply and distribution of services, i.e., water, telecommunication, electric and other power services, health and similar providers.

The importance of management science, decision analysis, and forecasting became ever more present in the supply of internet services to prevent unscrupulousactivities. These activities grow through the weakness in code utilized by the suppliers of these services. Their main goal is and was to build websites that are easy to use, provide reliable services for the clients of these firms and providers, fast and without error and security. They are often not due to a variety of causes laid done by the supplier services which are often expensive and later dispensed with, very difficult under present technology and sometimes just useless to customers.

Management science, decision analysis and forecasting software and experts may produce better services in the field of internet banking and commerce by providing the methods by which one may predict accurately the source of weaknesses in code that lead to unscrupulous activity. We observe the way in which these activities improve the quality of care and improvement in many industrial activities. Without hesitation, the scrutiny of new and existing code great demands experts who are not only code programmers but also educated in the sciences associated with the production of software. As a case for example , let use consider the software "Excel" which became the prime source of software used in commercial and often government software for business practice. This software replaced the many spread sheet software used by PC operators because of its greater variety of applications and the near monopoly of the producer in the industry.

Excel became the dominant method by which offices in agencies, business firms and the like presented and later would transfer data from one participant to another. As a professor who would teach students to use PC's for business and other purposes, the need to be fluent became mandatory for students to be able to work in modern industry which became so dependent on the internet. The ability to store, save and retrieve information became vital for internet banking and commerce to exist. Couple with transfer, storage and retrieval Excel became a useful tool for simple business computation. However, the demand for computation spread beyond the simple manipulations of computation within a cell. Many traditional uses of computers became dependent on the use of computers and Excel was available for this use on the PC's. The early developers of Excel knew its customers would use Excel for serious, difficult and time consuming calculations. Problems arose with cell based computations and many, early on, noted that solutions and computation in Excel were wrong. Serious errors associated rounding and sums of squares gave birth to the notion that spreadsheet were often wrong.

At the same time traditional optimization, data analysis and econometrics software saw their opportunity to survive and to survive well in the fiercely competitive field of management science, forecasting, quality control and improvement and some of these software became domination in the new markets for data mining and enterprise solutions. Within the "high tech" fields Excel did allow for solutions for others to develop add-on software to compete strongly its growing competitors. The problem with using Excel to do computer applications where it was not particularly intended to do became a problem for end-users. The demand for better use of PC's and other devises for accessing the internet is bringing on demand to induce better end-user software. We should note that Excel will not wither away but still has powerful uses. However, those of us who remember the withering away of machine dependent assembly languages and COBOL, change will occur.

CONCLUSIONS

The basic challenge to the internet banking and commerce industry is to develop newer and faster and more secure software to provide the end-user customers the ability to accomplish the applications they wish to achieve. Hence, the internet banking and commerce industry must demand new products from hardware and software producers to predict the problems associated with this growing and profitable industry. The implementation of management science, data analysis and forecasting in the programming of new software is important to see where unscrupulous activity may occur and where data bottlenecks may arise. No one will tolerate sitting at a computer or other device screen waiting for activity to occur. One place where you see the future not operating well because we have not developed the hardware and software well enough is to see customers at an automatic check-out counter in a market or hardware store. Technology developed so far is inadequate at these installations. No doubt that the internet industries will grow but the demand for newer and better technology need to grow first. We must use our scientific methods better. Voss [7] published his book where he outlined in detail methods by which business and logistics management (or "the supply chain") utilizes management science methods to improve methods of internet banking and e-commerce.

REFERENCES

1. Deming WE (1993) The new economics for industry, government and education. Massachusetts Institute of Technology Center for Advanced Engineering Study, Cambridge.
2. Mermod AY (2011) Customer's perspectives and risk issues on E-banking in Turkey; Should we still be online. Journal of Internet Banking and Commerce 16: 1-3.
3. Lustsik O (2003) E-Banking in Estonia: Reasons and benefits of the rapid growth. Kroon and Economy 3: 2-27.
4. Calisir F, Cigden AG (2008) Internet banking versus other banking channels: Young consumers view. International Journal of Bank Management 11: 87-114.
5. Courchrane M, Nickerson D, Sullivan R (2002) Investment in internet banking as a real option: Theory and tests. Journal of Multinational Financial Management 12: 347-363.

6. Xue M, Hitt LM, Chen P (2011) Determinants and outcomes of internet banking adoption. Management Science 57: 291-307.
7. Voss S (2009) Logistics-management: Systeme, methoden, integration. Physica-Verl: Heidelberg, Berlin.

7
CHAPTER

E-BANKING: PROBLEMS AND PROSPECTS

Ruby Shukla, Pankaj Shukla

Keywords: E-Banking, ATM, Internet Security

INTRODUCTION

The advent of E-Business accompanied with technological innovations and globalization is constantly propelling the businesses organization to redefine their business operations in terms of value chain reengineering and restructuring business models. Likely, the financial sector is metamorphosing under the impact of competitive, regulatory and technological forces. Financial institutions especially the banking sector is currently in a transition phase. The banks have put themselves in the World Wide Web to take advantage of the internet's power and reach, to cope with the accelerating pace of change of business environment. The famous quote by Bill Gates that banking is vital to a healthy economy, but banks themselves are not, highlights the crucial nature of the electronic forces that are affecting banks more than any other financial service provider group. This transition of business operations by banks have crated new mode of operation called E-Banking.

E-banking is the banking of new era. The term Internet Banking or E-Banking Internet both are used as supplement. Making banking products and other services available to wholesale and retail customers, through an electronic distribution channel is called e-banking. In other words E-Banking refers to the banking operations, which is done over World Wide Web. E-banking is the outcome of technological innovations and

Citation: Ruby Shukla, Pankaj Shukla, 2011. E-banking: problems and prospects, international journal of management and business studies, ISSN : 2330-9519.

competition. In fact, banks have been using electronic and telecommunication networks for delivering a wide range of value added products and services. The devices have been telephone, personal computers including Automated Teller Machines (ATM). The delivery channels have been direct dial up connections, private and public networks. To this newer edition of e-banking are being added e.g. Internet banking and mobile banking. The use of ATM's lead to the concept of 'anywhere' and 'anytime' banking. Through the use of ATM cards, one can operate his bank account to withdraw money from any of bank's ATM installed or available at the nearest site. This had broken down the time and space barriers. The new banks are providing some of the services exclusively through ATM's.

The growing popularity of personal computers, easy access to internet and world wide web (WWW), has increased the use of internet by banks as a channel for receiving instructions and also delivering their pros\ducts and services to the customers,. This is generally referred to as 'Internet banking' or I-banking or Net Banking. This is one of the newer forms e-banking which is gaining popularity. The other popular name for e-banking is on line banking.

A. Indian Scene: internet banking has gained wide acceptance internationally. In India also the things are changing fast. India is on the threshold of a major banking revolution with the introduction of 'Net-banking'. In year 2002, only a dozen or so banks are providing services at different levels. However, almost double those numbers are ready to make entry. Others may be compelled to follow.

B. Future Scene in India: The Indian banks lag far behind the international banks in providing online banking. In fact, this is not possible without creating sufficient infrastructure or presence of sufficient number of users. The experience of ICICI Bank Ltd. and HDFC Bank Ltd. shows that the number of transactions carried out on the Net are very limited.

No matter where online banking comes from or where it is today, it is most certainly here to stay. As a tool of modern living and as a lifestyle aid, it is absolutely indispensable. The fact is that many services that are now being offered with online banking are almost impossible to avail of in regular banking. This holds even truer for developments that the future of online banking will bring.

Judging by its current popularity and rate of implementation, online banking will increase in scope and user base in the future. Individuals and businesses that have refused to adopt it as a commercial tool before now will not really be left with much choice. As things stand now, using conventional methods of business inquiry, confirmation, order-placement and bill payment is retrograde at best. The speed (and reduced manpower) with which the same activities can be done online leaves the traditional methods completely in the shade.

The same holds true for normal vs. online business-related banking. In a domestic setting, too, shopping has been and will continue to be revolutionized by the Internet option.

Payments for goods bought online will almost always be done via a bank-related credit card or direct deduction from a bank account. However, traditional biases against online banking are not going to be overcome entirely by hard facts and figures in its favor. The rate at which this sector of banking will grow will depend on how many user-friendly facilities are incorporated the additional facilities that will be added and the way the concept is packaged for the general public. It is unfortunately a fact that banks and their customers have rarely agreed on what is a useful facility and what isn't. A lot of market research and customer polling will be required before the gap between what is needed in banking and what is available is filled. When that finally happens, the final frontier of online banking will indeed be explored.

STEPS FOR POPULARIZING E-BANKING

Department of telecommunication is making additional bandwidth available. Steps have been initiated to appoint Certification Authority. As Chief Vigilance Commissioner is insisting on more computerization and Credit Information Bureau is proposed to be set up, this will help I-banking. The payment gateways being created by ICICI bank and HDFC bank will give boost to I-banking. The RBI has set up a group to examine various issues regarding I-banking and technology. This will help in creating the right kind of infrastructure.

Internet Banking in India – Guidelines

Reserve Bank of India had set up a 'Working Group on Internet Banking' to examine different aspects of Internet Banking (I-banking). The Group had focused on three major areas of I-banking, i.e, (i) technology and security issues, (ii) legal issues and (iii) regulatory and supervisory issues. RBI has accepted the recommendations of the Group to be implemented in a phased manner. Accordingly, the following guidelines are issued for implementation by banks. Banks are also advised that they may be guided by the original report, for a detailed guidance on different issues.

TECHNOLOGY AND SECURITY STANDARDS

Banks should designate a network and database administrator with clearly defined roles as indicated in the Group's report. Banks should have a security policy duly approved by the Board of Directors. There should be a segregation of duty of Security Officer / Group dealing exclusively with information systems security and Information Technology Division which actually implements the computer systems. Further, Information Systems Auditor will audit the information systems. Banks should introduce logical access controls to data, systems, application software, utilities, telecommunication lines, libraries, system software, etc. Logical access control techniques may include user-ids, passwords, smart cards or other biometric technologies. At the minimum, banks should use the proxy server type of firewall so that there is no direct connection between the Internet and the bank's system. It facilitates a high level of control and in-depth monitoring using logging and auditing tools. For sensitive systems, a stateful inspection firewall is recommended which thoroughly inspects all packets of information, and past and present transactions are compared. These generally include a real time security alert. All the systems supporting dial up services through modem on the same LAN as the application server should be isolated to prevent intrusions into the network as this may bypass the proxy server. It is also recommended that all unnecessary services on the application server such as FTP (File Transfer Protocol), telnet should be disabled. The application server should be isolated from the e-mail server. Physical access controls should be strictly enforced. Physical security should cover all the information systems and sites where they are housed, both against internal and external threats. Banks should have proper infrastructure and schedules for backing up data. The backed-up data should be periodically tested to ensure recovery without loss of transactions in a time frame as given out in the bank's security policy. Business continuity should be ensured by setting up disaster recovery sites. These facilities should also be tested periodically.

LEGAL ISSUES

Considering the legal position prevalent, there is an obligation on the part of banks not only to establish the identity but also to make enquiries about integrity and reputation of the prospective customer. Therefore, even though request for opening account can be accepted over Internet, accounts should be opened only after proper introduction and physical verification of the identity of the customer.

From a legal perspective, security procedure adopted by banks for authenticating users need to be recognized by law as a substitute for signature. In India, the Information Technology Act, 2000, in Section 3(2) provides for a particular technology (viz., the asymmetric crypto system and hash function) as a means of authenticating electronic record. Any other method used by banks for authentication should be recognized as a source of legal risk.

In Internet banking scenario there is very little scope for the banks to act on stop-payment instructions from the customers. Hence, banks should clearly notify to the customers the timeframe and the circumstances in which any stop-payment instructions could be accepted.

REGULATORY AND SUPERVISORY ISSUES

As recommended by the Group, the existing regulatory framework over banks will be extended to Internet banking also. In this regard, it is advised that: Only such banks which are licensed and supervised in India and have a physical presence in India will be permitted to offer Internet banking products to residents of India. Thus, both banks and virtual banks incorporated outside the country and having no physical presence in India will not, for the present, be permitted to offer Internet banking services to Indian residents. The products should be restricted to account holders only and should not be offered in other jurisdictions. The services should only include local currency products. The 'in-out' scenario where customers in cross border jurisdictions are offered banking services by Indian banks (or branches of foreign banks in India) and the 'out-in' scenario where Indian residents are offered banking services by banks operating in cross-border jurisdictions are generally not permitted and this approach will apply to Internet banking also. The existing exceptions for limited purposes under FEMA i.e. where resident Indians have been permitted to continue to maintain their accounts with overseas banks etc., will, however, be permitted. Overseas branches of Indian banks will be permitted to offer Internet banking services to their overseas customers subject to their satisfying, in addition to the host supervisor, the home supervisor.

Risks

E-banking poses some different risks as compared to the traditional banking. These risks are more pronounced in the case of Internet banking. Firstly, the risk of technological changes has to be carefully watched. This is essential to update technologies and remain cost effective and customer friendly. The technologies are generally obtained from outside parties. The banks have to be careful about risks involved in such agreements. The security is an important area of risk. In fact it will be very crucial for the expansion of Net Banking. Another important area will emerge out of cross-border implications as 'Net Banking' breaks the geographical boundaries. Imposing regularity conditions on such transactions will be a difficult task.

Security Issues

While making online payments or transferring money from one account to another, the online bankers are always concerned about the hackers and anti-social elements. Hacking enables the unethical hackers to penetrate the accounts of online bankers, and spend their money. Availability of confidential information which is just secured by a user name and password makes it vulnerable to such threats. Most of the banks try to make their sites secured by implementing latest network security software. However, there have been plenty of cases in which web surfers were accidentally exposed to the financial details of online bankers. Internet security had a setback when in 2004, Morgan Stanley admitted a serious security flaw in the system of the latest online banking operation. This flaw allowed customers to access account details of other clients.

Necessity of the Internet

For availing the benefits of online banking one should have access to the Internet. For this purpose, he should own a desktop, laptop or PDA device, and an Internet connection. This reason limits the usage of online banking, as sometimes it's almost impossible to have an Internet connection, to serve the purpose. One might also face problems if the Internet connectivity breaks down during an ongoing transaction, or if someone eavesdrop his user name and password, while accessingitinacybercafe.

Customer Care Services

While carrying out online transactions there are many instances when the banker might need help of a representative, from the bank. The brick and mortar banks have customer care representatives who are easier to talk to, but in case of online banking, in which the banks provide customer care numbers, the bankers find it difficult to get their problems solved. Sometimes there is a congestion in the network and they have to wait for some time, in order to talk to the bank's representative at the other end. Once the line is put through, one may either get somebody helpful and knowled geable or may not, leaving him in a baffled and confused situation. Although online banking involves risk and imposes certain problems, there are many facilities provided by it. To avail these benefits, it is important for one to educate himself about the risks, and the steps he can take to protect his financial information. It is also necessary to understand the rights and responsibilities as an online banking consumer, in order to make a difference to one's own financial well-being.

Technical difficulties

Sometimes online banking Websites go down. When this happens, there's no backup branch that you can go to – and the phone lines will be clogged. To protect yourself, always keep a local bank or credit union account open with some emergency cash so you won't be penniless while they fix the problem.

Security Precautions

Customers should never share personal information like PIN numbers, passwords etc with anyone, including employees of the bank. It is important that documents that contain confidential information are safeguarded. PIN or password mailers should not be stored, the PIN and/or passwords should be changed immediately andmemorizedbeforedestroyingthemailers. Customers are advised not to provide sensitive account-related information over unsecured e-mails or over the phone. Take simple precautions like changing the ATM PIN and online login and transaction passwords on a regular basis. Also ensure that the logged in session is properly signed out.

CONCLUSION

E-banking offers a higher level of convenience for managing one's finances even from one's bedroom. However, it continues to present challenges to the financial security and personal privacy. Many people have had their account details compromised, as a result of online banking. Thus, if one is going to use it for financial transactions, he should be aware of the risks involved. Awareness of the risks and problems enables him to take precautions for a more secured online banking experience.

8

CHAPTER

FACTORS AFFECTING THE ADOPTION OF INTERNET BANKING AND THE CONTINUANCE USE: AN EXTENSION OF THE TECHNOLOGY ACCEPTANCE MODEL

Arian Eshraghi

INTRODUCTION

Information technology (IT) plays an important role in the lives of people around the world. Many activities are carried out electronically with the help of IT in the workplace and home, including the use of email, e-commerce, and e-government. The internet encompasses a considerable part of the everyday lives of people in both developing and developed countries; banking services and their response methods have experienced a revolution with the use of the internet.

The banking industry has invested a significantly in the use of IT. The banking and finance sector has done much to encourage customers to use electronic banking. The needs of customers have changed over the past three decades. In the past, if people needed money or to carry out other banking activities, they would go to a bank during working hours on the weekdays and queue for their turn with a bank teller. Automatic teller machines (ATM) were put into use in the late 1970's worldwide. This trend continued with the emergence of telephone banking and computer banking

The widespread use of online banking expanded with the development of the internet. Increased use of the internet and electronic commerce has prompted banks to encourage customers to use online banking services .The rapid growth in the amount and number of transactions of e-commerce in the late 1990s increased the use of electronic banking for commercial transactions.

Electronic banking created new ways to carry out e-commerce and increased the use of electronic shopping. By creating new substrate and providing the ability to trade outside of office hours, e-banking provided a new opportunity for commercial organizations.

Citation: Arian Eshraghi, (2016), Factors Affecting the Adoption of Internet Banking and the Continuance Use: An Extension of the Technology Acceptance Model.Journal of Internet Banking and Commerce.

Electronic banking is the use of electronic devices such as ATMs, bank machines, internet banking, and telephone banking to directly send funds and perform other financial activities from one account to another account instead of using checks and cash. Electronic banking represents a connection between personal computer users and a bank's internal networks. Electronic banking is synonymous with online banking and allows the use of banking services through internet browsers from a distance.

Electronic banking can be considered a responsive self-service channel which enables the customers to easily access to their financial and monetary activities at any time and place. Self-service electronic banking reduces costs for both banking services and the bank itself by creating virtual responsiveness and services. Today, customers in North and South America, Europe and Australia carry out more transactions via personal computers, tablets, and smartphones than in Asian countries.

Although electronic banking provides benefits such as comfortable 24-hour use of banking services at no cost, a large number of customers are hesitant to use electronic banking. The technology must become more accepted to encourage consumers to use electronic banking. Acceptance of technology is difficult because it requires detailed understanding of consumer behavior. Internet technology generally and internet banking services create challenges to learn the technology that combine with economic problems for customers in some countries, especially developing countries. Identifying customer attitudes towards the selection of e-banking is important to encourage them to use it.

Researchers believe that attitude has a strong, direct, and positive impact on customer feelings about their intention to use the technology. Despite the extensive research in developed countries, little research has been conducted on encouraging customers to use e-banking in developing countries. Understanding the reasons for customer resistance of technology and electronic banking can provide useful information for bank managers so that they can find ways of increasing its use. The current study provides a model for identifying customer attitudes and behavior towards electronic banking and ways of acceptably increasing its use.

LITERATURE REVIEW

Research on electronic banking can be divided into three categories: descriptive and relational articles and comparative articles. A series of studies have identified the characteristics and attitudes of those adopting electronic banking and the barriers to and attractive features of adoption. Sathye initially investigated the adoption of electronic banking and showed that security concerns, lack of awareness about electronic banking, and unreasonable costs were important factors deterring the adoption of electronic banking by Australian customers. Howcroft considered important factors such as low cost, recommendations by friends, 24-hour availability, time productivity, good quality of service, and coverage in the public media as important factors that encouraged the use of e-banking. Liao cited important factors including accuracy, speed of transaction, user experience, user involvement, and convenience.

Akinci cited reliability of the bank and privacy as important features. Hanifzadeh believed that the factors influencing adoption of e-banking are the same in different cultures. For example, Laforet studied Chinese customers and listed factors such as perception of risk, technology, and skills as very important; however, they observed that the Chinese tradition of carrying cash was the main barrier. Gerrard used data from an open questionnaire to determine the reasons for the lack of desire for electronic banking using content analysis. Their investigations identified eight factors that hinder the adoption of electronic banking: risk, lack of understanding of the need, lack of awareness of the services, inertia, lack of availability, lack of sensing, pricing concerns, and weakness in the technology.

Laukkanen examined the reluctance of Finnish customers to use e-banking and identified four groups: those without resistance, those who expressed functional resistance, those who had mental resistance, and those who showed dual resistance. Speece showed that the benefits and drawbacks of e-banking are similar among ordinary customers of big companies. In particular, they found that factors affecting the desire to adopt electronic banking in big companies consisted of information quality, availability of information, information sharing, and benefits of lower trading cost. Major obstacles to adoption of electronic banking were drawbacks in reliability, legal support, and organizational barriers.

Hanifzadeh examined relational studies investigating the various factors affect the adoption and use of electronic banking. The main difference between these studies with descriptive studies was their attempt to explain and predict adoption of electronic banking using existing models.

The dominant theories originated from psychology. Some of the most important are:

- Theory of reasoned action (TRA)
- Theory of planned behavior (TPB)
- Social cognitive theory (SCT)
- Self-trust theory (STT)
- Perceived risk theory (PRT)

Two initial theories (TRA and TPB) assume that a person's adoption behavior originates from his/her intentional behavior as a function of individual attitude and the influence of external factors such as community standards. SCT provides a framework with which to understand, predict, and change behavior. This theory identifies personal behavior as the interaction of personal, behavioral, and biological factors. The interaction between personal and behavioral factors affects an individual's mentality and reaction. The interaction between personal and biological factors is reflected in his/her beliefs and knowledge. STT and PRT represent the views that impair the adoption of electronic banking. STT cites a failure in commitment that causes loss of confidence. PRT finds that adopters of new technology should measure the benefits obtained against the potential risks resulting from its use. These risks are mainly related to the psychosocial nature of the adoption of e-banking. Many theories have promoted past theories and adapted them for e-banking.

The most important of these are:

- Innovation diffusion theory (IDT) .
- Technology acceptance model (TAM) .
- Decomposition theory of planned behavior (DTPB) .
- Developed technology acceptance models (TAM2) .
- Unified theory of acceptance and use of technology (UTAUT) .

IDT considers electronic banking as a social structure and is one of the first theories used to examine the adoption and encouragement of electronic banking. Liao tested IDT for adoption and encouragement of electronic banking in Hong Kong and showed that individual attitudes toward technology and perceived behavioral control are the most important predictive factors for the intention of individuals. Recent studies on IDT combined the model with other attitudes

TAM is a simple interpretation of technology acceptance beliefs in which a series of external factors have a strong effect on the usefulness and perceived ease of use. The theoretical basis understands the usefulness and the perceived ease of use. Understanding the perceived ease of use is related to the personal perception that there is no need to exert physical and mental effort to use computers because they are very easy to use. Perceived usefulness is related to personal perceptions about the results of using a specific technology to enhance the performance of people.

TAM was initially used by Bhattacherjee to encourage electronic banking. His research examined the role of TAM in the use of technology. Important research about the impact of TAM on acceptance of new banking systems were carried out by Suh in South Korea and Vatanasombut , who combined the CTA and TAM. TAM2 and DTPB theories were developed with the help of Hernandez and Chirani. Hernandez and Mazzon investigated Brazilian banks. Chirani researched customers in Gilan province of Iran and strengthened the link between the importance of the compatibility of the banking system and the individual characteristics of the users.

UTAUT has been the focus of recent attention by researchers in this field. One of the best examples is from Yuan on customers of banks in America, Australia, and Malaysia. Comparative studies from the perspective of Hanifzadeh have examined encouragement of customers to use e-banking by assessing and comparing key factors influencing acceptance. These studies take into consideration personal differences for demographic characteristics such as age, culture, society, and economics.

The newest and most efficient papers in this field were written by Sayar .They investigated factors influencing an increase in customer use of electronic banking in Turkey and UAE. Mirza compared factors encouraging customers of public and private banks in Iran and demonstrated that private banks have been more successful in this area. Dimitriadis studied electronic banking and telephone banks and showed that the effect of trust on the acceptance and encouragement for use of this technology is greater than for other indices. Rouibah compared the TAM, TPB, and TRA models for adoption of technology and found that TPB was more powerful for describing the increase in willingness to use electronic banking. These results were not decisive.

Yousafzai combined the three models and conducted experimental studies to show the effect of TAM model was greatest.

Research Model and Hypotheses

The TAM model was used as a framework for the conceptual model. This model is a simple interpretation of technology acceptance beliefs in which a series of external factors can have a strong effect on the usefulness and perceived ease of use. The theoretical basis of this model is its perceived usefulness and ease of use. Perceived ease of use relates to an individual's perception that there is no physical or mental effort required for the use of the computer system, which is actually very easy to use.

Perceived usefulness relates to an individual's perception of the results of using a specific technology to enhance performance. Initial research has focused on the factors effecting customer decisions and has considered the acceptance of e-banking as adoption of innovative technology. The conceptual model can be understood by studying the research of Nikghadam

CONCEPTUAL MODEL

Understanding Security

As for all software, customers are concerned about the risk of leakage of private information such as social security numbers, account numbers, and account information. Customers are concerned about exposure and identification of private transactions; thus, understanding the security and confidentiality of information is important and is an influential factor in adoption of electronic banking. Researchers believe that security and confidentiality are the most important factors in adoption of e-banking. Understanding security is more significant for the individual service market than the product market.

Previous studies have examined the issue of understanding security measures. Eight factors were used to ascertain this:

1. Importance of username and password security;
2. Clear and safe guidelines and procedures;
3. Security of electronic transactions;
4. Bank compensation policy for damages;
5. Reliability of the bank;
6. Ethical and professional behavior;
7. Provision of a menu for solving problems on the web site for e-banking;
8. Reliability of bank when modifying the wrong deals.

Perceived Risk

Peter used perceived risk to describe consumer behavior. Lim defined perceived risk as a factor which effected consumer decision-making. Perceived risk is defined as the possibility of loss while pursuing profit. Lee suggested six types of perceived risk. The major components are financial, performance, social, physical, privacy, and time lost. Lee believed that online banking poses no danger to humans and requires no measures to protect against physical risk.

Perceived ease of use

Davis explained perceived ease of use as the level at which people believe that use of a system will be free from effort. Whichever system is easiest to use is more easily accepted. The TAM model explains perceived ease of use in information systems as being different from IBSs. The new model is based on the TAM model and focuses on adoption of IBSs. Tsai inferred that if an IBS conforms to existing knowledge, it is perceived as easy to use. Research about this factor includes Straub, Taylor, Szajna, and Mathieson. The following factors were considered for perceived ease of use:

1. User-friendly site;
2. Easily carried-out electronic transactions;
3. The desire to adopt the technology;
4. Ease of accessible at anytime and anywhere;
5. A setup fee and annual fee;

Perceived usefulness

Davis used perceived usefulness (PU) in the TAM model. Seddon defined this as the degree with which people believe that using a specific system will enhance job performance. People show interest in a technology that is beneficial for performing a particular task. PU is an important factor for the TAM model that effects the attitude toward acceptance of IS. Yousuf examined the relationship between PU and IS in an e-library and Suki did so in a 3G mobile network. All of these showed a direct relationship on between PU and IS.

Demographics

Factors such as age, gender, occupation, and education level are demographic characteristics. Demographics play an important role in the adoption mode. Hojjati said demographic factors such as previous banking experience, previous computer experience, and previous mobile experience also have important effects on adoption of internet banking. Akinci said that age is an important factor for adoption of internet banking. They studied consumers in Turkey and showed that middle-aged consumers use IBSs more than younger and older consumers.

Gender is an important factor influencing usage of IBSs. Lichtenstin believed that male customers are more comfortable with IBSs than women. Another study about the important role of demographics was carried out by Stavins . He showed that geographic location affected adoption of IS. Gan found local residents of a region are more likely to adopt internet banking. Married, affluent, highly educated consumers are also likely users of IBSs. It can be concluded that demographics is a major index of adoption of internet banking.

Responsiveness

Responsiveness is the perception that the service provider will provide the information necessary for customers to carry out transactions at an appropriate speed and on time. Shaza defined quick responses to complaints and problems as responsiveness. Responsiveness originates from cognitive learning theory. It is evident that customers will more easily adopt IBSs when the service provider shows responsiveness and empathy for customer needs. Lichtenstein and Williamson believed that support and responsiveness is needed to achieve trust from a customer. They also believed that support is needed for initial registration and set-up, followed by responsiveness to ongoing concerns. It can be concluded that responsiveness is a major index of the adoption internet banking.

Internet experience

IBSs are carried out in an internet environment; if an individual is familiar and experienced with working with the internet, he/she will more easily accept IBSs. The TAM model states that perceived ease of use influences the attitude toward system usage. An individual with internet experience will perceive IBSs as easy to use; this relates to perceived ease of use on TAM model. Nikghadam cited factors such as extent of internet use, internet use at the workplace, experience with e-finance, and experience with online purchases for internet experience.

Training

Training is another factor in adoption of IBSs. Research shows that for individual perception of IS and IBSs, acceptance increases with appropriate training from the bank. Research done by Ansar Bank in Iran showed that 70% of customers cited lack of proper training was a reason not to use IBSs. To work with IBSs, it is necessary to understand what practitioners need. Venkatesh believed banks should provide computer training programs to the consumer. He also asserted that training has a direct effect on self-efficacy. Torkzadeh, Barbeite and Hasan suggested that training programs enhance customer perceived ease of use and usefulness. It can be concluded that training is a major index of adoption of internet banking.

Advertising

Effect of advertising was introduced by White. Ennew believed that factors such as transparency, honesty of brand, brand reputation, and interaction with dissatisfied customers are important impetus factors in e-advertising of the banking industry. Seni emphasized word-of-mouth advertising and defined this as a context that transmitted positive things about IBSs to other people. Marketers said advertising is a powerful instrument, especially from a familiar person. In research on bank branch managers, 58% believed that most customers who do not use IBSs, have no knowledge about it, and are not aware of its features. Serni believes that the effect of loyalty on advertising effects attitudes toward adoption of internet banking. It can be concluded that advertising is a major index of adoption of internet banking.

User satisfaction

Perceived risk, perceived usefulness, perceived security, perceived ease of use, demographics, responsiveness, internet experience, training, and advertising can change attitudes toward acceptance of internet banking. These factors improve the attitude of the customer toward the use of IBSs. After using IBSs, customers are either satisfied or dissatisfied. This feeling is very important and will cause new attitudes toward IB. Customer satisfaction is a major consequence of qualit. Researchers suggest user satisfaction is important to encouraging customers to continue use of IBSs .

User satisfaction increases when the customer interacts with the system in the bank without error and conveniently. If bank service is a good fit for the customer and performs well for the customer, it will increase a sense of satisfaction. If the system is perceived to be useful, it has a higher level of satisfaction for customers. Lee et al. believed that if the system is perceived as easy to use, it can increase the sense of satisfaction. Based on these arguments, user satisfaction can affect the attitude toward adoption of internet banking.

Continuous usage intention

Customers who feel a sense of satisfaction will decide to continue to use the internet. This is a business success factor. Research has shown a relationship between the intention for continuous usage and user satisfaction. It is evident that when customers are satisfied with the service, they will continue to use it. Studies on this subject include Eriksson, Benamat , Akhlaq, and Ling Yu. For example, Akhlaq show that there is relationship between trust and continuous usage. A customer develops trust when they feel a sense of satisfaction from IBSs and develop expectations of IBs. Tsai believed that customer loyalty can promote continued use of IBSs. They believed there is a relationship between continuous usage, PU, PEOU, and perceived compatibility.

Hypotheses

The following hypotheses were found using the research model:

H0: Perceived security and attitude have a positive relationship.

H1: Perceived risk and attitude have a positive relationship.

H2: Perceived ease of use and attitude has a positive relationship.

H3: Perceived usefulness and attitude have a positive relationship.

H4: Demographics factors and attitude have a positive relationship.

H5: Responsiveness and attitude have a positive relationship.

H6: Internet experience and attitude have a positive relationship.

H7: Training and attitude have a positive relationship.

H8: Advertising and attitude have a positive relationship.

H9: User satisfaction and attitude have a positive relationship.

H10: Attitude and Intention to use have a positive relationship.

H11: Continuous usage intention and user satisfaction have a positive relationship.

H12: Continuous usage intention and attitude have a positive relationship.

H13: User satisfaction and intention to use have a positive relationship.

RESEARCH METHOD

Data Collection

Field studies were used to verify the model. Information was collected from bank managers, clerks, and customers. Table 1 shows the number of interviews carried out in 25 branches of the bank. A total of 16 bank managers, 35 bank clerks, and 53 customers were interviewed.

Table 1: Bank details.

Number of bank's branches	Number of bank's manager	Number of clerk	Number of customer
25	16	35	53

Table 1: Bank details.

A proposal was prepared and presented to Ansar Bank for which the bank emailed the questionnaires to the respondents and allowed distribution of questionnaires at the bank branches. Ansar Bank is registered as a company and industrial property according to the rules of non-governmental banks and related regulations under registration # 374528 dated 29 May 2010. The banking operation license # 89/59204 was issued by the Central Bank of Iran on 10 June 2010. We chose Ansar bank because of its purpose in 5 years later. This bank will want growing in Online Banking. As a result, Ansar bank was welcome for our study. This bank has 800 branches across Iran, of which 33 branches were chosen. A total of 450 questionnaires were distributed, of which 370 were internet banking users. To encourage to participation, gifts were distributed to participants who completed the questionnaires. Table 2 shows the demographic profile of the sample.

Table 2: Demographic profile

Measure	Items	Freq	%
Number of user	Internet Banking User	270	82%
Gender	Male	261	58%
	Female	189	42%
Age	18~24	126	28%
	25~31	139	31%
	32~38	95	21%
	39~44	57	13%
	>44	31	7%
Education	High school	58	13%
	39~44	57	13%
	>44	31	7%
Education	High school	58	13%
	College/ university	297	66%
	Master	85	19%
	PhD	9	2%
Years using online banking	<1 year	140	31%
	1~3 year	175	39%
	3~5 year	90	20%
	> 5 year	45	10%

Measure

The questionnaire contained three parts. The first part used a five-point Likert scale and parts 2 and 3 used nominal scales. Part one ranged from disagree strongly to agree strongly and addressed perceived security, perceived risk, perceived ease of use, percei ved usefulness, attitude, intention to use, responsiveness, training, and satisfaction. Part 2 addressed internet experience, perceived ease of use, advertising, intention to use, and intention to continue usage. Part 3 addressed demographics.

Perceived security was adapted from criteria determined by Ming-Chi Lee, Chengcand Featherman . Perceived risk was adapted from criteria determined by Featherman, Littler, and Ming-Chi Lee. Perceived ease of use and attitude were adapted from criteria determined by Ming-Chi Leeand Cheng. Perceived usefulness was adapted from criteria determined by Ming-Chi Lee.

Intention to use was adapted from criteria determined by Tsai and Ming-Chi Lee Responsiveness was adapted from criteria determined by Patsiotis. User satisfaction was adapted from criteria determined by Zhou and Oliver.

Part 2 used nominal scales. Internet experience was adapted from criteria determined by Karjaluoto and Nikghadam . Perceived ease of use was adapted from criteria determined by Nikghadam and Lee. Type of internet connection was used as an indicator of perceived ease of use addressed in this part. Advertising experience, intention to use and intention to continue usage were adapted from criteria determined by Nikghadam. Before distributing the questionnaires, they were emailed to university faculty members for their comments and were revised based on the results.

CONCLUSION

The current study developed a model for usage of online banking services that was based on models of previous studies. The study combined various opinions about IB. Ansar Bank in Iran was selected as the focus of the study. Questionnaires were distributed and showed that users of IBSs were effected by different factors to continue using IBSs. The study successfully integrated the TAM model to obtain a new model for adoption of online banking. Advertising and training were introduced as new factors affecting adoption of IBSs. The current study focused on online banking, but future research could study a subset of online banking, such as mobile banking. The study examined the attitudes of Iranian customers, but this could be generalized to other Middle Eastern countries.

FUTURE RESEARCH

Although we studied this study in Iran, we can focus on adoption IB in Middle East or Asia. Even, future studies can extend this by examining the difference in the relationship between trusting beliefs, trustworthiness, and trust in internet banking across different countries reflecting distinct cultural orientations.

9
CHAPTER

MOBILE BANKING ADOPTION

Manoranjan D, Snigdha S and Bhusan PB

Keywords: Technology acceptance model (TAM), Assertive, Aggressive, Passive

INTRODUCTION

Over time, definition of bank as an organization taking deposits, lending and helping customers in managing risk has been changed due to time pressure and competition in global banking which has created multifaceted group comprising of diverse products and services operating across various business lines. The supreme modernization in banking that has occurred due to the payment system which has taken momentum in the developed world and also well accepted in the budding market. The rapid penetration of mobile devices in the cashless society has significant effects on every day activities of people. Disruptive technology in context to mobile technology, provided dynamics in delivering health services which has changed the societal value and communication eco system. New horizons of life have been integrated to societal well beings. The possession of cell phone by users is more than PCs in India. The bankers are trying to take advantage of these devices for distributing their banking and financial services.

In the present banking scenario in India, mobile banking registration is increasing 50% more than the Internet banking as per the data revealed by different private and public sector banks in India. In comparisons to the internet transaction over mobile transactions if growth of mobile banking sustain over a period of time it will cross internet transaction. Banks are providing location based offers for customers for getting notification through their iWatch and are adding tag feature to introduce the concept of 'tap and pay' without customer having to reach for his wallet. Mobile banking is an approach for providing financial services through ICT. Mobile phones offer the

Citation: Manoranjan D, Snigdha S, Bhusan PB (2016) Mobile Banking Adoption. J Internet Bank Commer 21:153.

advantage of using financial services 24/7 at any place. It creates a stronger relationship between banks and customers. Physicians are providing mobile health services to patients, so that their work may be better supported, and obtain useful information and guidance to manage their health services better.

Despite the potential benefits of mobile healthcare services, physicians have inevitably encountered numerous difficulties and challenges in transacting their financial transaction through mobile devices. The omnipresence and multifunctional core of these devices along with their features allows mobile users to add different applications to their mobile devices and customize them based on preferences as well as use them to address their needs. Therefore, factors that influence the adoption of mobile banking services by physicians must be investigated. The objective of this study is to analyze the behavior style of physicians on the attitude towards the adoption of mobile banking. In the research we tried to integrate behavioral variables with TAM Model.

MOBILE BANKING IN INDIA

As research report, by 2018, 130 million markets will be created by Smart Wearable devices, and these will provide massive opportunities to cash on by the Banks in delivering their banking transactions. Banks in the future will be using smart watches and Google glass to create a niche market for mobile banking. Internationally mobile banking situation is favourable as evident from user adoption statistics across all different regions.

In Australia,5 million mobile banking customers in 2013 Banks reported that 60% of transactions were done using NFC contactless payments in 2013, In Europe, 38% of the European mobile consumers have adopted mobile banking Stable adoption rate 56% of the mobile banking users are from Turkey and 38% from the UK. In, Asia, China and India record the highest banking app users at 73% and 59% respectively 19% banking app users in Japan indicates relatively slow adoption of mobile banking. Chinese mobile transaction value was around US$360 billion.

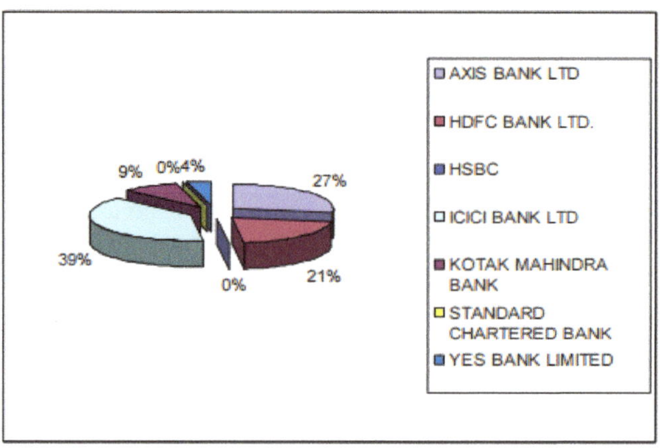

Figure 1: Top private sector bank wise mobile banking transactions for the month of October 2015 in India.

Among private sector banks the leading top players are ICICI Bank Ltd, Axis Bank followed by HDFC Bank Ltd in mobile banking transaction in volume (actual to value in Rs.'000) (Figure 1,2) (Table 1,2).

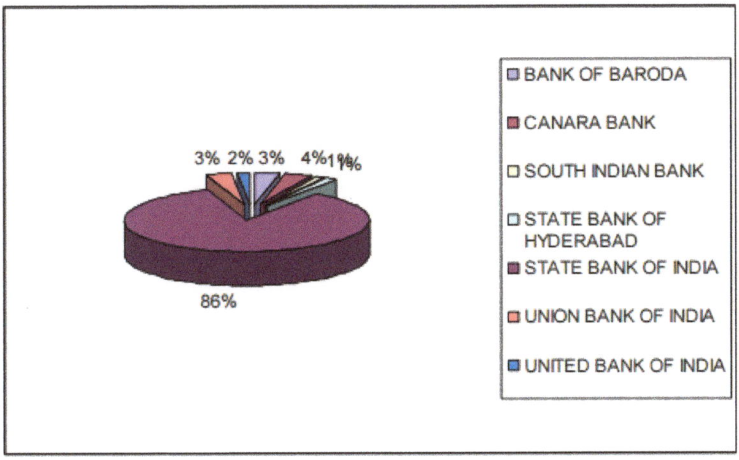

Figure 2: Public sector bank wise mobile banking transactions for the month of October 2015 in India.

Table 1: Top private sector bank wise mobile banking transactions for the month of October 2015 in India

Bank Name	Volume (Actual)	Value(in Rs'000)
AXIS BANK LTD	4429296	55277546
HDFC BANK LTD.	3361701	77664825
HSBC	8846	350570
ICICI BANK LTD	6314628	85730160
KOTAK MAHINDRA BANK	1508124	20670932
STANDARD CHARTERED BANK	104	13160
YES BANK LIMITED	609960	3093137

Among public sector banks the leading top players are SBI, Canara Bank followed by Union Bank of India in mobile banking transaction in volume (actual to value in Rs.'000).

In comparison to Sep-2015 the volume (actual to Value (in Rs.000) has been increased month wise which indicates there is trend towards conduction banking transaction through mobile month by month (Table 3,4).

Web transaction and mobile transaction seems to be comparable which can surpass the internet transactions in future ahead. The growth of the usage of mobile forces the banks to deliver their financial services though these devices with the changes of dynamism of customer expectation in conduction banking services.

Table 2: Public sector bank wise mobile banking transactions for the month of October 2015

Bank Name	Volume (Actual)	Value(in Rs'000)
BANK OF BARODA	443961	1784848
CANARA BANK	516101	3103862
SOUTH INDIAN BANK	153739	387558
STATE BANK OF HYDERABAD	195151	69977
STATE BANK OF INDIA	11872596	39998538
UNION BANK OF INDIA	466532	2947132
UNITED BANK OF INDIA	212889	242465

Table 3: Bank wise mobile banking transactions for the month of September 2015

Sr. No.	Bank	Volume (Actual)	Value(in Rs'000)
	Total	27105418	269602075.89
Total (Volume in million, Value in billion)		27.11	269.60

Table 4: Bank wise mobile banking transactions for the month of October 2015.

Sr. No.	Bank	Volume (Actual)	Value (in Rs'000)
	Total	32484266	305677166.39
Total (Volume in million, Value in billion)		32.48	305.68

LITERATURE REVIEW

TAM (Technology Acceptance Model) traces its root from TRA (Theory of Reasoned Action) to psychology to information system (IS) and is widely used for studying the use and acceptance of technology. As specified by Davis [1] the TAM model PEOU a PU is the key variables for the determinant for the behavioral intention to use the technology as argued by the model and has strong control on attitude. The TAM model have been enriched by IDT (Innovation Diffusion Theory) by different researchers. Different research conducted in different countries in context to adoption of mobile banking applied Diffusion of Innovation (DOI) Model, Theory of Planned Behaviour (TPB), Technology Acceptance Model (TAM) model constructs. Lee and Mattila discussed the importance of perceived risk on adoption behavior and has found Jacoby and Kaplan's six risk dimensions applicable to adoption behavior in the Mobile banking context.

Behavioral intention is the main determinant of one's actual behaviour which is determined by attitude [2]. Legris critically examined the external variables and found they are the drivers of technology. Many researchers have explored the effect of external variables on technology usage as well as relationship between individual differences and acceptance of technology. Mattila found adopters of mobile banking relatively young and majority of them belong to 25-34 years and non-adopters display different socio-demographic characteristics. TAM uses perceived usefulness and perceived ease-ofuse as key determinants to explain users' acceptance of IT [3]. Adopters are willing to use mobile banking when they perceive it to be useful and helpful for the efficiency of their work. So PEOU, PU constructs have a direct effect on behavioral intention. Adams [4], Agarwal [5], Venkatesh [6] and Venkatesh [7] found a significant relationship between individual differences and technology acceptance. Lee found that innovative attributes are related to consumers' attitudes toward adoption. Mattila [8] pointed out availability of mobile services as an important factor in the adoption of mobile banking. Nor [9] found risk, trust, social norms, perceived usefulness, attitude, self-efficacy and perceived ease of use are the key determinants in adoption of Internet banking.

According to TRA, an individual's behavioral intention, which results in actual behavior, is influenced by his/her subject norm and attitude, and the attitude is influenced by individual beliefs [10]. However, despite the growing interest in the field of mobile banking, there has been limited empirical literature that explored the customers' attitudes and intentions toward mobile banking in context to the behavioral style with attitude formation. PEOU refers to the degree to which a person believes that using a particular system would be free of effort. Malhotra, Gefen and Matheison argued in their study PEOU is one of the main variables influencing other variables on adoption of technology Agarwal and Prasad [5], Davis [3] provided evidence of PEOU having a significant effect on behavioral intention for adoption of technology.

PU is defined as the degree to which a person believes that using a particular technology will enhance his performance. Araujo, Noteberg, Gefen, Matheison and Malhotra considered PU as an important variable in TAM. Perceived Usefulness has been confirmed as an important variable that influences user technology acceptance and therefore has received a great deal of attention from prior researchers. Davis [11] defined perceived usefulness as the individual's perception that using the new technology will enhance or improve her/ his performance. Chau [12] in the study on understanding physician's usage of telemedicine adoption used the TAM model which explained the telemedicine adoption.

Perceived usefulness was found to be the most significant determinant of Behavioral intention to use and Attitude in the model. Mathwick defined perceived usefulness as the extent to which a person deems a particular system to boost his or her job performance. Agarwal [13], Davis [3], Venkatesh [14,15]. TAM suggests that attitude is based on the salient beliefs which a person has about the consequences of a given behavior and his or her evaluation of those consequences. Understanding the determinants of consumer's attitude, it is argued that this attitude has a strong, direct, and positive effect on customers.

Assertive behavior is usually honest, direct, expressive, spontaneous, and self-enhancing. Assertive persons make their own choices, are confident, and feel good about themselves while being assertive and afterward. They usually achieve their goals; when they don't, they still feel good about themselves because they know they have been straightforward. Assertive behaviors among the physicians uphold personal self-respect and cultivate health relationship with others.

Assertiveness describes having a positive attitude towards yourself, and others. It is about being honest, respecting yourself and with others. When you are self confident and your behavior is assertive, you are open to others and their views event though they may be different from your own. Your opinion, beliefs and feelings is important for you as well as for others. Assertive behaviour is all about, being honest, mutual equilibrium and benefit in a relation ship, getting more social responsibility, and showing respect to others.

Passive behavior: The person who behaves non-assertively in a situation does not assert his/her basic rights, instead he/she allows others to disobey upon them. Passive Behavior includes not expressing feelings, needs, and ideas; ignoring personal rights; and allowing others to disobey upon them.

Nonassertive behavior is usually emotionally dishonest, indirect, inhibited, and self-denying. Nonassertive persons often let other people choose for them and end up feeling disappointed in themselves and angry with them.

Aggressive behavior: The person who behaves aggressively in a situation asserts his/her basic rights at the expense of the other person's rights. He/she does not respect that other person has rights.

Negative attitude and passive behaviour

- Low self esteem and Lack of self confidence.
- Lack of self respect
- Negative feelings and thoughts about yourself
- Feelings of inferiority compared to others
- Like others to be in control of people and situations
- Demotivated

Negative attitude and aggressive behaviour

- Lack of self confidence and low self esteem
- Lack of respect towards others
- Put others down
- Feelings of superiority
- Don't listen to or ask questions

Positive attitude assertive behaviour

- Self confidence and high self esteem
- Respect for self and towards others
- Take responsibility for self

- Motivated to do a good job
- Interested in others' feelings and thoughts
- Ask questions
- Honest and direct
- Listen to others

RESEARCH MODEL

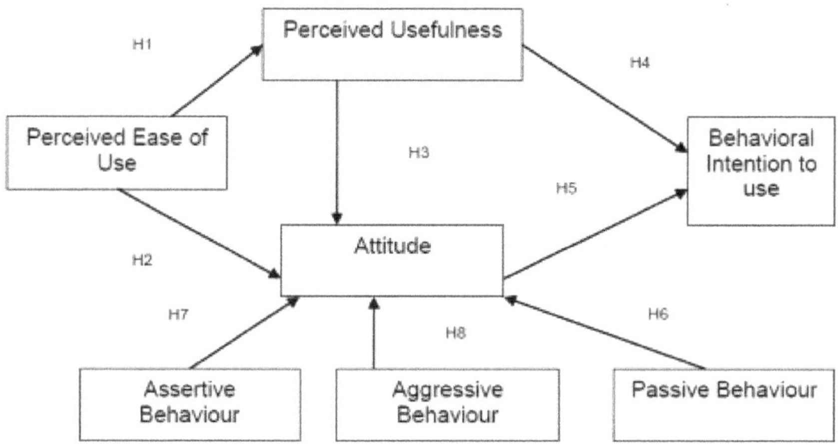

Figure 3: Proposed research model

The research model depicted below is an effort to consist of external variables to effect the attitude formation. The model is specifically to answer the following research question (Figure 3):

How TAM does related factors and different behavioral styles impact the attitude.

H1: Physician's Perceived Ease of Use has a positive significant impact on perceived usefulness of mobile banking.

H2: Physician's Perceived Ease of Use has a positive significant impact on attitude towards using mobile banking.

H3: Physician's Perceived Usefulness has a positive significant impact on attitude towards using mobile banking.

H4: Physician's Perceived Usefulness has a positive impact on behavioral intention towards using mobile banking.

H5: Physician's Attitude towards using Mobile banking has a significant impact on behavioral intention to use it.

H6: Physician's Passive behavior has a significant impact on attitude towards mobile banking.

H7: Physician's Assertive behavior has a significant impact on attitude towards mobile banking.

H8: Physician's Aggressive has a significant impact on attitude towards mobile banking.

METHODOLOGY

Sampling and data collection

This study was conducted in three private medical colleges and one public hospital consisting of health care professional's i.e., physicians, nurses and para medical staff located in the capital of Odisha, India. The survey was confined to the physicians and the data was collected from them. Systematic random sampling was used and had given a response rate of 41% from the potential sample of 700. Practically around 92% of the population of physicians are having a practical exposure to the smart phones and are very well conversed with the devices. 85% are familiar with the social media tools i.e., whatsapp and facebook and using different apps for their online shopping and payment. Averagely 65% on an average are familiar with the personal computers, 45% of them use their email daily i.e., confined to the physicians working in the private hospitals. Physicians confined to private hospital in teaching are using daily their personal computers for email and other search engine for searching their medical information. 10% of the physicians use their social media for communicating with the patients through mobile. Physicians were asked to rate their knowledge of using electronic health care system or telemedicine system or online consulting on a scale of from 0 to 5, none to expert. Mean value of 1.28 is obtained indicating physicians are having poor knowledge or very less exposure to the online consulting or remote health care system. Physician in private hospital have more exposure to the electronic health system than the physicians working in public hospitals. Demographically, majority of the respondents were male (73%) and female (27%) with a mean age of 49 years. The sampling frame was compared with other state in India which indicated representation of distribution of sex, age and specialization is well justified which indicates sample is a proper representation of the population.

Variables and measures

Five-point Likert scale from 1 = "Strongly Disagree" to 5 = "Strongly Agree" was used for measuring the items. Items used are adopted from sales validated by previous researchers in context to adoption of mobile banking in different countries, thus leading to the validation through content validity. TAM scale items were adopted from Davis [3], Chau [12] and Venkatesh [6]. Factor analysis using SPSS statistical software was used to test reliability and to test hypotheses. Cronbach's alpha values were used to test the reliability of the measurement scale adopted for the study. The reliability coefficients for all the predictors are above 7 [16]. Principal Component analysis was employed for the factor analysis. Factor loading of .5 are taken into consideration which are very significant in this study [16].

Result measurement model analysis

Hypotheses based on SEM were tested using PLS multivariate technique (partial least squares) approach. This evaluate both structural and measurement model. Smart PLS software with bootstrapping method was used to analyse the data. Average variance extracted was greater than .5. Structural model depict the causal relationship among the constructs, path coefficients and the R2 value. Path coefficients and R2 indicate how well the data support the hypothesized model. PLS (Partial Least Square is used to evaluate the model. It assesses reliability and validity by calculating the internal composite reliability (ICR) and the average variance extracted (AVE). ICR of 0.7 and above is taken into consideration and AVE greater than .50 is taken into consideration. In PLS model path coefficients represent standard beta values while R2 represent the amount the variance explained. A correlation analysis was conducted on all variables to explore the relationship between the variables. The bivariate correlation procedure was subject to two tailed tests of statistical significance at two different levels highly significant ($p < 0.01$) and significant ($p < 0.05$). The result of correlation analysis for all the variables is shown in (Table 5) (Figure 4).

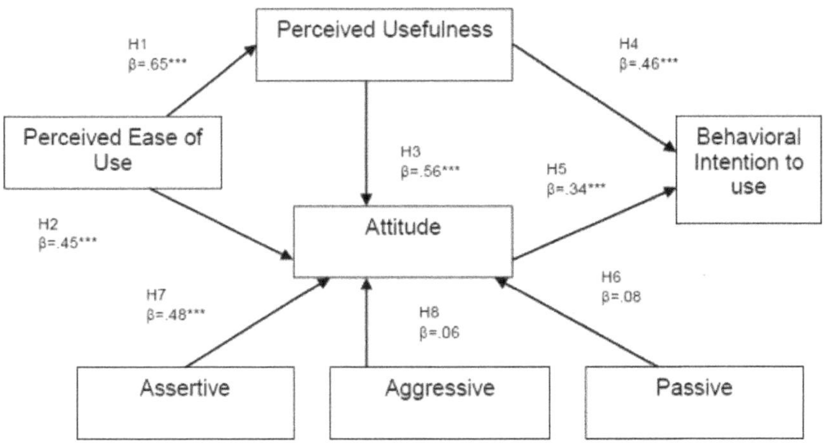

Figure 4: Research model results.

Table 5: Correlation matrix

		ATT	PU	PEOU	Assertive	Passive	Aggressive
ATT	Pearson Correlation	1					
	Sig. (2-tailed)	.					
	N	300	300				
PU	Pearson Correlation	0.718**	1				
	Sig. (2-tailed)	0.000	.				
	N	300	300				
PEOU	Pearson Correlation	0.749**	0.897**	1			
	Sig. (2-tailed)	0.000	0.000	.			
	N	300	300	300			
Assertive	Pearson Correlation	0.186	0.076	0.227*	1		
	Sig. (2-tailed)	0.153	0.192	0.029	.		
	N	300	300	300	300		
Passive	Pearson Correlation	0.198**	0.243**	0.420**	0.356**	1	
	Sig. (2-tailed)	0.001	0.000	0.000	0.000	.	
	N	300	300	300	300	300	
Aggressive	Pearson Correlation	0.699**	0.754**	0.759**	0.130*	0.184**	1
	Sig. (2-tailed)	0.000	0.000	0.000	0.026	0.002	.
	N	300	300	300	300	300	300

** Correlation is significant at the 0.01 level (2-tailed).

• Correlation is significant at the 0.05 level (2-tailed).

It examines the correlations among perceived usefulness, perceived ease of use, Attitude, Behavioral Intention to Use, Assertive, Aggressive and Passive.

Hypothesis -1 (Perceived Ease of Use (PEOU) → Perceived Usefulness (PU))

PEOU is found to be statistically significant with PU where $\beta = 0.65$, $p < 0.001$, R2 = 0.34. This suggests that Physicians, perceive mobile banking is easy to use will prove to be useful for them. The findings suggested that, sample of Physicians who have perceived in easy in using mobile banking perceive usefulness of mobile banking for conducting their banking transaction or payment.

Hypothesis -2 (Perceived Ease of Use (PEOU) → Attitude (ATT))

PEOU is found to be statistically significant with ATT where $\beta = 0.45$, $p < 0.001$, $R2 = 0.48$. This suggests Physicians attitude is significantly affected by the perceived ease of use of mobile banking. Another implication of this as physicians is familiar with the smart phone devices which also forms a positive attitude towards mobile banking.

Hypothesis -3 (Perceived Usefulness (PU) → Attitude (ATT))

PU is found to be statistically significant with ATT, where $\beta = 0.56$, $p < 0.001$, $R2 = 0.35$. Physicians derived their usefulness from mobile banking usage which is forming a positive attitude towards it.

Hypothesis -4 (Perceived Usefulness (PU) → Behavioral Intention to Use (BIU))

PU is found to be statistically significant with BIU, where $\beta = 0.46$, $p < 0.001$, $R2 = 0.65$. Usefulness of mobile banking is leading to the intention of using mobile banking in future. It can be viewed as more the usefulness of the users more will be the intention of using mobile banking.

Hypothesis -5 (Attitude (ATT) → Behavioral Intention to Use (BIU))

ATT significantly impact on the behavioral intention to use where $\beta = 0.34$, $p < 0.001$, $R2 = 0.45$. Physicians maintain a positive attitude towards mobile banking usage and also satisfied with ease of use and usefulness they derive from the mobile banking.

Hypothesis -6 (Passive Behaviour → Attitude (ATT))

Passive behaviour characteristics of physicians are not having a positive attitude towards use of mobile banking and this is not statistically significant as per the analysis results. Passive behaviour is not significant on attitude where $\beta = 0.08$, $p > 0.001$, $R2 = 0.55$. Aggressive behavior people having low self esteem, lack of self confidence, lack of self respect and negative feelings and thoughts are having a negative attitude formation towards mobile using mobile banking.

Hypothesis -7 (Assertive Behaviour → Attitude (ATT))

Assertive behaviour characteristics of physicians are having a positive attitude towards use of mobile banking and this is statistically significant as per the analysis results. Assertive behaviour is significant on attitude where $\beta = 0.48$, $p < 0.001$, $R2 = 0.65$. Aggressive behavior people having high self esteem, high self confidence, have high self respect and positive feelings and thoughts are having a positive attitude formation towards mobile using.

Hypothesis -8 (Aggressive Behaviour → Attitude (ATT))

Aggressive behaviour characteristics of physicians are having a negative attitude towards use of mobile banking and this is statistically not significant as per the analysis results. Passive behaviour is not significant on attitude where $\beta = 0.06$, $p > 0.001$, $R2 = 0.15$. Aggressive behavior people having lack of self confidence, lack of self respect and negative feelings and thoughts are having a negative attitude formation towards mobile using mobile banking.

DISCUSSION AND MANAGERIAL IMPLICATIONS

Banking will be using predictive behaviour model in minimizing the risk of delivering their financial services. The research contributes to the existing literature on mobile banking adoption among customers with special focus on physician's adoption. TAM model has power in explaining the technology acceptance by users. In one eye theoretical knowledge is enriched with practical contribution to the field of banking as well as health sector. It has tried to find out the factors in particular to behavior of customers. It has found how the behavioral characteristics are affecting the attitude which in turn influences behavioral intention to use mobile banking.

As per the study, behavioral characteristics play a vital role for attitude formation. PU and PEOU, ATT are the main predictors of technology acceptance. The hypothetical model was constructed and validated to predict factors which affect mobile banking adoption among physicians. The Partial Least Squares Path Modeling a variation of Structural Equation Modeling (SEM) was employed to validate both measurement and structural model. Furthermore, results displays that perceived usefulness, perceived ease of use, attitude, and assertive behavior of physicians are the main predictor for the adoption of mobile banking.

From the banker's point of view, bank should promote positive attitude towards mobile banking among customers. Mobile banking adoption is driven by attitude and personality style of physicians. As attitude is built among physicians then they become an effective customer for mobile banking. Assertive behavior of physicians has the skills to state their opinion, try to influence others while the aggressive behavior physicians will force their opinion on others for the usage of mobile banking. Assertive people have a better chance of gaining the respect of those around them as they are able to stand up for themselves while considering the needs and views of others. Aggressive people can be unapproachable, show they don't have positive attitude towards the mobile banking. This significant relationship suggests that physicians who perceive mobile banking as a useful channel for doing banking activities more likely prefer to use it.

Physicians using mobile banking save time by using the service effectively and efficiently. Physicians prefers mobile banking because they are charged less for performing banking transaction compared to in branch services. Additionally, customers might use mobile banking to have greater control over their financial activities from anywhere at any time without going to bank branches and standing in queue. Aggressive people may show irritated manner at others while assertive people appear relaxed in stressful situation which shows a positive attitude for adoption of mobile banking. They have a negative attitude and forget to carry out tasks. Assertive is the healthiest and most effective style of communication, and have the confidence to communicate without restoring manipulations. Different mobile banking strategy for segment strategy. Positive assertiveness among the physicians indicate their leadership ability, reduce conflict, Increase the quality of the relationships both at work and in their personal life, and to get more of what they want in life. This indicates a positive attitude towards adoption of mobile banking. They are good communicators to know their needs and expectations by communicating them clearly. Customer expectations, technological innovations; effect of regulation with attitude formation towards the technology acceptance plays a vital role for the adoption of mobile banking. Significant influences of ease of use on mobile banking suggest bankers that physicians will use if they feel comfortable to operate and for them it will be easy to use. User friendly interface, easy instruction to follow will promote the physicians in adoption of mobile banking.

Bankers should focus more on this aspect while designing the channel for distribution of financial services. More and more physicians are inclined for use of mobile devices rather than for internet banking due to the small devices they carry with it. From this study bank should consider the behavioral characteristics of customers in different group segment while designing their strategy for distribution of financial services. In the study assertive behavior among physicians' is much more prevalent still then many physicians even familiar with smart devices don't adopt mobile banking where the behavioral style of physicians play a important role in the attitude towards adoption of mobile banking.

CONCLUSION

This study represented as distinctive research in the adoption of mobile banking that integrated the behavioural style factors with TAM model. The findings discovered the assertive behaviour of physician's forma positive attitude towards adoption of mobile banking. Aggressive and passive behaviour forms negative formation towards the behavioural intention to use mobile banking. Perceived usefulness, perceived ease of use, assertive factors is significant in affecting physician's attitude which leads to the behavioral intention to use mobile banking. Study also found attitude plays vital role in the intention to use mobile banking or with the continued use of mobile banking in future. Further study can be enhanced by taking into the consideration of culture factor with the personality behavior style of physician's in formation of attitude towards the adoption of mobile banking. The study was an attempt to attract a particular segment of the society which is highly educated and occupying a noble possession to pass message to society to create cash less society where patient, doctor and other stakeholders in the health sector transact each other in financial issues as well as other banking transaction.

REFERENCES

1. Davis FD (1989) Perceived usefulness, perceived ease of use, and user acceptance of information technology. MIS Quarterly 13: 319-340.

2. Yang KC (2005) Exploring factors affecting the adoption of mobile commerce in Singapore. TelemInform 22: 257-277.
3. Davis FD, Bagozzi RP, Warshaw PR (1989) User acceptance of computer technology: A comparison of two theoretical models. Management Science 35: 982-1003.
4. Adams DA, Nelson RR, Todd PA (1992) Perceived usefulness, ease of use, and usage of information technology: A replication. MIS Quarterly 16: 227-247.
5. Agarwal R, Prasad J (1999) Are individual differences Germane to the acceptance of new information technologies? Decision Sciences 30: 361-391.
6. Venkatesh V (2000) Determinants of perceived ease of use: Integrating control, intrinsic motivation, and emotion into the technology acceptance model. Information System Research 11: 342-365.
7. Venkatesh V, Morris MG, Davis GB, Davis FD (2003) User acceptance of information technology: toward a unified view. MIS 27: 425-478.
8. Mattila M (2003) Factors affecting the adoption of mobile banking services. Journal of Internet Banking and Commerce 8: 24-36.
9. Nor KM, Pearson JM (2008)An exploratory study into the adoption of internet bankingin a developing country: Malaysia. Journal of Internet Commerce 7: 29-73.
10. Ajzen I, Fishbein M (1980) Understanding attitudes and predicting social behavior. Englewood Cliffs, Prentice-Hall.
11. Davis FD, Bagozzi RP, Warshaw PR (1992) Extrinsic and intrinsic motivation to use computers in the workplace. Journal of Applied Social Psychology 22: 1111-1132.
12. Chau PYK, Hu PJ (2001) Information Technology Acceptance by Professionals: A Model Comparison Approach. Decision Sciences 32: 699-719.
13. Agarwal R, Prasad J (1998) A conceptual and operational definition of personal innovativeness in the domain of IT. Information Systems Research 9:204-215.
14. Venkatesh V, Davis FD (1996) A model of the antecedents of perceived ease of use: Development and test. Decision Sciences 27: 451-481.
15. Venkatesh V, Davis FD (2000)A theoretical extension of the technology acceptance model: F our longitudinal field studies. Manage Sci 46: 186-204.
16. Hair J, Anderson J, Norman J, Black W (1995) Multivariate Data Analysis with Readings 4th (edn.). Prentice-Hall, New Jersey.

10
CHAPTER

FACTORS AFFECTING CUSTOMER'S ADOPTION OF MOBILE BANKING SERVICES

Amola Bhatt, Shahir Bhatt

Keywords: Mobile banking, Customer perception, Usage patterns

INTRODUCTION

The last two decades have witnessed a technology deluge with the integration of information and communication technology (ICT) in routine transactions at the corporate and retail level. Several reasons can be attributed to this phenomenon, ranging from costeffectiveness on the part of service providers to convenience and timeeffectiveness on the end of consumers. Suoranto [1] has confirmed that factors contributing to the adoption of mobile banking are related to convenience, access to the service regardless of time and place, privacy and savings in time and effort. However, the fact is that the adoption of new technology is not growing at the same pace as the introduction of the same. Consumers are refraining from using these technologically advanced services, partly because of lack of awareness and partly due to other concerns of security, device functionality, etc. Mobile banking, which allows the user to perform financial transaction using a mobile device, is not an exception to resistance faced from consumers. Weisbaum [2] quotes that 86% of the people who did not use mobile banking services in US were of the opinion that their banking needs were being met without mobile banking and nearly two-thirds of people who did not use mobile banking cited security concerns, such as data interception, phone hacking or lost phone. Another article by Marous [3] states that 22% people owning mobile phones and having a bank account were not aware of mobile banking. In India, as quoted by an RBI report [4], 64 banks (out of 80 permitted banks) have commenced mobile banking operations

Citation: Bhatt A, Bhatt S (2016) Factors Affecting Customer's Adoption of Mobile Banking Services. J Internet Bank Commer 21: 161.

and there are 22 million active mobile banking users (out of 30 million subscribed as of October 2013). However, customer enrollment related issues like mobile number registration, M-PIN generation process, security-related concerns, bank-staff education and customer awareness and education, and technical issues faced by banks including access channels for transaction, cumbersome transaction process and coordinating with Mobile Network Operators (MNOs) in mobile-banking eco-system are inhibiting the adoption of mobile banking.

But, all is not lost as this report foresees a bright future for mobile banking, provided the issues are sorted out. The report displays a growing trend of mobile banking with the volume and value of transactions having risen at 108.5% and 228.9% from Financial Year 2012 to 2013 respectively. Reserve Bank of India (RBI) further reports that there were around 870 million mobile connections in India by June, 2013 and around 450 million bank accounts. Hence, the scope of mobile banking is bound to increase and it shall also serve as a tool for financial inclusion by bringing unbanked people with mobile phones in the rural areas in the net. As per International Data Corporation (IDC) [5] estimates, the smartphone usage in India will increase at a CAGR of 36% from 2014 to 2019 amounting to 651 million smartphone users. This by itself manifests as a growth opportunity for mobile banking as it is found that most of the growth in mobile banking users directly stems from smartphone purchases [3]. Hence, at this juncture it becomes pertinent to know the customer segment using mobile banking along with their usage patterns and to further map their perceptions, so that improvisations in the service can be made and the reach can be increased. Such studies in the Indian context are few in number and hence, this study will address a knowledge gap in this field of study. Moreover, the study goes beyond and attempts to draw a relation between certain demographic characteristics of m-banking users and their perceptions, so that appropriate communication strategy can be used for the target audience. Thus, the study will give an empirically drawn observation on m-banking users' perceptions towards the service and help the banks in increasing the penetration by focusing on the factors drawn out of this study, especially in the context of a fast developing country like India.

LITERATURE REVIEW

Mobile banking model and services

The mobile banking platform combines payments, banking, and real-time, two-way data transmission for on-the-move, ubiquitous access to financial information and services [6]. Mobile banking is the financial service innovation offered through the use of Information and Communications Technology (ICT) [7]. Mobile Banking can be broadly classified into Bank-led model and Mobile Service Provider Led Model. In the bank led model, only customers of a bank can avail the mobile banking service from the bank and perform various banking activities. While, in the Mobile Service Provider Model, unbanked customers can also perform banking transactions through their mobile service provider.

Mobile banking services can be classified into SMS Banking, Application (Software) oriented, Browser (Internet) based model and Mobile Apps. The common activities which can be performed through mobile banking are balance enquiry, mini statement, money transfer, payment of bills, etc.

Awareness level of mobile banking

Devadevan [8] conducted a survey on 65 respondents, and found that 84.6% of the same had tested the mobile banking facility while the rest were unaware of the same. Li [9] points out a low level of awareness in China as far as mobile banking was concerned. In view of the same, Laukkanen [10] tested the impact of information and guidance offered by the bank. They found that the information and guidance offered by a bank has the most significant effect on perceived functional usability of mobile banking and also significantly increases the positive image associated with the innovation. The results also suggested that information and guidance significantly increase the perceived value added provided by mobile banking and decrease the perceived risks related to the innovation. However, information and guidance have no significant impact of psychological barriers like tradition.

Effect of demographics on usage of mobile banking

It is usual to include demographics characteristics in models about technology use and adoption [11]. The impact of demographics on the adoption of various electronic devices has been extensively studied [12]. Howcroft et al. [13] revealed that younger consumers value the convenience or time saving potential of online and mobile banking more than older consumers. These authors further found the educational levels of respondents did not affect the use of telephone or online banking. Capgemini [14], Goh [15] and Laukkanen [12] also found that younger customers, who are more technology savvy, are placing greater importance on mobile banking than senior people. Karjaluoto et al. [16] found a typical user of online banking in Finnish market highly educated, relatively young and wealthy person with good knowledge of computers and, especially, the internet. Li [9] noted that a typical user of mobile banking in China was male, aged upto 44 years and belonged to the high-income group. Further, respondents' level of education was not found to influence mobile banking adoption in China. According to Crabbe [17], demographic factors play a significant role in adoption decisions. They find that social and cultural factors, such as perceived credibility, facilitating conditions, perceived elitism, and demographic factors, significantly affect adoption decisions for m-banking in Ghana. Similarly, a survey conducted in Malaysia [18] reveals that both demographic and psychographic variables affect the adoption of new innovations such as m-banking-in particular, age, gender, personal income, and education. Finally, in their investigation of the influence of demographic factors on the adoption of m-banking and its applications, Teo [19] also incorporate demographic factors and subjective norms with the Technology Adoption Model (TAM) to assess intentions to adopt in Malaysia. As indicated by Goswami [20] Mobile-savvy college students, who are using their mobile devices for services beyond voice, will drive adoption of innovative mobility services, including mobile banking. Similarly, a study conducted by KPMG [21] found that mobile phone users aged between 16 and 34 were most comfortable using mobile phones for financial transactions, while majority of respondents in 65 and above age group were not at all comfortable.

Customer's adoption of technology in banking

There are various studies which highlight the customer adoption of technology in banking and map their satisfaction levels thereof. A study done by Polatoglu [22] indicates that early adopters and heavy users of internet banking were more satisfied with this service compared to other customers. Others also argued that the delivery of technology services appears to be correlated with high satisfaction where these services were most important to customers [23]. Efficiency, convenience and safety were viewed as desired end-state goals when using mobile banking [24]. Chung [25] found that system and information quality significantly influenced customer satisfaction, while information presentation did not significantly influence customer satisfaction. Also, trust can play a crucial intervening role in the relationship between perceived value (system and information quality) and customer satisfaction. In a recent study conducted on adoption of m-banking in China among customers of four state owned banks of China, ease of use was found to have significant impact on trust [26]. Chen [27], in their attempt to examine the effect of perceived risk on the adoption of Mobile Banking, found it as the key factor affecting attitude. Perceived usefulness has been found to have a significant positive effect on both attitude and usage intention toward use of Mobile Banking Services [11,28].Thakur [29] found that mobile interface usability (quick response time and easy navigation) and service had a positive effect on customer satisfaction. The results also confirmed that loyalty of m-banking customers was directly affected by satisfaction from m-banking services. On similar lines, a study by Deb [30] also found that perceived usefulness, perceived ease of use and social influence were related to positive attitude towards m-banking. Moreover, a positive relationship existed between attitude towards m-banking and intention to adopt m-banking. These results coincided with the findings of Chen [27] who reported that consumers who enjoyed wireless banking transactions and those who found mobile banking services easy to use displayed a positive attitude towards usage of mobile banking. Lee et al. [31] point out that once service providers are able to deliver user friendly, and consumer-satisfying services, then Mobile Banking will be adopted by consumers [32].

ISSUES AND CHALLENGES

The major reasons behind non-usage of mobile banking were security concerns and technical problems of getting the MPIN [8]. Similar results were noted by Li [9], who stated that among security concerns, hackers and fraud were responsible for non-adoption of online and mobile banking in China. This is also proved in studies done by Brown [31], Luarn [33], Chen [27]. Moreover, Chen [27] claims that frequent users of mobile banking were more concerned with psychological risks and the infrequent users were more concerned with financial risk as well as psychological risk. Previous studies indicate that perceived financial cost [33] and perceived complexity [34] inhibits the use and adoption of mobile banking services. Suoranta [1] found that mobile services were not used since they were perceived as impractical and not sufficiently diversified. In the case of the mobile phone, the small screen with small amount of information makes the device very difficult to use in fund transfer [35]. According to a study conducted by KPMG [21], respondents mentioned that their decision to use m-banking in future would depend on security or privacy and ease of use.

Objectives

- To study the usage pattern of mobile banking services
- To determine the factors which influence the adoption of mobile banking services
- To find relationship, if any between the demographics, usage pattern and the factors brought out from the study

Research Methodology

The research design for the study is descriptive in nature and the sampling unit were people having a bank account and using mobile banking services. The total sample size was 200, of which, deliberately, equal number of public bank account holders and private bank account holders were sampled. The questionnaire constructed for the study included several questions which were continuous and categorical in nature. The survey consisted of three sections, wherein the first section reported the demographic details, the second section explored the usage pattern and knowledge about mobile banking services, and the third section comprised of variables of mobile banking service and their agreement levels thereof. The scale pertaining to measuring perceptions of mobile banking consumers was adopted from a Dissertation by A. Prameela [36] and the relevant statements were retained for the current study. These statements were measured on a 5-point Likert scale ranging from highly agree to highly disagree. This questionnaire was administered on 200 respondents in the cities of Ahmedabad and Gandhinagar in Gujarat state. Using convenience sampling, the survey was conducted from January 2015 to March 2015. Convenience sampling is a type of non-probability sampling method and it involves collecting data from respondents who are a part of the population as desired under the study and are conveniently available to participate in the study. However, care was taken that the selected respondents were holding a bank account and using mobile banking services.

DATA ANALYSIS AND INTERPRETATION

Demographic details of the respondents

People who used mobile banking formed the sample, which also gives a general idea on the demographics of consumers of mobile banking in Gujarat. Almost 73% of the respondents belonged to the age-group of 18- 25 years and 77% of the sample were males. About 73% of the respondents were graduates, suggesting that most consumers of mobile banking were literate. Also, majority respondents were students (44%), followed by people engaged in private sector (33%). Majority of the respondents earned below Rs. 10,000 (48%) followed by earnings in the range of Rs. 10,000 to Rs. 30,000 (41%). This might be the case as a significant part of the sample comprised of students. About 56% of the respondents were married, with the balance being unmarried (Tables 1 and 2).

Table 1: Demographics of the respondents

Demographic factors		Frequency	Percentage
Age	18–25	147	73.5%
	26–30	40	20.0%
	31–40	8	4.0%
	41–50	5	2.5%
Gender	Male	154	77.0%
	Female	46	23.0%
Education	Under-graduate	7	3.5%
	Graduate	147	73.5%
	Post-graduate	46	23.0%
Occupation	Govt. employee	17	8.5%
	Private service	66	33.0%
	Business	20	10.0%
	Student	89	44.5%
	House-wife	8	4.0%
Monthly income	Below 10,000	97	48.5%
	10000-30000	83	41.5%
	30000-50000	15	7.5%
	Above 50,000	5	2.5%
Marital Status	Married	113	56.5%
	Unmarried	87	43.5%
Source: Primary data collected through questionnaire.			

Table 2: Banking related information of the respondents

Bank details		Frequency	Percentage
Name of Bank	SBI	49	24.5%
	BOB	52	26.0%
	ICICI	49	24.5%
	HDFC	50	25.0%
Operation of Bank Account	Self	197	98.5%
	Others	3	1.5%
Type of Bank Account	Savings	180	90.0%
	Current	11	5.5%
	Both	9	4.5%
Source: Primary data collected through questionnaire.			

Banking related information of respondents

As mentioned in the previous section, almost equal number of respondents was chosen from the leading public sector and private sector banks of India. The State Bank of India and Bank of Baroda were chosen from the public sector, while ICICI and HDFC banks were chosen from the private sector. The statistics reveal that almost all respondents self-operated their bank account and 90% of the respondents held Savings accounts with these banks.

Usage frequency of respondents

The above table reports the usage frequency of various modes of banking available to the customers. For majority respondents, branch banking, internet banking, telephone banking and mobile banking invite less than 3 visits every month. However, respondents frequently visit the ATMs for conducting banking transactions. Branch banking is losing its appeal in light of technological advancements. However, security and operational issues have also deterred the usage of internet and phone / mobile banking. Hence, as a mid-way option, customers prefer using ATMs for common transactions (Table 3).

Table 3: Usage frequency of the respondents

Usage frequency per month	**< 3 times**		**4–8 times**		**> 8 times**	
Mode of Banking	**Frequency**	**Percentage**	**Frequency**	**Percentage**	**Frequency**	**Percentage**
Branch Banking	164	82.0	32	16.0	4	2.0
ATM Banking	91	45.5	100	50.0	9	4.5
Internet Banking	137	68.5	54	27.0	9	4.5
Telephone (Landline) Banking	186	93.0	13	6.5	1	0.5
Mobile Banking	148	74.0	44	22.0	8	4.0
Source: Primary data collected through questionnaire.						

Factors affecting customers' adoption of mobile banking services

To determine the important factors affecting the usage of mobile banking, the factorability of 18 items was examined, and the respondents were asked to rate these variables using a 5-point Likert scale, which ranged from 'strongly disagree' to 'strongly agree'. Firstly, the internal consistency of the items was checked using Cronbach's alpha. The Cronbach's alpha value came to 0.817 for the entire scale of 18 items which was considered to be excellent, as the closer the reliability coefficient gets to the value of 1 the better is the reliability of the measures. Moreover, deletion of any item could not significantly improve the reliability results. Next, the Bartlett's test of sphericity was found to be significant (Chi-Square 1203.615, p-value < 0.0001). The Kaiser-Mayer-Olkin (KMO) measure of sampling adequacy was high at 0.823. The KMO value of 0.823 was excellent since it exceeded the recommended value of 0.6. The two results of (KMO and Bartlett's) suggested that the data was appropriate to proceed with the factor analysis using all the 18 items of the scale. The principal component analysis with varimax rotation was used as the basic idea was to identify the factors, thereby narrowing the scope and computing factor loadings for the same.

Exploratory factor analysis (EFA) was performed and it was found that all the items carried an eigenvalue of more than 1. Hence, all the factors were retained as they were considered significant to the study. The result was that there were a total of 5 factors, which explained 57.09% of the total variance. The Table 4 gives the rotated component matrix dimensions for better understanding of the factors.

Table 4: Factors influencing customers for adoption of mobile banking services

	1	2	3	4	5
Factor 1: Time-effective					
The current software enables m-banking smoothly	0.716				
Login process is fast	0.769				
Bill payment can be done in less time	0.749				
Service charges are reasonable	0.798				
Clearing services are fast	0.670				
Factor 2: Convenience					
Prepaid mobile recharge can be done easily		0.709			
Transaction Status can be known easily		0.633			
Secure transactions		0.563			
Factor 3: Safety					
Bill payments is secure			0.649		
Account to account transfer is secure			0.618		
Statement request can done easily			0.676		
Disallows third party tampering			0.599		
Factor 4: Operational simplicity					
SMS alerts about specific information				0.503	
Fast responses				0.538	
Simple steps in processing				0.764	
Less possibilities of hacking				0.652	
Factor 5: Ease of navigation					
Less waiting time					0.757
Login/signoff are easy					0.623
Source: Primary data collected through questionnaire.					

Factor 1 has an eigenvalue of 5.602 and has five variables clubbed under it. This factor can be labelled as "time-effective" as the underlying variables indicate the benefits of using mobile banking in saving time, like faster logins, bill payments and clearing services. At the same time, it also indicates the smooth functioning of this platform. The items received a mean score of 2.28 on a scale of 1 to 5 where majority agreed that mobile banking services are time-effective and this factor can influence the usage of the same.

Factor 2 labelled as "Convenience", having an eigen value of 2.278 reflects the ease of conducting various transactions using mobile banking. This factor clubs statements like ease of performing mobile recharges, knowing the status of transactions. The items received a mean score of 1.93 on a scale of 1 to 5 where majority agreed that convenience can be an important factor in adoption of mobile banking. This finding is supported by Mathew [37] who found that usefulness and facilitating conditions had the most influence in discriminating between mobile banking user and non-user.

Factor 3 has an eigenvalue of 1.302 and has four variables clubbed under it. This factor can be termed as "Safety" since it primarily talks about the security features offered by mobile banking. The variables under this factor talk about security in bill payments, transfer of funds, account statements and disallowance of third party tampering. The items received a mean score of 1.94 on a scale of 1 to 5 where majority agreed that contrary to traditional views, mobile banking ensures adequate safety measures and this feature should be publicized so as to gain greater acceptance among non-users. This finding is in line with a study conducted by Singh [38], which states that factors influencing customer perceptions of mobile banking can be labelled as security/ privacy, reliability, efficiency and responsiveness.

Factor 4 loaded on four variables carries an eigen value of 1.268 and is labelled as "Operational Simplicity". The underlying variables portray the processes involved in mobile banking and their corresponding simplicity. These variables relate to SMS alerts about specific information, faster responses, simpler steps in processing and fewer possibilities of hacking. The items received a mean score of 1.97 on a scale of 1 to 5 where majority agreed that operational simplicity could influence people in adopting m-banking. Olasina [39] finds a positive correlation between perceived ease of use and adoption of m-banking.

Factor 5 has an eigenvalue of 1.091 and has two variables clubbed under it. This factor can be termed as "Ease of Navigation" as it comprises of statements which indicate less waiting time and ease of login and signoff. The items received a mean score of 2.07 on a scale of 1 to 5 where majority agreed that in addition to simpler operational steps, ease of navigation is critical for adoption of m-banking. On similar lines, a study by Yu [40] indicates security, interactivity, relative advantage, ease of use and interface creativity as determinants affecting the perceptions of customers post-adoption of mobile banking services.

Hypothesis testing

The study tested the following hypothesis:

Hypothesis 1: Ho: There is no significant relationship between factors influencing m-banking adoption and the demographics

H1: There is significant relationship between factors influencing m-banking adoption and the demographics

One-way ANOVA (analysis of variance)/independent sample t-test is used to test the hypothesis. On a variable of interest, ANOVA tests the significance of differences between two or more groups, while t-test looks at differences between two groups. Of the independent variables relating to demographics, gender and marital status contain only two groups each while the other variables like age, occupation and monthly income consist of more than two categories. Hence, t-test is applied for gender and marital status, while ANOVA is used for the remaining variables. Data is normally distributed and homogeneity of variance is checked using Levene's statistic which can be seen in Table 5. Post-hoc tests (Tuckey/Games Howell) are also carried out to further analyze the data wherever significant relationship is established.

Table 5: Relationship of factors with demographics

		Age	Education	Occupation	Monthly Income	Gender	Marital Status
Time-effective	Levene Statistic	1.613	2.106	2.695	2.703	3.995	9.812
	Levene Sig.[1]	0.188	0.124	0.032	0.047	0.047	0.002
	ANOVA/Welch F Statistic[2]	0.915	2.873	3.190	6.668		
	ANOVA/Welch Sig[3]	0.434	0.059	0.025	0.003		
	t-statistic					2.229	-3.011
	t sig					0.028	0.003
	Ho Rejected	No	No	Yes	Yes	Yes	Yes
Convenience	Levene Statistic	1.215	1.554	1.653	0.593	5.119	0.707
	Levene Sig.	0.305	0.214	0.163	0.621	0.025	0.401
	ANOVA/Welch F Statistic	0.530	0.106	1.174	0.518		
	ANOVA/Welch Sig	0.662	0.899	0.324	0.670		
	t-statistic					-0.490	0.150
	t sig					0.626	0.881
	Ho Rejected	No	No	No	No	No	No
Safety	Levene Statistic	2.141	0.426	2.403	1.754	0.003	0.209
	Levene Sig.	0.096	0.654	0.051	0.157	0.959	0.648
	ANOVA/Welch F Statistic	0.159	3.014	0.991	1.893		
	ANOVA/Welch Sig	0.924	0.051	0.414	0.132		
	t-statistic					0.022	-1.441
	t sig					0.983	0.151
	Ho Rejected	No	No	No	No	No	No
Operational Simplicity	Levene Statistic	1.688	0.110	0.652	1.270	0.064	1.055
	Levene Sig.	0.171	0.896	0.626	0.286	0.800	0.306
	ANOVA/Welch F Statistic	2.505	0.084	1.385	0.881		
	ANOVA/Welch Sig	0.060	0.919	0.240	0.452		
	t-statistic					0.273	0.510
	t sig					0.785	0.611
	Ho Rejected	No	No	No	No	No	No
Ease of Navigation	Levene Statistic	0.679	0.386	0.559	1.042	0.022	0.298
	Levene Sig.	0.566	0.680	0.693	0.375	0.883	0.586
	ANOVA/Welch F Statistic	0.694	2.057	1.279	0.979		
	ANOVA/Welch Sig	0.557	0.131	0.280	0.404		
	t-statistic					1.057	-1.658
	t sig					0.292	0.099
	Ho Rejected	No	No	No	No	No	No

[1]Levene's test is used for determining the homogeneity of variances. In the given table, the significance value of Levene's test is shown. If this significance value is less than 0.05, the null hypothesis of equal variances is rejected. [2]ANOVA test indicates whether there is an overall difference between the groups. However, it can only be used if the data meets the assumption of homogeneity of variance (as indicated by Levene's

test). If the data does not satisfy the assumption of homogeneity of variance, Welch F-test is run to identify the overall difference between the groups. The t-test is also used to find the difference between the groups, when the groups are limited to two.In this case for "gender" and "marital status", t-test is run as groups are only two. If the groups exceed two, then ANOVA is used. The statistics in this row relate to ANOVA or Welch F or t-test as applicable under the given constraints.

[3]The significance value given in this row is used to accept or reject the null hypothesis tested using ANOVA or Welch or t-test.

- Time-effective and Occupation: The assumption of homogeneity of variance is violated and therefore, the Welch F-ratio is reported. There is a statistically significant difference between groups as determined by Welch ($F(4,195) = 3.19$, $p = 0.025$). The null hypothesis can be rejected here. The Games- Howell post-hoc test does not rely on homogeneity of variance and so this was chosen. This test revealed that time-effectiveness is statistically higher for students ($2.44 \pm .799$) than for people engaged in private service ($2.06 \pm .556$). It can be concluded that for the given data there is a relationship between time effectiveness and occupation. It can be stated that people occupied in private service believe that savings in time benefit can be a critical factor influencing the usage of mobile banking.
- Time-effective and Monthly Income: The assumption of homogeneity of variance is violated and therefore, the Welch F-ratio is reported. There is a statistically significant difference between groups as determined by Welch ($F(3,196) = 6.67$, $p = 0.003$). The null hypothesis can be rejected here. The Games-Howell post-hoc test revealed that time-effectiveness is statistically higher for people with monthly income below Rs. 10,000 ($2.39 \pm .769$) than for people in the income-bracket of Rs. 31000-50000 ($1.99 \pm .480$) as well as for people with income higher than Rs. 50000 per month ($1.68 \pm .335$). It can be concluded that for the given data there is a relationship between time-effectiveness and monthly income. It can be stated that people belonging to higher income brackets believe that savings in time benefit can be a critical factor influencing the usage of mobile banking.
- Time-effective and Gender: The results of Independent Sample t-test ($t = 2.229$, $p = 0.028$) confirm that there exists a relationship between time-effectiveness and gender. Further, the descriptive statistics confirmed that time-effectiveness is statistically higher for males ($2.33 \pm .748$) than females ($2.11 \pm .539$). Hence, it can be stated that females perceive timeeffective mobile banking services could be a more influential factor in adopting the same.
- Time-effective and Marital Status: The results of Independent Sample t-test ($t = -3.011$, $p = 0.003$) confirm that there exists a relationship between time-effectiveness and marital status. Further, the descriptive statistics confirmed that timeeffectiveness is statistically higher for unmarried people ($2.46 \pm .803$) than for married people ($2.15 \pm .600$). Hence, it can be stated that married people perceive time-effectiveness to be an important factor behind influencing people to use mobile banking services.

Hypothesis 2: Ho: There is no significant relationship between the type of bank ownership and factors influencing m-banking adoption

H1: There is significant relationship between the type of bank ownership and factors influencing m-banking adoption

Independent sample t-test is used to test the hypothesis, as it looks at differences between two groups on a variable of interest. In the current context, bank ownership was classified as public and private. Data is normally distributed and homogeneity of variance is checked using Levene's statistic which can be seen in Table 6.

Table 6: Relationship of Factors with Type of bank ownership

Factors	Levene Statistic	Levene Sig.	t-statistic	t sig	H0 Status	Mean Values	
						Public Bank	Private Bank
Time-effective	26.055	0.000	7.303	0.000	Rejected	2.62	1.96
Safety	0.362	0.548	3.073	0.002	Rejected	2.05	1.83
Convenience	0.000	0.998	2.385	0.018	Rejected	2.02	1.84
Operational Simplicity	0.521	0.471	3.011	0.003	Rejected	2.08	1.85
Ease of navigation	0.378	0.539	2.764	0.006	Rejected	2.19	1.95

The test results make it evident that all the factors brought out from the study which influence a respondent to adopt mobile banking bear a statistically significant relationship with the type of bank ownership. It needs to be recalled here that deliberately equal number of respondents were taken from both the categories of banks, so as to remove the bias created by the sample size. Further analysis of the descriptives reveals that consumers of private banks perceive the factors, viz. time-effective, safety, convenience, operational simplicity and ease of navigation as potential drivers for adoption of mobile banking. Hence, it can be suggested that public sector banks need to improve their customer experience of m-banking services.

Hypothesis 3: Ho: There is no significant relationship between the frequency of using mobile banking and factors influencing m-banking adoption

H1: There is significant relationship between the frequency of using mobile banking and factors influencing m-banking adoption

One-way ANOVA (analysis of variance) is used to test the hypothesis, as it tests the significance of differences between two or more groups on a variable of interest. Data is normally distributed and homogeneity of variance is checked using Levene's statistic which can be seen in Table 7. In the cases, where the assumption of homogeneity of variance is violated, Welch F is used as an alternative. Post-hoc tests (Tuckey/Games Howell) are also carried out to further analyze the data wherever significant relationship is established.

Table 7: Relationship of Factors with Frequency of using mobile banking

Factors	Levene Statistic	Levene Sig	F/Welch Statistic	Sig.	H0 Status
Time-effective	11.109	0.000	17.464	0.000	Rejected
Safety	1.165	0.314	4.808	0.009	Rejected
Convenience	0.164	0.849	4.044	0.019	Rejected
Operational Simplicity	0.724	0.486	5.648	0.004	Rejected
Ease of navigation	0.881	0.416	3.609	0.029	Rejected

The above results suggest that the null hypothesis is rejected for all the factors and there is a significant relationship between frequency of usage of mobile banking and factors influencing the adoption of m-banking. The post-hoc tests further suggest that in the case of time-effective, operational simplicity and ease of navigation, people using mobile banking for 4 to 8 times in a month agree more than people using mobile banking for less than 3 times. On similar lines, people using mobile banking for more than 8 times a month on an average believe safety and convenience to be critical factors affecting the adoption of m-banking, as compared to people using m-banking for less than 3 times. Hence, it can be inferred that respondents using mobile banking more frequently perceive that the above-mentioned factors can actually rope in people to adopt m-banking as an alternative channel of banking. This inference assumes importance as the heavy users would have experienced the benefits of m-banking and their responses are more authentic.

CONCLUSION

The market for mobile phones, especially the smart phones is assuming great heights and the banks want to ride on this growth by offering mobile banking as an alternative channel of providing services. However, consumers are wary of the new technology and literature is replete with papers which discuss the initial resistance exhibited by consumers towards technological developments. As a matter of fact, the usage pattern reveals that people frequent ATMs more than using internet banking or mobile banking. In light of this, the current study offers insights on the perceptions of mobile banking users and tries to unearth the factors which could influence more people into adopting mobile banking. The factors brought out from the study are labelled as Time-effective,

Safety, Convenience, Operational simplicity and Ease of navigation. Additionally, it was revealed that users who were females, engaged in private sector, belonged to high income class, and were married stated time-effectiveness to be a critical factor for influencing the usage of m-banking. Respondents holding accounts in private banks could relate to all the factors as being important for adoption of m-banking. Similarly, frequent users of mobile banking could also identify with the above-mentioned factors and agreed that these could be the driving forces for increasing the reach of m-banking in the region. Hence, spreading awareness about m-banking based on these factors would certainly help the banks.

REFERENCES

1. Suoranta M (2003) Adoption of mobile banking in Finland. Doctoral thesis, Jyva skyla, Finland,
2. Weisbaum H (2015) Why has Mobile banking growth stalled? Blame Hackers.
3. Marous J (2015) Has Mobile Banking Usage Reached a Plateau? The Financial Brand.
4. (2014) Report of the Technical Committee on Mobile Banking. RBI.
5. http:/www.slideshare.net/zinnov/smartphone-market-in-india
6. Jacob K (2007) Are mobile payments the smart cards of the aughts? Federal Reserve Bank of Chicago, Chicago.
7. Mishra V, Bisht SS (2013) Mobile banking in a developing economy: A customer-centric model for policy formulation. Telecommunications Policy 37: 503-514.
8. Devadevan V (2013) Mobile Banking in India – Issues and Challenges. International Journal of Emerging Technology and Advanced Engineering 3: 516-520.
9. Laforet S, Xiaoyan Li (2005) Consumers' attitudes towards online and mobile banking in China. International Journal of Bank Marketing 23: 362-380.
10. Laukkanen T, Kiviniemi V (2010) The role of information in mobile banking resistance. International Journal of Bank Marketing 28: 372-388.
11. Shaikh AA, Karjaluoto H (2015) Mobile banking adoption: a literature review. Telematics and Informatics 32: 129-142.
12. Laukkanen T, Cruz P (2012) Cultural, individual and device-specific antecedents on mobile banking adoption: a cross-national study. Proceedings of the 45th IEEE Hawaii International Conference on System Sciences (HICSS), Hawaii.
13. Howcroft B, Hamilton R, Hewer P (2002) Consumer attitude and the usage and adoption of home-based banking in the United Kingdom. International Journal of Bank Marketing 20: 111-121.
14. Capgemini (2013) World retail banking report. European Financial Management and Marketing Association.
15. Goh TT, Suki NM, Fam K (2014) Exploring a consumption value model for Islamic mobile banking adoption. Journal of Islamic Marketing 5: 344-365.

16. Karjaluoto H, Mattila M, Pento T (2002) Factors underlying attitude formation towards online banking in Finland. International Journal of Banking Marketing 20: 261-272.

17. Crabbe M, Standing C, Standing S, Karjaluoto H (2009) An adoption model for mobile banking in Ghana. International Journal of Mobile Communication 7: 515-543.

18. Sulaiman A, Jaafar NI, Mohezar S (2007) An overview of mobile banking adoption among the urban community. Int J Mobile Commun 5: 157-168.

19. Teo A, Tan GW, Cheah C, Ooi K, Yew K (2012) Can the demographic and subjective norms influence the adoption of mobile banking? International Journal of Mobile Communication 10: 578-597.

20. Goswami D, Raghavendran S (2009) Mobile-banking: can elephants and hippos tango? Journal of Business Strategy 30: 14-20.

21. (2009) Consumer taking charge, consumers and convergence III – survey report. KPMG International.

22. Polatoglu VN, Ekin S (2001) An empirical investigation of the Turkish consumers' acceptance of internet banking services. International Journal of Bank Marketing 19: 156-165.

23. Joseph M, Stone G (2003) An empirical evaluation of US bank customer perceptions of the impact of technology on service delivery in the banking sector. International Journal of Retail and Distribution Management 31: 190-202.

24. Laukkanen T (2007) Internet vs mobile banking: comparing customer value perceptions. Business Process Management Journal 13: 788-797.

25. Chung N, Kwon S (2009) Effect of trust level on mobile banking satisfaction: a multi-group analysis of information system success instruments. Behaviour and Information Technology 28: 549-562.

26. Zhou T (2012) Examining mobile banking user adoption from the perspectives of trust and flow experience. Information Technology and Management 13: 27-37.

27. Chen C (2013) Perceived risk, usage frequency of mobile banking services. Managing Service Quality: An International Journal 23: 410-436.

28. Purwanegara M, Apriningsih A, Andika F (2014) Snapshot on Indonesia regulation in mobile internet banking users attitudes. Procedia – Social and Behavioral Sciences pp: 147-155.

29. Thakur R (2014) What keeps mobile banking customers loyal? International Journal of Bank Marketing 32: 628-646.

30. Deb M, Lomo-David E (2014) An empirical examination of customers' adoption of m-banking in India. Marketing Intelligence and Planning 32: 475-494.

31. Lee H, Harindranath G, Oh S, Kim DJ (2015) Provision of mobile banking services from an actor-network perspective: implications for convergence and standardization. Technological Forecasting and Social Change 90: 551-561.

32. Brown I, Cajee Z, Davies D, Stroebel S (2003) Cell phone banking: predictors of adoption in South Africa – an exploratory study. International Journal of Information Management 23: 381-394.

33. Luarn P, Lin HH (2005) Toward an understanding of the behavioral intention to use mobile banking. Computers in Human Behavior 21: 873-891.

34. Lee MSY, McGoldrick PF, Keeling KA, Doherty J (2003) Using ZMET to explore barriers to the adoption of 3G mobile banking services. International Journal of Retail and Distribution Management 31: 340-348.

35. Laukkanen T, Sinkkonen S, Kivijarvi M, Laukkanen P (2007) Innovation resistance among mature consumers. Journal of Consumer Marketing 24: 419-427.

36. Prameela (2013) Technology in banking: an impact study in the operations of public and private sector banks with reference to Andhra Bank and ICICI bank – Vizag city. Shoshganga.

37. Mathew M, Sulphey MM, Prabhakaran J (2014) Perceptions and Intentions of Customers towards Mobile Banking Adoption. Journal of Contemporary Management Research 8: 83-101.

38. Singh S (2014) Customer Perception of Mobile Banking: An Empirical Study in National Capital Region Delhi. Journal of Internet Banking and Commerce 19: 1-22.

39. Olasina G (2015) Factors Influencing the Use of M-Banking by Academics: A Case Study of SMS-Based MBanking. African Journal of Information Systems 7: 56-79.

40. Yu T, Fang K (2009) Measuring the Post-Adoption Customer Perception of Mobile Banking Services. Cyberpsychology and Behavior 12: 33-35.

11
CHAPTER

RISK AND INTENTION OF ADOPTING INTERNET BANKING

Fadare OA, Ibrahim MB and Edogbanya A

Keywords: Perceived risk, Internet banking, Social risk, Performance risk

INTRODUCTION

The word internet banking implies the delivery of information and services rendered from bank to its clients, with the aid of a computer. More advanced amenity is one which grants clients with the opportunity to enable them in gaining access to their accounts, performs transactions, and also buy product online with the aid of the internet [1]. Internet banking is another opportunity for banks to convey their amenities and for clients to be able to receives services [2]. This implies those customers that use internet banking are connected via computer internet, while those customers making use of mobile banking are through wireless devices [3].

In the developing countries, numerous features can be cited for the practices and non-usage of internet banking services. Ezeoha [4] contend with the adoption of internet services in Nigeria is so sluggish compared to that of developed countries and some part of African continent. In Nigeria, internet banking services is categorized as a new innovation. Therefore a sensible topic to be treated for the quality and quantity in Nigeria banking sector can be heightened for future purpose. Despites the facts that online banking offers numerous benefits like quicker transaction, speediness and subordinate supervision dues [5], there are still large number of clients who did not support the adoption of internet banking.

Citation: Fadare OA, Ibrahim MB, Edogbanya A (2015) Risk and Intention of Adopting Internet Banking. J Internet Bank Commer 21:144.

Pavlou [6] stated that perceived risk is suggested as a projecting obstacle to customer acceptance of internet banking [7]. In the setting of internet banking, risk can be seen either via system and information exchange attacks or it can also be seen via illegal access to the account by untruthful or imperfect verification. Therefore, perceived risk may be concerned with numerous problems from economic losses to confidentiality issues.

Likened to online purchase, adoption of internet banking is classically more multifaceted, as it pledges a lengthy tenure connection among the user and internet banking services. A considerable measure in question for clients as they consider going into business link with reserved, unidentified internet banking services, while costumer perception towards the risks of adopting internet banking have already been deliberated on by several researchers [8,9] perceived risk mutable it has already been exhibited been a sole concept which have flops to imitate the actual features of perceived risk and clarify the reasons in which customers fight banking services. Although, numerous study projects already engrossed the causes which influence the adoption of information technology or the internet during the past era Heijden [10]; Taylor et al. [11] partial experiential work which captures the achievement aspects or the positive aspects in internet banking in other to be of help to form a tactical agenda.

Based on several study such as Westin et al. [12]; Cranor et al. [13] secrecy problems already verified vital barricades to the usage of internet services. Users like to direct what sort of information is been collected, and for what purposes, to what extent, how long the information is documented, and what is the main purpose their files are treated [14]. For a solid theoretical source to be provided for inspecting the adoption of internet baking services the study emphasize on two thoughts of reasonable act technology acceptance model (TAM). Davis et al. [15] the theory of planned behaviour (TPB) Azjen [16] posit five types of risk; which are security risk, financial risk, social risk, time or convenience risk, and performances risk. All these risks are associated with internet banking. The problem internet banking as discussed Durkin et al. [17], Haque et al. [18] stated that the acceptance and usage of internet banking services by most banking clients is still inconsequential regardless of the massive savings on the internet banking know-how by countless monetary institutions all over the world. The inconsequential result is due to the perceived risk intricate in using the internet banking services

LITERATURE REVIEW

Internet banking

Internet banking also known as electronic banking, It can also be termed online banking. Internet banking system offers electronic distribution of banking products and services to all its clients comprise computerized teller machine (ATM) exchanges, web banking exchanges, phone banking, and online account opening. Internet banking is essential for long period existence of banks in the realm of electronic commerce [19]. Internet banking business sector is predicted to rise as fast as possible in the few years to come, anticipated to ascend as quick as could reasonably be expected in the few years to come, influencing the game changer benefit by customary branch banks [8,20].

Internet banking is consequently accepted to progress consumer loyalty as it can offer earlier, cooler, calmer and other more dependable administrations through a solitary stage, if access the bank website. Actually, investigation by Arthur [21] discovered that crudely 50% of consumer would first investigate with their current banker in case if they are in need of a new monetary product. Hence, if properly allied, internet banking provides a superb chance for cross retailing banking facilities and goods and therefore, enriches the banks modest location, experiences shopper requests better, generates fresh spreading channel, also expand the business picture and lessen price Currie [22], Lam et al. [23].

From the Figure 1, Sai [24] listed are some of the internet banking transaction which involves ATM, telephone banking, smart card, internet banking, mobile banking, and electronic transfer, it insufficient for a bank to reason concerning the welfare of internet banking neither is it adequate for a bank to discourse internet banking enlargement problems.

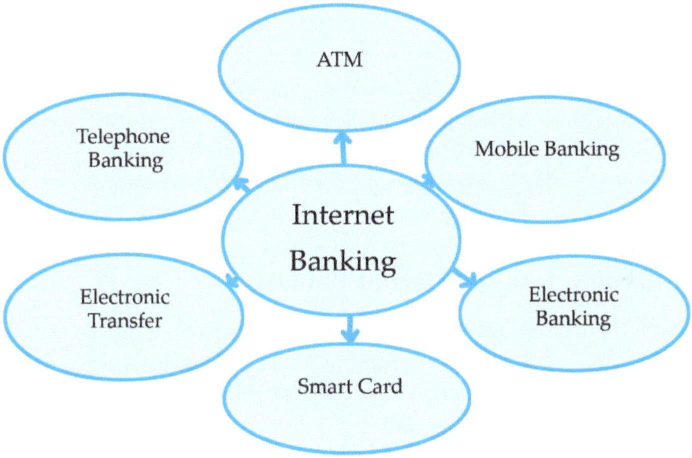

Figure 1: An overview of internet banking [24]

One of the advantages of banks going online is the prospective reserve funds in the expense of conserving an old-style branch network [25]. Turban et al. [26] specified that internet banking is tremendously advantageous to clients due to the fund in expenses, period and space it provides, its swift answer to grievances, and its distribution of better-quality facilities, in which all the benefit makes it easier for convenient banking. Internet banking acceptance already multiplied exceptional consideration in educational studies study in the most recent five years; for example, banking diaries have dedicated distinct matters on the subject. The Technology Acceptance Model, TAM [27] already turn out to the qualify model of IT acceptance, predicting the magnitude to the extent of which a crispy IT is utilized. Suh et al. [28] directed an enquiry based on the technology acceptance model (TAM) to examine client acceptance of internet banking. They demanded TAM as a suitable model for describing acceptance in the circumstance of internet banking.

Factors influencing the adoption of internet banking

Internet banking services channels of customer intention to adopt online banking have been affected by the front position of numerous study works in the advance world [29,30]. By and by, there is all that much restricted distributed works that explore the influences affecting the adoption of internet banking from the perspective of clients in the setting of increasing nations like Nigeria. Until now there are still no much studies on the adoption of IB, a significant exemption to this study is directed by Gardachew [31] who concentrated on electronic banking practices, chances and difficulties in Ethiopia.

Grethen posit that privacy, honesty, and also verification are vital structures in the banking sector and they have been positively succeeded the world over in pre-internet period, communication crossway on an open and thus unconfident station in a way that the internet might not be the superlative base for customer relations as reliance might partly be misplaced. Here are the selected disadvantages of online banking which include: bank relationship, transaction issues, services issues, security [32]. It is getting to be progressively hard to disregard Technology Acceptance Model (TAM) as an apparatus to test technology adoption in the surviving literature. Essentially TAM is already being mostly utilized to test clients' aim, intention to acknowledge or to decay the utilization of a specific innovation and for the matter of internet banking adoption [33].

Customer Intention to Use Internet Banking

Aderonke et al. [34] discovered that most internet customers make use of it just because of its convenience and saves time and suitable for all their transactions desires. More so, the network security and the security of the system when it comes to confidentiality are the main disquiets of the consumers and institute restriction to potential users.

Customer intention to use internet banking might be unhurried with the proclamation: "I have intention or desire to utilize Online Banking whenever I step outside to pay my bill online later on. Aderonke [34] focused on the acknowledgement and utilization of the internet banking benefits by managing an account client. This is unimportant notwithstanding the tremendous ventures on the online technology by different monetary establishments everywhere throughout the world.

Customers already started in perceiving the service of internet banking through the use of the internet as a major good-looking feature than any other key manufactured goods features of the bank, customer already begin in assessing the banks based on the suitability and luxury it offers to them [35]. Bankers now start in emerging numerous product structures and services making use of internet application. It has been expressed that apparent handiness and convenience are the most discriminating serious variables in anticipating whether an innovation has a tendency to be utilized or not [36]. It was observed that convenience had a fundamentally solid connection with intention to use internet banking technology [27,37].

Perceived risk

Several researchers requested that consumer's perceived risk is a type of a multi-dimensional concept, perceived risk is term as consumer personal prospect of misery, a loss in chase of a preferred result, also as internet banking which is subjectively strong-minded hope of loss by an online bank user in considering a precise deal. Jacoby et al. [38] Roselius [39] Roboff [40] realised that individuals have a feeble knowledge of internet banking risks while they are mindful of the dangers. To be more exact, privacy and security were originate to be substantial hindrances to the adoption of internet banking in Australia [41]. The notion of customer perceived risk has been extensively managed in e-channel utilizing IT devices and has been revealed to impact clients intention and attitude [42].

Progressing monetary dealings on the internet present countless risks for consumers, above and over the deal procedure itself being perceived as risk [43]. In the internet surroundings, unlawful deeds can be achieved with tremendously high haste, furthermore, deficient with regards to any physical contact [44]. Whenever an unofficial fellow is capable to get in touch to a consumer's internet banking folder, terrific economy information can cause a lot of economic losses. The most vital aspects of internet banking are probable to be security risk associated to the possible loss because of shortages in the functioning system or embezzlement of resources via illegitimate exterior entry [45-48].

Performance risk

Clients assessment of performance risk is taking into account their understanding and reasoning capacities in a convinced item area [45]. Asymmetry in internet banking data and the absence of individual contact avert the customer from properly assessing the attributes of the item, lessening certainty. Probability of the failing and not executing as it was considered and promoted and therefore deteriorating the preferred benefit [49]. A way product and services deliver benefits as perceived by a consumer [50] can also be referred to as a terror of loss that can also be incurred when a variety, product or dealer do not accomplish as projected [51]. Performance risk implies losses sustained by shortages or faulty of internet banking websites. Customers are frequently anxious that collapse of system servers or termination from the web will transpire while leading transaction because the circumstances might outcome in unanticipated fatalities [52].

Social risk

Social risk is the anxiety of the likelihood of enticing in unfavourable consideration and reaction from obtaining a specific item. The social wellbeing of the client who utilizes internet banking administrations may be influenced due to the positive or negative impression of internet banking administrations by people, family, or companions [45].

Clients state of mind to the diverse technique for obtaining rely on upon their attributes, the individuals who most regard social connections being the most hesitant to build up an uplifting mentality or optimistic approach to internet banking. The absence of human collaboration can be an obstruction to the utilization of innovation centred facilities.

Social risk denotes the option that making use of internet banking might outcome in condemnation of one's family or group, it also an impending loss of rank in one's communal gathering as an outcome of adopting item and administration, looking untrendy. It is likely that one's social stand-up might be improved or reduced subject on how internet banking is regarded. It can be those individuals have unfavourable or positive perception of internet banking. In other words, the opinions of its adopters not accepting internet banking might have negative or positive implications.

Time risk

Combination of time lost and effort consumed in acquiring any item and services [53]. At the point when additional time is mandatory in a way to study how to get to any certain administration, risk perception upsurge. Customers are also said to perceived risk when currency transferal is not comprehended in time and errors take place during the period of the transaction turning to period loss perception [45].

Inconvenience and time may refer to a loss sustained because of the postponement of getting payment or the effort of steering (discovery suitable services and hyperlinks). Two foremost reason of displeasing internet banking experiences that may be considered as a time risk involving a confused site and pages which are so lazy it couldn't be possible download [54]. It can be interrelated to the dimension of time included in holding up the knowledge how to perfume internet banking websites, time may be lost when consumer is settling on a terrible buying choice by squandering time looking into and making the purchase, learning ways of using the product just to have substitute it if it do not accomplish to anticipations.

Financial risk

Financial Risk also implies monetary risk which is the likelihood of economic losses during the process in online purchase or shopping [55]. In another way round FR is the loss of money as an outcome of buying product and facilities [56]. Risk insight of internet banking users mainly cultivates out of the IT gaps and the subsequent losses experiences in deceitful entrance to customer accounts [45].

It is also referred to as prospective for economic loss payable to transaction mistakes or the bank account misappropriation. For instance, untrustworthy merchants convey insufficient items or even neglect to convey items to clients. Sometimes, people spend cash to overhaul challenging items. Then again, Master card details of people can be lifted when deal happen over the Internet [58].

Security risk

Security risk has been expressed in various studies that the utmost trial to the internet banking will be captivating the belief of clients concerning the problems of security

[59,60]. Security risk happen when customers is about to transfer money from their account or from their secluded economic information which can be view by others deprived of their consents, this concern create security risk [45].

Security risk is the core hindrance in making use of the internet banking. PolatoÃÂlu et al. [61] has already been recommended that better quality security in defending individual information can escalate the partiality for making use of internet banking. Security/privacy risk is categorised as a prospective forfeit owed to fraud or a hacker bargaining the security of an internet bank user [62]. Phishing is an alternate original misconduct aptitude in which phishers tries to deceitfully obtain delicate data, for example, usernames, passwords and MasterCard subtle elements, as a dependable object in an automated message.

Effect of Perceived Risk on Intention to Use Internet Banking

Studies indicated perceived risk as a critical factor and its relationship to the internet banking adoption [61,63,64]. Past study has discovered the risk connected with fatalities misfortunes from the internet banking exchange is more noteworthy than in customary situations [65-67].

Bauer [68] initially presented the idea of perceived risk. He characterized risk as far as the instability and outcomes connected with a consumer' activities. For instance, consumer investigators characterize perceived risk as a customer's view of the indecision and unfriendly outcomes connected with purchasing an item (or facility) [69]. Perceived risk increments with vulnerability and size of the related negative result.

Perceived risks in a few studies have been regarded as a multidimensional theory. Prior effort has demonstrated that perceived risk comprises of various sorts of risk, containing performance risk, social risk, time risk, monetary risk and security risk [38,39,70]. Zimund affirmed the significance of risk connected with the chance expense of settling on a purchase choice. It was realised that clients require more data to settle on further risky choice [71].

Research Conceptual Framework

This research is centred on perceived risk and intention of adopting internet banking among the postgraduate student of UUM. Past researchers have identified relationships among the independents variables of this study perceived risk, performance risk, social risk, time risk, financial risk, and security risk and the dependent variable intention to use. The framework provided below explains the relationship between the risks perceived in using the internet banking and the intention to use the internet banking. This research is of the opinion that the increase in the risk perceived by the potential customers will decreased the intention to utilize the internet banking services. Thus, it is hypothesized that there is a negative relationship between perceived risk and the intention to use internet banking services (Figure 2).

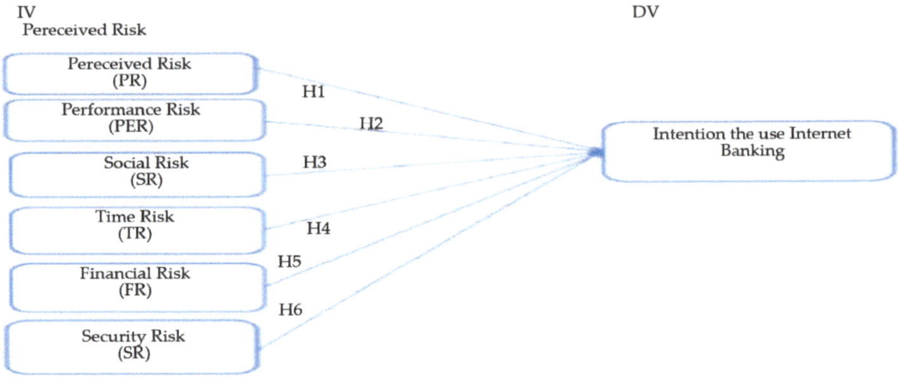

Figure 2: Research framework

Research Hypotheses

The following are the specific hypothesis that depicts the framework of this research:

H1: Perceived risk negatively influences intention towards the use of internet banking.

H2: Performance risk negatively influences intention towards the use of internet banking.

H3: Social risk negatively influences intention towards the use of internet banking.

H4: Time risk negatively influences intention towards the use of internet banking.

H5: Financial risk negatively influences intention towards the use of internet banking.

H6: Security risk negatively influences intention to use online banking.

RESEARCH METHODOLOGY

Sekaran [72] stated that the choice of research design in a study depends on the nature of the research questions being considered by the researcher. As a result of the nature of the questions addressed in this research, a quantitative research design is considered appropriate for this study. Research methodology involves four different phases: the definition of the problem, data collection, data analysis, and reporting. Therefore, gathering information about the problems or issues of the research involves an exploratory study which is conducted via thorough literature review to gain familiarity about the research issues. As such, the definition of the problem in this study involves an exploratory study via literature review to understand the background to the study after which a research proposal is drafted. These are designed and tailored to precisely answer the research questions, test the hypotheses and achieve the research objectives. Data Collection instrument is done by using an adapted questionnaire from the previously related study Ming-Chi Lee [62].

Population and sampling

The population used in this study is Nigeria graduate students of Universiti Utara Malaysia (UUM) comprising of both the Master students and PhD students. The population comprises of Nigeria post graduate students with internet banking. According to Krejcie et al. [73] a population range between 180-190 will have a sample size of 120. After confirming the total number of the UUM student from the student affairs department Unit Perancangan Korporat 2011 which revealed that there are 5,389 postgraduate students studying in UUM and the total number of Nigeria postgraduate's student is 670. Therefore, a representative sample of 120 students was surveyed in UUM. This is justified by Sekeran [74].

Respondents profile

The very initial stage of this study analysis is to understand the demographic background of the respondents. Thus the necessity for analysing the questions that is included in the questionnaire purposefully to examine respondent demographic profile. Age was included as one of the questions needed to understand respondents' demographic features and the descriptive result revealed that 59 (49.2%) students among the respondents are between the ages of 19 to 30. 56 (46.7%) fall in the age of 31 to 45.4 (3.3%) students among the respondents are between the age of 46 to 60 and just 1(.8%) respondents are greater than 60 years old and above. Hence, the descriptive analysis of gender revealed that 90 (75.0%) males responded to the administered questionnaire and 30 (25.0%) are females out of those that responded to the administered questionnaire. Amongst the demographic features is the education level of the respondent is 120 (100.0%).

The descriptive analysis of marital status revealed that 54 (46.7%) single responded to the administered questionnaire and 66 (53.3%) are married out of those that responded to the administered questionnaire. Based on the survey, descriptive analysis of occupation shows that 66 (55.8%) employed responded to the administered questionnaire and 54 (44.2%) are unemployed out of those that responded to the administered questionnaire. According to the survey, result shows that 120 (100%) of the respondents' do have a bank account. It is also revealed that 111 (92.5%) are students who make use of internet banking, while 9 (7.5%) are students who do not use internet banking.

A none-structured question was also asked in the Part A of the study questionnaire, purposefully for the respondents to record their internet usage habits. The research recorded and examines computed frequencies of the internet usage habits recorded by the respondents. It is revealed that 55 (45.9%) are student respondents who usually make use of internet banking transaction (IBT), while 65 (54.1%) are student response who frequently make use of internet banking transaction (IBT). It was found that 82 (68.3%) students do normally access there internet banking in the school (AOIB), in filling the questionnaire and the remaining 38 (31.7%) students do normally access there internet banking at home (AOIB). It is revealed that 73 (60.8%) are student respondents who make use of personal computer to have access to their computer (DTC), while 47 (39.2%) are student response who make use of mobile phone to have access to their computer (DTC).

It was also realised that 71 (59.2%) students respondents who do encounter problem frequently in using their Internet Banking (PEIB), in filling the questionnaire and the remaining 49 (40.8%) students respondents who do not encounter problem frequently in using their Internet Banking (PEIB). According to the survey, result shows that 84 (70.0%) of the respondents' do make use of internet banking from more than one bank frequently (UIB), Meanwhile the remaining 36 (30.0%) respondent's do not make use of internet banking from more than one bank frequently (UIB).

TEST FOR MULTI-COLLINEARITY

Multicollinearity demonstrates a circumstance in which there is high linear relationship between the independent variables [75]. The presence of Multicollinearity does not show a good regression model. Multicollinearity can be identified by inspecting the tolerance value, variance inflated factor (VIF) and the condition index. The tolerance value of 0.1 or lower and a VIF value higher than 10 shows Multicollinearity threat [76]. In this study, the tolerance value are higher than the threshold value of 0.1, the VIF value is lower than the threshold value 10, while the condition index are lesser than 30, which shows that Multicollinearity is not a threat in this study.

PEARSON CORRELATION ANALYSIS

Correlation analysis indicates the strength and the direction of a bivariate relationship [77]. Pearson moment correlation coefficient, in this study, was used in determining the bivariate relationship among the independent variables (perceived risk (PR), performance risk (PFR), social risk (SR), time risk (TR), financial risk (FR), security risk (SER) and the dependent variable, intention to use (IU). Correlation co-efficient of value indicates no strength, 0.1 – 0.3 is weak, 0.4 – 0.6 is moderate, 0.7 -0.9 is strong, while 1 indicates a perfect relationship [78]. Table 1 presents the findings of the Pearson correlation analysis.

Table 1 shows the correlation coefficient result of the hypothesized relationships. Perceived (r = 0.258) has a weak positive relationship with intention to use (IU) with correlation coefficient. Performance risk (r = 0.221) was found to possess a significant weak positive relationship with intention to use. Also social risk (r = 0.125) has a weak positive relationship with intention to use (IU). In addition, time risk (TR) has a weak negative relationship with intention to use (IU). Financial risk (0.155) has a weak positive relationship with intention to use (IU) while, security risk (r = 0.035) has a weak positive relationship with intention to use (IU).

Table 1: Pearson Correlation

		IU
Intention to Use	Pearson Correlation	1
	Sig. (2-tailed)	
	N	120
Perceived Risk	Pearson Correlation	.258**
	Sig. (2-tailed)	.005
	N	120
Performance Risk	Pearson Correlation	.221*
	Sig. (2-tailed)	.015
	N	120
Social Risk	Pearson Correlation	.125
	Sig. (2-tailed)	.173
	N	120
Time Risk	Pearson Correlation	-.179
	Sig. (2-tailed)	.050
	N	120
Financial Risk	Pearson Correlation	.155
	Sig. (2-tailed)	.090
	N	120
Security Risk	Pearson Correlation	.035
	Sig. (2-tailed)	.703
	N	120

Multiple regression analysis

Upon the completion of the correlation analysis, multiple regressions was also employed by the researcher to determine the effect of each independent variable (PR, PFR, SR, TR, FR and SER) to explaining the variances in the dependent variable (IU). The multiple regression analysis result shows R2 Adjusted = 0.169 which reveals that the predictors contributed 16.9% variance level in explaining intention to use. The result of the F-test revealed a significant relationship between the independent variables and the dependent variable representing the overall model by the equation: (F (7, 120) = 5.033, $P < 0.05$). As depicted by Table 2 below, the result shows that perceived risk (PR) indicated by a beta value of (β = 0.287) has a larger contribution to explaining the variance in intention to use than performance risk (PFR), social risk (SR), time risk (TR), financial risk (FR), security risk (SER) with beta value (β = 0.244, -0.82, 0.351, 0.227, and 0.215) respectively.

Table 2: Multiple regression analysis

Model	Unstandardized Coefficients	Standardized Coefficients	T	Sig.	
	B	Std. Error	Beta		
(Constant)	3.669	0.542		6.766	0
PR	0.317	0.105	0.287	3.033	0.003
PFR	0.295	0.121	0.244	2.434	0.016
SR	-0.083	0.1	-0.082	-0.827	0.41
TR	0.349	0.103	0.351	3.64	0
FR	0.227	0.106	0.227	2.153	0.033
SER	0.219	0.104	0.215	2.146	0.004

Model	R	R2	Adj. R2	Std. Error	F Change	Sig.
1	.459a	0.211	0.169	1.454	5.033	0

Furthermore, the regression analysis shows a significant effect of perceived risk (PR) ($\beta = 0.287$, $t = 3.033$, $P < 0.05$) on intention to use while performance risk (PFR) show an evidence of significant relationship ($\beta = 0.244$, $t = 2.434$, $P < 0.05$) with intention to use. Additionally, social risk failed to show an evidence of significant relationship ($\beta = -0.082$, $t = -0.827$, $P > 0.05$) with intention to use. Also time risk (TR) show an evidence of significant relationship ($\beta = 0.351$, $t = 3.640$, $P < 0.05$) with intention to use. Likewise, financial risk (FR) show an evidence of significant relationship ($\beta = 0.227$, $t = 2.153$, $P < 0.05$) with intention to use. Moreover, security risk (SER) show an evidence of significant relationship ($\beta = 0.215$, $t = 2.146$, $P < 0.05$). Thus, Hypotheses H1, H2, H4, H5, and H6 are accepted while hypothesis H3 not accepted. Table 2 presents the result of regression analysis.

DISCUSSION

The discussion of the findings in this study will be discussed based on the hypothesized relationship in this study. The following section presents the discussion on the relationship between perceived and intention to use IB.

The effect of perceived risk on the intention to use internet banking

In pursuit of this objective, hypothesis H1 which posited that perceived risk negatively influences intention towards the use of internet banking, the regression analysis shows a significant effect of perceived risk (PR) ($\beta = 0.287$, $t = 3.033$, $P < 0.05$) on intention to use which was accepted in this study, also the result from the descriptive analysis shows that the respondent slightly agree to have intention to use internet banking. While, the result from the Pearson correlation analysis found that perceived risk has a weak positive significant relationship with intention to use internet banking. This study is in line with previous researches of Roselius [39]. Roboff et al. [40] realised that individuals have a weak knowledge of internet banking risks while they are mindful of the dangers. So many diverse of study already exhibited perceived risk as a very vital factors which influence internet banking adoption which has been negatively related [63].

The effect of performance risk on the intention to use internet banking

In pursuit of this objective, hypothesis H2 which posited that performance risk negatively influences intention towards the use of internet banking, the regression analysis shows an evidence of significant effect of performance risk (PFR) ($\beta = 0.244$, $t = 2.434$, $P < 0.05$) on intention to use which was accepted in this study, also the result from the descriptive analysis shows that the respondent slightly agree to have intention to use internet banking. While, the result from the Pearson correlation analysis found that performance risk has a weak positive significant relationship with intention to use internet banking. This study is in line with previous researches of Kuisma [52] performance risk implies losses sustained by shortages of internet banking websites. Customers are frequently anxious that collapse of system servers or termination from the web will transpire while leading transaction because the circumstances might outcome in unanticipated fatalities.

The effect of social risk on the intention to use internet banking

The third hypothesis H3 in this study social risk negatively influences intention towards the use of internet banking, Additionally, the regression analysis for social risk failed to show an evidence of significant relationship ($\beta = -0.082$, $t = 0.827$, $P > 0.05$) with intention to use in which it was not accepted which, also the result from the descriptive analysis shows that the respondent are neutral to have intention to use internet banking. While, the result from the Pearson correlation analysis found that performance risk has a weak positive significant relationship with intention to use internet banking. The findings indicate that there is no relationship between social risk and intention to use internet banking. Few researchers' assertion that technology based services has in-built preventive influences by not offering collaborating impact with individuals [45]. This is the opportunity of derogate self-esteem and curiosity [53].

The effect of time risk on the intention to use internet banking

In pursuit of this objective, hypothesis H4 which posited that time risk negatively influences intention towards the use of internet banking, the regression analysis shows an evidence of significant relationship of time risk (TR) ($\beta = 0.351$, $t = 3.640$, $P < 0.05$) with intention to use internet banking, which was accepted in this study, also the result from the descriptive analysis shows that the respondent are neutral to have intention to use internet banking. While, the result from the Pearson correlation analysis found that time risk has a weak negative significant relationship with intention to use internet banking. Time risk can also be identified with the period included in managing with wrong dealings.

The effect of financial risk on the intention to use internet banking

In pursuit of this objective, hypothesis H5 which posited that financial risk negatively influences intention towards the use of internet banking, Likewise, the regression analysis shows an evidence of significant relationship of financial risk (FR) ($\beta = 0.227$, $t = 2.153$, $P < 0.05$) with intention to use which was accepted in this study, also the result from the descriptive analysis shows that the respondent slightly agree to have intention to use internet banking. While, the result from the Pearson correlation analysis found that performance risk has a weak positive significant relationship with intention to use internet banking. This study is in line with previous researches of Kuisma [52] says customers are frightened losing their money while carrying out transaction from their account via the utilization of the internet, it is also referred to as prospective for economic loss payable to transaction mistakes or the bank account misappropriation.

The effect of security risk on the intention to use internet banking

Lastly, the hypothesis H5 in this study security risk negatively influences intention towards the use of internet banking. Moreover, the regression analysis shows an evidence of significant relationship of security risk (SER) ($\beta = 0.215$, $t = 2.146$, $P < 0.05$) with intention to use internet banking, which was accepted in this study, also the result from the descriptive analysis shows that the respondent slightly agree to have security risk in internet banking. While, the result from the Pearson correlation analysis found that security risk has a weak positive significant relationship with intention to use internet banking. Littler [45] assertion security risk is the core hindrance in making use of the internet banking. The belief of so many consumers is that there are susceptible to identity theft whenever they are making use of the internet services [7].

Executive Summary of the Findings

In relation to the five hypothesized relationships in this study, statistical analysis was used to test the relationship and the result found that four hypotheses were supported, while two hypotheses were not supported. Specifically, the result found a statistical weak positive significant relationship between perceived risk (PR) and intention to use (IU), a significant weak positive relationship between performance risk (PFR) and intention to use; also there is a significant weak positive relationship between social risk (SR) and intention to use (IU), there exist significant negative relationship between time risk (TR) and intention to use; while, a significant weak positive relationship between financial risk (FR) and intention to use; lastly, there occur a significant weak positive relationship between security risk (SER) and intention to use. In addition, the findings shows that perceived risk (PR) among all other variables contributes more in explaining intention to use indicating that it is the most important among the factors that influence intention to use among the postgraduates student. The Table 3 below presents the hypothesis of the study.

Table 3: Summary of the findings

	The hypotheses	Decision
H1	There is relationship between perceived risk and intention to use internet banking.	Accepted
H2	There is relationship between performance risk and intention to use internet banking.	Accepted
H3	There is no relationship between social risk and intention to use internet banking.	Not Accepted
H4	There is relationship between time risk and intention to use internet banking.	Accepted
H5	There is relationship between financial risk and intention to use internet banking.	Accepted
H6	There is no relationship between security risk and intention to use internet banking.	Accepted

Implication of the Study

This study contributes both theoretically and practically. Theoretical, this study has been able to examine the link between perceived risk intentions to use. As such, it has donated to the group of knowledge by supporting the previous studies on the established relationship between perceived risk and intention to use internet banking. In addition, it has been able to expand literatures on the issues and trends of internet banking today and indicates the influences that can enhance intention to use internet banking among UUM postgraduate students. More so, the empirical findings of the study have been able to discuss on previous literature study concerning technology acceptance model (TAM) and theory of planned behavior (TPB)

Practically, this study has provided an avenue for Nigeria government and banking authority to instil and improve on customer adoption on internet banking in Nigeria by pointing out to the bank authorities that perceived risk is an important factor that determines intention to use internet banking users. As such, stable availability of network or circulation of information during maintenance of system should be given optimum attention in order to enhance the intention of customers towards the usage of internet banking.

CONCLUSION

This study was conducted among the Nigeria postgraduate student of UUM and the study make use of perceived risk and it dimension. The researchers were able to draw their conclusion. Under Pearson correlation that perceived risk has a weak relationship with intention to use, Performance risk was found to possess a significant weak positive relationship with intention to use. Also social risk has a weak positive relationship with intention to use (IU). In addition, time risk (TR) has a weak negative relationship with intention to use (IU). Financial risk has a weak positive relationship with intention to use (IU) while, Security risk has a weak positive relationship with intention to use (IU). The findings shows that perceived risk (PR) have the highest value (0.258) among all other variables that exist in Pearson correlation coefficient in which it contributes more in explaining intention to use indicating that it is the most important among the factors that influence intention to use among the Nigeria postgraduates student in UUM.

Also, the multiple regression analysis from this study, also ascertain that perceived risk, performance risk, time risk, financial risk and security risk were all accepted, while social risk is not accepted, so therefore the study argued that the five risk which are accepted are the most important, while social risk is unimportant. the result shows that perceived risk (PR) indicated by a beta value of ($\beta = 0.287$) has a larger contribution to explaining the variance in intention to use than performance risk (PFR), social risk (SR), time risk (TR), financial risk (FR), security risk (SER) with beta value ($\beta = 0.244$, -0.82, 0.351, 0.227, and 0.215) respectively.

Lastly, student should be exposed to internet system which lay emphasis on developing internet banking skills and knowledge. Banks administrators and the government should team up to produce and promote a good image of bank as a choice of career. To improve students' intention to use, certain method needs to be adopted and the internet banking policy makers should add more value and reliability to their online transaction for customers by integrating the elements that boost the development of internet banking.

Recommendation for Future Study

There have been some notable limitations that this are beyond the control of this present study. Future researchers are recommended to delve deeper on the effect of perceived risk on intention to adopt internet banking. It is also expected that future studies should survey bigger sample size to enable wider generalization of the study findings. Additionally, future researchers are recommended to validate this present research theoretical framework with a multivariate analytical tool such as SEM or path analysis. Lastly, future researchers are recommended to structure their scope of study longitudinally for the purpose of understanding the influences and changes in students' responses through the change of time.

REFERENCES

1. Daniel E (1999) Provision of Electronic Banking in the UK and the Republic of Ireland. International Journal of Bank Marketing 17: 72-82.
2. Scornavacca,Hoehle (2007) Mobile Banking in Germany: A Strategic Perspective. International Journal of Electronic Finance 1: 304-320.
3. Riquelme HE (2010) The Moderating Effect of Gender in the Adoption of Mobile Banking. International Journal of Bank Marketing 28: 328-341.
4. Ezeoha AE (2006) Regulating Internet Banking in Nigeria: Problems and Challenges. Journal of Internet Banking and Commerce 10: 1-3.

5. Kalakota R, Whinston AB (1997) Electronic Commerce: A Manager's Guide. Addison Wesley.
6. Pavlou P (2001) Integrating Trust in Electronic Commerce with the Technology Acceptance Model: Model Development and Validation. AMCIS Proceedings, Boston.
7. Lee MC (2009) Factors Influencing the Adoption of Internet Banking: An integration of TAM and TPB with Perceived Risk and Perceived Benefit. Electronic Commerce and Applications 8: 130-141.
8. Liao S (1999)The Adoption of Virtual Banking: An Empirical Study. International Journal Information Management 19: 63-74.
9. Tan M, Teo TSH (2000) Factors Influencing the Adoption of Internet Banking. J Association Information System 1: 1-42.
10. Heijden HV (2003) Factors Influencing the Usage of Websites: The Case of a Generic Portal in the Netherlands. Inform Manage40: 541-9.
11. Taylor S, Todd P (1995) Assessing IT Usage the Role of Prior Experience. MIS Quarterly 19: 561-570.
12. Westin AF, Maurici D (1998) E-commerce and Privacy: What the Net Users Want. Privacy and American Business, New York.
13. Cranor S, Ackerman (1999) Beyond Concern: Understanding Net Users' Attitudes about Online Privacy. The Internet Upheaval: Raising Questions, Seeking Answers in Communications Policy.
14. Kobsa A (2001) Tailoring Privacy to Users' Needs.Computer SciencePp: 301-313.
15. Davis FD, Bagozzi RP,Warshaw PR (1989) User Acceptance of Computer Technology: A Comparison of two Theoretical Models. Management Science 35: 982-1003.
16. Azjen I (1985) From Intentions to Actions: A Theory of Planned Behaviour. Action ControlPp: 11-39.
17. Durkin M, Jennings D, Mulholland G, Worthington S (2008) Key Influencers and Inhibitors on Adoption of the Internet for Banking. Journal of Retailing and Consumer Services 15: 348-357.
18. Haque A, Osman J, Ismail A (2009) Factors Influencing Selection of Islamic Banking: A Study of Malaysian Customer Preferences. American Journal of Applied SciencesPp: 922-928.
19. Burnham B (1996) The Internet's Impact on Retail Banking. Booz-Allen Hamilton Third Quarter.
20. Duclaux D (1996)The Call of the Web ABA Banking Journal, Financial Times. Internet Poses Growing Threat to Traditional Banks.
21. Arthur Grubb (2000) Myth vs Reality in Financial Services: What your Customers Really Want. Deloitte Consulting.
22. Currie W (2000)The Global Information Society. Wiley.

23. Lam R, Burton S (2005) Bank Selection and Share of Wallet among SMEs: Apparent Differences between Hong Kong and Australia. Journal of Financial Services Marketing Pp: 204-213.
24. Sai Om (2004) A Study on Customer Attitude towards the Use of e-banking Services in Kerala. Journal of Commerce and Management.
25. Shih, YY, Fang K (2004) The Use of a Decomposed Theory of Planned Behaviour to Study Internet Banking in Taiwan. Internet Research14: 213-219.
26. Turban E, Lee J, King D, Chung HM (2000) Electronic Commerce: A Managerial Perspective. Prentice-Hall, NJ.
27. Davis FD (1989) Perceived Usefulness, Perceived Ease of Use, and User Acceptance of Information technology. MIS Quarterly 13: 319-340.
28. Suh B, Han I (2003) The Impact of Customer Trust and Perception of Security Control on the Acceptance of Electronic Commerce. International Journal of Electronic Commerce7: 135-161.
29. Lassar WM (2005)The Relationship between Consumer Innovativeness, Personal Characteristics, and Online Banking Adoption. International Journal of Bank Marketing23: 176-199.
30. Kolodinsky JM, Hogarth JM (2004)The Adoption of Electronic Banking Technologies by US Consumers. The International Journal of Bank Marketing22: 238-259.
31. Gardachew FM (2010) Electronic-Banking in Ethiopia- Practices, Opportunities and Challenges. Journal of Internet Banking and Commerce.
32. Gonzalez ME (2008) An Alternative Approach in Service Quality: An E-Banking Case Study. Quality ManagePp: 41-48.
33. Pikkarainen T,Karjaluoto H, Pahnila (2004) Consumer acceptance of online banking: an Extension of the technology Acceptance Model. Internet ResearchPp: 224-235.
34. Aderonke, Charles (2010) Empirical Investigation of the Level of Users Acceptance of E-Banking in Nigeria. Journal of Internet Banking and Commerce 2: 418-430.
35. Wilson GW, Sasseville DR (2004) A Study on Customer Perception in Online Banking. John Wiley.
36. Davis FD (19 93) User Acceptance of Information Technology: System Characteristics,User, Perceptions and behavioural impacts. International Journal of Man-Machine Studies 38: 475-87.
37. Eriksson K, Kerem K, Nilsson D (2005) Customer Acceptance of Internet Banking in Estonia. International Journal of Bank Marketing23: 200-216.
38. Jacoby J, Kaplan L (1972)The Components of Perceived Risk. Advances in Consumer Research, Chicago.
39. Roselius T (1971) Consumer Rankings of Risk Reduction Methods. J Market35: 56-61.

40. Roboff G, Charles C (1998) Privacy of Financial Information in cyberspace: Banks Addressing what Consumers want. Journal of Retail Banking Services 20: 51-56.

41. Sathye M (1999)Adoption of Internet Banking by Australian Consumers: An Empirical Investigation. International Journal of Bank Marketing17: 324-334.

42. Krauter SG, Faullant R (2008) Consumer Acceptance of Internet bBanking: the Influence of internet trust. International Journal of Bank Marketing26: 483-504.

43. Einwiller S, Will M (2001) The Role of Reputation to Engender Trust in Electronic Markets. Proceedings of the 5th International Conference on Corporate Reputation, Identity, and Competitiveness, France.

44. Cheung CMK, Lee MKO (2006) Understanding Consumer Trust in Internet Shopping: A Multidisciplinary Approach. Journal of the American Society for Information Science and Technology 57: 479-492.

45. Littler D, Melanthiou D (2006) Consumer Perceptions of Risk and Uncertainty and the Implications for Behaviour towards Innovative Retail Services. The Case of Internet Banking13: 431-43.

46. Rotchanakitumnuai S, Speece M (2003) Barriers to Internet banking adoption: A Qualitative Study among Corporate Customers in Thailand. International Journal of Bank Marketing 21: 312-323.

47. Kim C, Mirusmonov M, Lee I (2010) An Empirical Examination of Factors Influencing the Intention to Use Mobile Payment. Computers in Human Behaviour26: 310-322.

48. Schneier B (2011) Secrets and Lies: Digital Security in a Networked World. Wiley, Indiana.

49. Grewal D, Gotlieb J, Marmorstein H (1994)The Moderating Effects of Message Framing and Source Credibility on the Price-Perceived Risk Relationship. Journal of Consumer Research 21: 145-153.

50. Neal CM, Quester PG, Hawkins D (2002) Consumer Behaviour, Implication for Marketing Strategy (3rdedn.). Australia.

51. Horton RL (1976)The Structure of Perceived Risk. Journal of the Academic of Marketing Sciences4: 694-706.

52. Kuisma T, Laukkanen T,Hiltunen M (2007) Mapping the Reasons for Resistance to Internet Banking: AMmeans-End Approach. Int J Inform Manage27: 75-85.

53. Murray KB, Schlacter JL (1990) The Impact of Services versus Goods on Consumer's Assessment of Perceived Risk and Variability. Journal of the AcademyMarketing Science 18: 51-65.

54. Forsythe SM, Shi B (2003) Consumer Patronage and Risk Perceptions in Internet Shopping. Journal of Business Research 56: 867-75.

55. Lim, Nena (2003) Consumer's Perceived Risk: Sources versus Consequences. Electronic Commerce Research and Applications2: 216-228.

56. Laroche, Michael, McDougall, Gordon HC, Bergeron (2004) Exploring How Intangibility Affects Perceived Risk. Journal of Service Research6: 373-389.
57. OECD (1999)The Economic and Social Impact of Electronic Commerce. Preliminary Findings and Research Agenda.
58. Lee D, Park J (2001) On the Explanation of Factors Information Affecting commerce Adoption. Proceedings of the 22nd International Conference on Information SystemsPp: 109-120.
59. Bestavros A (2000) Banking Industry Walks 'Tightrope' in Personalization of Web Services. Bank System Technology 37:54-6.
60. Furnell SM, Karweni T (1999) Security Implications of Electronic Commerce: A survey Of Consumers and Businesses. Internet Research 5:372-82.
61. PolatogluV, Ekin S (2001) An Empirical Investigation of the Turkish Consumer'sAcceptance of Internet Banking Services. International Journal of Bank Marketing 19: 156-165.
62. Lee MC (2008) Predicting Behavioural Intention to Use Online Banking. Proceedings of the 19th International Conference on Information Management.
63. Gerrard P, Cunningham JB (2003) The Diffusion of Internet Banking among Singapore Consumers. The International Journal of Bank MarketingPp: 16-28.
64. Hewer P, Howcroft B (1999) Consumers Distribution Channel Adoption and Usage in The Financial Services Industry: A Review of Existing Approaches. Journal of Financial Services Marketing 344-58.
65. Bradley L, Stewart K (2003) Delphi Study of Internet Banking. Marketing Intelligence and Planning21: 272-281.
66. Mukherjee A, Nath P (2003) A Model of Trust in Online Relationship Banking. International Journal of Bank Marketing 21: 5-15.
67. Wang Y, Lin H, Tang T (2003) Determinants of User Acceptance of Internet Banking: An Empirical Study. International Journal of Service Industry Management14: 501-519.
68. Bauer RA (1960) Consumer Behaviour as Risk Taking. Proceedings of the 43rd Conference of the American Marketing AssociationPp: 389-98.
69. Cunningham SM (1976) The Major Dimensions of Perceived Risk. In: Cox DF, editor Risk taking, and information handling in consumer behaviour. Harvard University Press, Boston.
70. Kaplan LB, George JS, Jacoby J (1974) Components of Perceived Risk in Product Purchase. Journal of Applied Psychology59: 287-91.
71. Dowling R, Staelin R (1994) A Model of Perceived Risk and Intended Risk-Handling Activity.Journal of Consumer Research21: 110-34.
72. Sekaran U (2003) Research Methods for Business – A Skill Building Approach. 4th Edition, John Wiley and Sons.
73. Krejcie RV, Morgan DW (1970) Determining Sample Size for Research Activities. Educational and Psychological Measurementpp: 607-610.

74. Sekaran G (2008) Characterization of an Alkaline Active–Thiol Forming ExtraCellular Serine Keratinase by The Newly Isolated Bacillus Pumilus. Journal of Applied Microbiology 104: 411-419.
75. Hair JF, Black WC, Babin BJ, Anderson RE (2010) Multivariate Data Analysis. 7th edition, Upper Saddle River, New Jersey.
76. Hair JF, Hult GT, Ringle CM, Sarstedt M (2013) A Primer on Partial Least Squares Structural Equation Modeling (PLS-SEM). Sage Publications Ltd, Thousand Oaks, Carlifornia.
77. Pallant Y (2011) SPSS Survival Manual: A Step by Step Guide to Data Analysis Using SPSS for Windows. 3rd edition, McGraw Hill Open University Press, England.
78. Dancey C, Reidy J (2004) Analysis of Differences between Two Conditions: The T-test. Statistics without Maths for Psychology: Using SPSS for Windows Essex, England.

12
CHAPTER

IMPACT OF DIMENSIONS OF MOBILE BANKING ON USER SATISFACTION

Bharti M

Keywords: Mobile banking, Efficacy, Security, Satisfaction

INTRODUCTION

Technology has opened up new markets, new products, new services and efficient delivery channels for the banking industry. Specifically, banking industry has undergone radical changes as a consequence of the breath-taking developments in this technological revolution. Banks have changed from paper-based banking solutions provider to the latest of the technologies like online-banking, mobile-banking, etc. Also, to cater to the ever increasing consumer expectations and demand, the banking industry has these technologies to offer banking services at the convenience and comfort of its customers. New business models, processes and revolutionized distribution channels are the outcome of technical advances in the banking industry.

Mobile commerce is a natural successor to electronic Commerce. Mobile banking is a revolution that is driven by the world's one of the fastest growing sectors mobile communication technology. Mobile banking is defined as an interaction in which a customer is connected to a bank via a mobile device such as cell phone, smartphone or personal digital assistant (PDA) [1]. Mobile banking can also be considered as the convergence of mobile technology and financial services [2]. M-banking is a subset of banking as it allows everyone easy access to their banking activities via mobile handsets [3]. According to Palani et al. [4] Mobile banking in India is in growth; approximately 43 million urban Indians used their mobile phones to access banking services during

Citation: Bharti M (2016) Impact of Dimensions of Mobile Banking on User Satisfaction. J Internet Bank Commer 21:152. doi:10.4172/1204-5357.1000152s.

quarter ending August, 2009, a reach of 15% among urban Indian mobile phone user. Technology providers and financial institutions believe that m-payment will reach critical mass in the next few years [5].

RATIONALE

Adoption of mobile-banking has received more attention in recent years, because there are more phone users than computer users in the market. Mobile services and their consumption have lately become a burning issue among information systems (IS) and marketing scholars [6]. At the same time, many service providers are making substantial investments to take advantage of the business opportunities offered by wireless technology. Despite the rapid rollout of mobile services over the past decade, mobile transactions, including mobile banking and payments, have not been used as much as expected [7] and the services are marginally adopted [8]. Studies by Amin [9], Luarn [10] and Mattila [11] have also documented the need of mobile banking services in the society.

Mobile banking in India is still at a growing stage, so there is a need to understand the bank customers' acceptance of this service and to examine the factors affecting their intentions to use mobile banking. It has been found that in India not even 20% of the population use E-channels [12] only 6% out of 3100 samples of consumer surveyed across India are using the internet for banking services. Kwiatkowski [13] confirms the prediction by reporting that up to now usage of mobile banking is decidedly low, even within developed markets where mobile devices have become nearly ubiquitous. However, technology providers and financial institutions believe that m-payment will reach critical mass in the next few years [5].

As the Internet banking is still in its growing stage, mobile banking has emerged as the next advance way of doing banking. Mobile phones make it simple to communicate with the target market and establish a stronger relationship as banks provide market compelling-needed services [14]. But, like in any emerging technology, there exist barriers to the adoption of mobile banking services. There are many reasons why technology has not been able to ride the acceptance wave and cross the hurdle and become an acceptable feature in banking. This paper is an attempt to understand the effect of different factors of mobile banking on the satisfaction related to mobile banking. In this paper, we have used Structural Equation Modeling through Smart PLS software to find out the relationship of the usage of mobile banking services with its determinants.

LITERATURE REVIEW

Mobile phones are likely to evolve as ubiquitous payment devices [15]. According to Donner [16] there is no universal form of m-banking; rather, purposes and structures vary from country to country. Goyal [17] presented a classification framework for m-banking research based on 65 m-banking papers published between 2000 and mid-2010. Rao analyzed the impact of new technology on banking sector. The technology is changing the way the business is done and opened new vistas for doing the same work differently in most cost effective manner. Tele-banking and internet banking are making forays such that branch banking may give to home banking. He provided some policies to protect their profitability. Shastri [18] studied the emergence of IT in banking sector. He highlighted some challenges faced by banks regarding IT implementation. This paper also highlighted future outlook of IT oriented banks. Uppal [12] studied the impact of Information Technology on various parameters of bank performance and concluded that Indian banking industry is fastly moving towards IT. The future of e-channels is very bright.

There are many advantages that mobile banking brings to customers. The systems offer a variety of financial functions, including micropayments to merchants, bill-payments to utilities, P2P transfers between individuals, and long-distance remittances. Mobile banking provides a new opportunity to banks to extend their services to customer and improve their competitiveness [19] includes value-added mobile services [20] offers an interactive banking transaction [21] and helps the banks in cost- saving in its operations. As such with mobile services, a bank will need to hire even less employees as people will no longer need to visit bank branches apart from certain occasions. With Indian telecom operators working on offering services like money transaction over a mobile, it may soon be possible for a bank to offer phone based credit systems. The prime benefit is the anywhere/anytime characteristics of mobile services. Mobile payments can become a complement to cash, cheques, credit cards and debit cards. It can also be used for payment of bills with access to account-based payment instruments such as electronic funds transfer, internet banking payments, direct debit and electronic bill presentment. The customers can also request for additional information. They can have information about the deposits and withdrawals as they occur and also pre-schedule their payments. Similarly, other banking transactions like stop cheque or issue of a cheque book can be easily done via a mobile phone. This will make credit cards redundant and also aid in checking credit card fraud apart from offering enhanced customer convenience. The use of mobile technologies is thus a win-win proposition for both the banks and the bank's customers. Also, through mobile messaging, banks provide value added services to the customer at nominal costs. Mobile phone handsets, which were initially used almost exclusively for voice calls are now often used to transmit data and undertake commercial transactions [22]. Sharma [23] identified 3 factors related to mobile banking which include access problems, dissatisfaction and inability to provide knowledge. Ewe [24] showed that perceived advantage over other mediums, perceived risk, usage complexity, past experience and awareness are potentially influencing the adoption of mobile banking.

Previous studies indicate, that factors contributing to the adoption of mobile banking are related to convenience, access to the service regardless of time and place, privacy and savings in time and effort [25]. Among the various factors determining adoption of mobile banking include levels of perceived risk [2,16] interaction [3] perceived uncertainty [26], perceived usefulness, ease of use, credibility, self efficacy, perceived system quality [7,10], experience [2], financial cost [27], time saving [7,26], security and privacy [10,28], Information quality [29,30], compatibility and risk [31] perceived financial cost [10], perceived risk [32], security issues [10,33].

RESEARCH METHODOLOGY

The research is exploratory in nature and the data used for the analysis is primary in nature. The data was collected using a self structured questionnaire having 55 questions. The questionnaire was designed following a wide review of the literature on mobile banking. In a pilot study of 100 consumers of mobile banking, the analysis of collected data was done by Statistical Package for Social Science (SPSS 15.0) and MS Excel 2007. Initially, item-total correlation was calculated for all 55 items to identify insignificant items not contributing towards perception regarding mobile banking. After first iteration, 4 items showed correlation values less than 0.196 (standard coefficient of correlation value for 100 or more respondents) and were thus found insignificant and were not considered for the analysis. Out of 55, Over-all reliability was evaluated for the scale by assessing the internal consistency of the remaining 51 items using Cronbach's Alpha. The instrument had a reliability of 0.83 which proves that it is reliable and can be used for further analysis. The data was then tested for Kaiser-Meyer-Olkin Measure of sampling adequacy and Bartlett's test of sphericity. High value of KMO i.e., 0.829>0.05 indicate that sample is sufficient for factor analysis. The Bartlett's test of sphericity is 0.000 which is less than 0.05 indicating that there exists significant relationship among the variable. Therefore all 51 items were accepted for the final scale and subjected to Principal Component Method of Factor Analysis using Varimax Rotation. This resulted into 17 factors of usage of mobile banking namely: Effortless Recoverability (% of Var.=6.470), Easy Accessibility (% of Var.=5.950), Distinguished Methodology (% of Var.=5.820), Functional Navigation (% of Var.=5.130), Improved Flexibility (% of Var.=4.985), Privacy Assurance (% of Var.=4.877), Environmental Collaboration (% of Var.=4.816), Ever Accessibility(% of Var.=4.514), Cost-Effective (% of Var.=4.248), Timely Updates (% of Var.=4.0350), new Technology Affable (% of Var.=4.028), Friendly User Interface (% of Var.=3.940), Ecological Friendly (% of Var.=3.887), Enhanced Customization (% of Var.=3.758), Knowledge Integration (% of Var.= 3.723), Effective Risk Measurement (% of Var.=3.481) and Interactive Technology (% of Var.=3.305). The total percent of variance for factors was 76.968% and the Eigen values for each factor was more than one.

These 17 factors when subjected to second order factor analysis, resulted into seven imperative dimensions of e-Books. These dimensions are Effective Distinctiveness (% of Var.=10.890%), Professed Security (% of Var.=8.663%), Immense Efficacy (% of Var.=8.238%), Supportive Access (% of Var.=8.122), Innovative Virtual Environment (% of Var.=7.736), Enhanced Personalization(% of Var.=7.298) and Improved Timely Updates (% of Var.=6.661). The total percent of variance for dimensions was 58.2% and the Eigen values for each dimension was more than one. The details of these factors tabularized with their item loads, Eigen values and percent of variances and shown in Annexure.

Finally, a total of 1000 respondents were administered this questionnaire containing 51 questions and responses were generated to determine satisfaction of user related to mobile banking.

Development of Hypothesis

Effective distinctiveness

The first dimension namely Effective Distinctiveness consisted of four factors namely Ever-Accessibility (Factor Load=0.655), Easy Accessibility (Factor Load=0.635), Environmental Collaboration (Factor Load=0.587) and Ecological Friendly (Factor Load= 0.559). Mobile devices improve the quality of the service because clients can perform transactions at their convenience wherever and whenever they want it provided there is a connection [26]. Ramdhony [34] identified Convenience, time and effort savings, privacy, ubiquitous access to banking services, compatibility with lifestyle and banking needs as the main factors motivating m-banking adoption. Suoranta et al. [21] identified different mobile banking facilities such as account balance retrieval, transaction history retrieval, transfer of funds between an individual's own accounts or third party accounts, stock trading, portfolio management, and bill settlements, etc. Skeldon [35] affirms that the general and widespread acceptance of mobile applications, the increasing use of mobile phones as a tool and means for paying bills, and lifestyle are the factors driving the adoption of m-banking. Ubiquitous access, convenience and mobility are the main benefits that m-banking confers to customers [36]. Advantages of mobile banking are availability of facilities of balance checking, access to account and card statement, checking recent transactions, ordering of cheque books, blocking of lost cards [37], checking of account history, SMS alerts, access to card statement, balance check, mobile recharge etc. via mobile phones [38]. The services today enable bank customers, for example, to request their account balance and the latest transactions of their accounts, to transfer funds between accounts, to make buy and sell orders on the stock exchange and to receive portfolio and price information. Previous studies indicate, that factors contributing to the adoption of mobile banking are related to convenience, access to the service regardless of time and place, privacy and savings in time and effort [25]. Mobile banking means that users adopt mobile terminals to conduct payment such as balance enquiry, transference and bill payment at anytime from anywhere [39]. Mobile banking frees users from spatial and temporal limitations, and enables them to conduct ubiquitous payment. Mobile banking means that users adopt mobile terminals to conduct payment such as balance enquiry, transference and bill payment at anytime from anywhere [40-42]. Shin defined mobile services as the range of services provided and accessed by a mobile device. The value of mobile banking for consumers is in its immediate location-free access to banking services enabling time savings, real-time information, and enhanced feelings of control [43]. Thus, it is reasonable to assume that:

H01: Effective Distinctiveness dimension of mobile banking does not have an association with satisfaction of user related to mobile banking.

Professed security

The Second dimension namely Professed Security consisted of three factors namely Effortless Recoverability (Factor Load=0.648), Effective Risk Measurement (Factor

Load=0.599) and Privacy Assurance (Factor Load=0.585). Kahandawa et al. [44] identified perception of risk and user's life style and current needs as the important factor of mobile banking. Zhihong et al. [45] considered perceived risk and system usability as the important factors. According to Kleijnen [7] Mobile banking and payments, have not been used as much as expected. This might be also due to the virtual look and lack of control that mobile banking involves great uncertainty and risk. Users need to build trust in order to adopt and use mobile banking [46]. Since mobile banking is the new banking gadget, the issue of security and privacy become important in understanding mobile banking acceptance among bank customer [10,28]. There is considerable amount of empirical research to suggest that users' intention to adopt mobile banking is inhibited by the perceived complexity of the innovation [40,47,48]. Ensuring security and confidentiality are the fundamental prerequisites before any banking activity involving sensitive information can take place Jayawardhena [49]. The significance of security and privacy for the adoption of online banking figured in many banking studies [50-53]. Lack of privacy and security found to be significant obstacles to the adoption of online banking [50]. They found that people have inadequate understanding of online banking security risks although they are aware of the risks. It was noted consumer's confidence in technology was weak. Consumers are becoming more concerned about security and privacy issues have proven important barriers to the use of online services.

The results of the study by Nicole [31] indicated that compatibility, perceived usefulness, and risk are significant indicators for the adoption of m-banking services and mobile phone banking includes using mobile devices to conduct personal financing via SMS and the mobile internet. Wolfinbarger [54] observed that reliability is an important factor for customer satisfaction. People refrain from using m-banking because it involves payments [10] such as SMS fee [55], security issues [33] and small keyboards and display screen of smart phone [26]. Particularly in banking services the perceived risk associated with the financial product itself as well as with electronic delivery channel is higher than in basic consumer goods, and hence increasing the importance of this attribute of innovation [56].

Generally, it has been found that Relative advantage, compatibility, trialability and observability are positively related to adoption of an innovation and the remaining two, complexity and perceived risk, negatively related. These innovation attributes and their influence on adoption of mobile banking services are detailed under empirical implications. Kim et al. [57] found that trust is also an important factor and should be taken into consideration by the Service providers; if consumers do not feel secure they will be reluctant to use the services. It is also found that people have less trust in the mobile banking services and personal disposition to trust played a positive role in developing initial usage in mobile banking. To some extent the success of acceptance of M-commerce transactions depends on the customer as well as vendor's trust. Kim et al. [57] and Majali [58] also discussed that if customers believe that a mobile banking firm is able to develop effective service delivery strategies and provide adequate protection from fraud and violation of privacy, then adoption (or continue-touse) intentions of the mobile phone users will increase. Thus, we can predict that:

H02: Professed Security dimension of mobile banking does not have an association with satisfaction of user related to mobile banking.

IMMENSE EFFICACY

The Third Dimension namely Immense Efficacy consisted of 2 factors namely Cost-Effective (Factor Load=0.770) and Improved Flexibility (Factor Load=0.574). Farhana [59] found that customers consider cost as the important factor Adewoye [60] found that Mobile banking improve banks service delivery in a form of transactional convenience, savings of time, quick transaction alert and save of service cost which has recuperate customer's relationship and satisfaction.

Mobile phone banking includes using mobile devices to conduct personal financing via SMS and the mobile internet. Mobile banking means that users adopt mobile terminals to conduct payment such as balance enquiry, transference and bill payment at anytime from anywhere [41,42]. The value of mobile banking for consumers is in its immediate location-free access to banking services enabling time savings, real-time information, and enhanced feelings of control [43]. Thus, we can predict.

H03: Immense Efficacy dimension of mobile banking does not have an association with satisfaction of user related to mobile banking.

Supportive Access

The Fourth Dimension namely Supportive Access consisted of 2 factors namely Knowledge Integration (Factor Load=0.756) and Distinguished Methodology (Factor Load=0.755). According to Alter [61] the amount of information consumers have about mobile banking is also identified as an important factor influencing the adoption. There is considerable amount of empirical research to suggest that users' intention to adopt mobile banking is inhibited by the perceived complexity of the innovation [40,47,48]. The results of the study by Nicole [31] indicated that compatibility, perceived usefulness, and risk are significant indicators for the adoption of m-banking services. Thus, we can assume that:

H04: Supportive Access dimension of mobile banking does not have an association with satisfaction of user related to mobile banking.

Innovative virtual environment

The Fifth Dimension namely Innovative Virtual Environment consisted of 3 factors namely easy Interactive style (Factor Load=0.643), Technology Affable (Factor Load=0.618) and Functional Navigation (Factor Load=0.585). High system quality and information quality are critical to ensure users' trust due to mobile banking unable to involve face-to-face contact customers [29]. Technical infrastructure, and design of technology are reported as individual barriers in a number of studies in inhibiting users' intention to adopt mobile banking [20,40,47,48,62,63].

Shoriful [64] explores the issues in mobile banking perceived critical for adoption by both mobile banking users as well as non-users. The study identified certain issues pertaining to banks, mobile handsets and telecom operator's viz. mobile handset operability, security/ privacy, standardization of services, customization, Downloading and installing application software and Telecom services quality. According to Sadi [65] facilitating Condition is also an important attribute, hence it is necessary to improve the facilitating conditions of mobile application services like connection speed, secure systems and easy transaction method. Chaipoopirutana et al. [66] claimed that the adoption of mobile banking is 'complex' as it has the negative relation with intention to adopt mobile banking. Mobile banking service quality assessment requires analysis of the full interface design. A good mobile system service will promote users' adoption intention; contrarily, a poor mobile system service will decrease users' adoption intention [67]. High system quality and information quality are critical to ensure users' trust due to mobile banking unable to involve faceto- face contact customers [29]. Technical infrastructure, and design of technology are reported as individual barriers in a number of studies in inhibiting users' intention to adopt mobile banking [20,40,47,48,62,63]. Thus, it is reasonable to assume that:

H05: Innovative Virtual Environment dimension of mobile banking does not have an association with satisfaction of user related to mobile banking.

The Sixth Dimension namely Enhanced Personalization consisted of 2 factors namely Friendly user interface (Factor Load=0.788) and Enhanced Customization (Factor Load=0.631). Personalization is the extent to which the device can be customized to fit a specific users needs. Personalization significantly impacts the ability to transfer knowledge since it presents presorted knowledge based on individual needs. Thus, we can assume that:

H06: Enhanced Personalization dimension of mobile banking does not have an association with satisfaction of user related to mobile banking.

The Seventh Dimension namely Improved Timely Updates consisted of only one factor namely timely updates (Factor Load =0.885). Mobile banking services through a variety of electronic pipeline to serve the consumer to create more opportunities, and has also been made to create added value for customers [68,69]. Thus, this leads to the development of the following hypothesis:

H07: Improved Timely Updates dimension of mobile banking does not have an association with satisfaction of user related to mobile banking.

Smart PLS was used to test the hypothesized relationships among the study variables. The choice was motivated by several considerations. PLS is a non-parametric estimation procedure [70]. Its conceptual core is an iterative combination of principal components analysis relating measures to constructs, and path analysis capturing the structural model of constructs. The structural model represents the direct and indirect causal relationships among constructs. It can be used to estimate models that use both reflective and formative indicators, is more appropriate for analyzing moderating effects because traditional techniques cannot account for measurement error in exogenous constructs allows for modeling latent constructs under conditions of non-normality, and is appropriate for small to medium sample sizes [71-73].

RESULTS AND DISCUSSION

The model was designed to study the effect of different dimensions of mobile banking on the user satisfaction (Figure 1). To assess the psychometric properties of measurement model, individual item loadings, internal consistency, convergent validity, and discriminant validity was examined of the reflective first-order factors (Effective Distinctiveness, Professed Security, Immense Efficacy, Supportive Access, Innovative Virtual Environment, Enhanced Personalization, and Improved Timely Updates).

The loadings of the measurement items on their respective factors were examined (Figure 2). Finally, the model included the items whose loading were above the threshold value on their respective factor and were statistically significant at the 0.001 level, which provides support for convergent validity (Figure 3). 1 item namely functional Navigation was deleted.

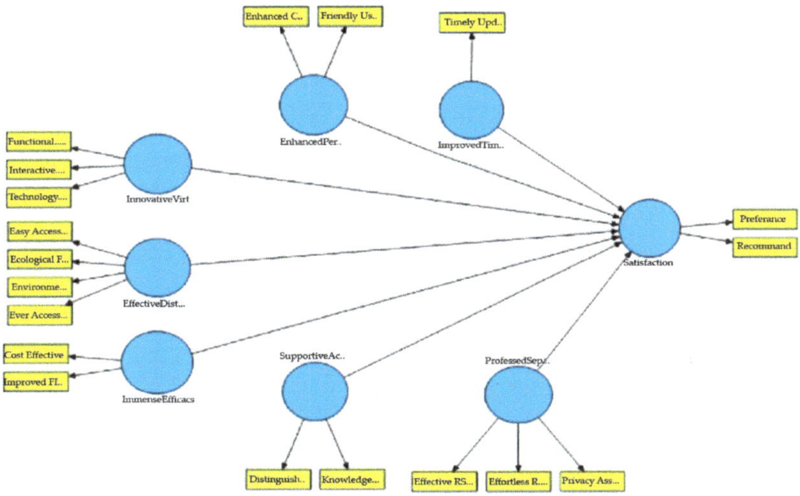

Figure 1: Initial model displaying relationship between dimensions of mobile banking on user satisfaction related to mobile banking.

The study assessed convergent validity by examining composite reliability and average variance extracted from the measures. Although many studies have used 0.5 as the threshold reliability of the measures, 0.7 is a recommended value for a reliable construct [71,72]. For the reflective measures, rather than using Cronbach's alpha, which represents a lower bound estimate of internal consistency due to its assumption of equal weightings of items, a better estimate can be gained by using the composite reliability measure [74]. As shown in Table 1, the internal consistency of all reflective constructs clearly exceeded 0.70, suggesting strong reliability. For the average variance extracted by a measure, a score of 0.4 indicates acceptability. From the table it is clear that AVE by all reflective measures is greater than 0.4, which is above the acceptability value.

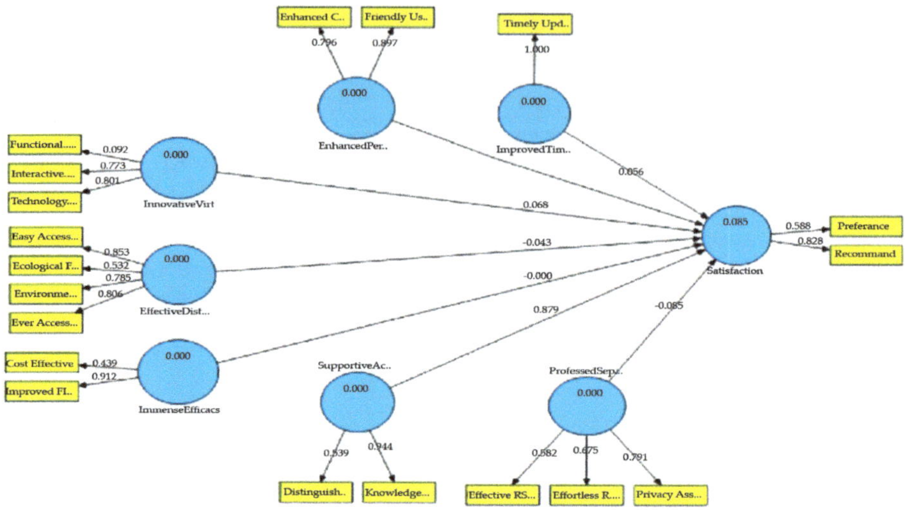

Figure 2: Initial values on the model displaying relationship between dimensions of mobile banking on user satisfaction related to mobile banking.

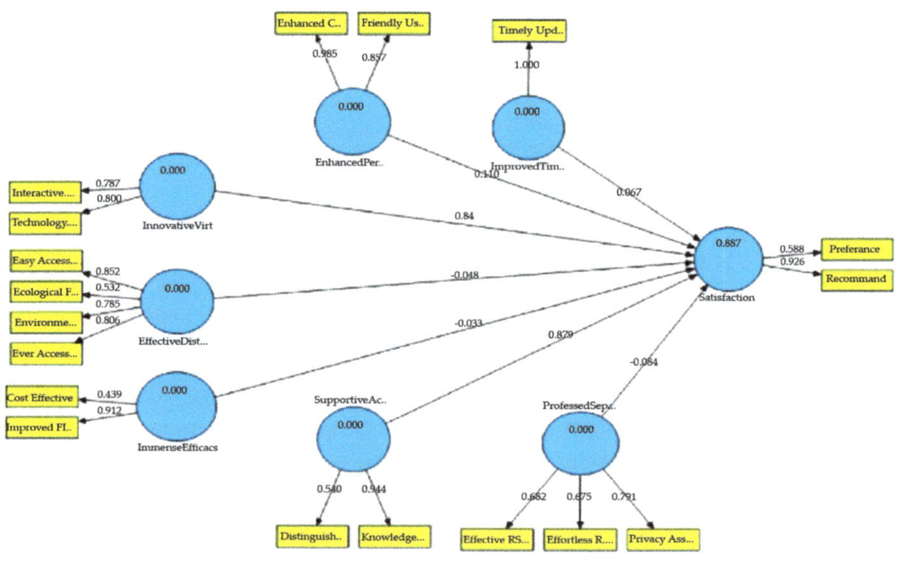

Figure 3: Model displaying relationship between dimensions of mobile banking on user satisfaction related to mobile banking after removal of some items.

Table 1: Verification of convergent validity

	AVE	Composite Reliability	Cronbachs Alpha
EffectiveDistinctiveness	0.49361	0.791807	0.651186
EnhancedPersonalization	0.683384	0.811699	0.539127
ImmenseEfficacy	0.511902	0.651348	0.060054
ImprovedTimelyUpdates	1	1	1
InnovativeVirtualEnvironment	0.629218	0.772406	0.4108
ProfessedSecurity	0.465779	0.719639	0.457007
Satisfaction	0.591387	0.732217	0.360159
SupportiveAccess	0.590731	0.728796	0.374417

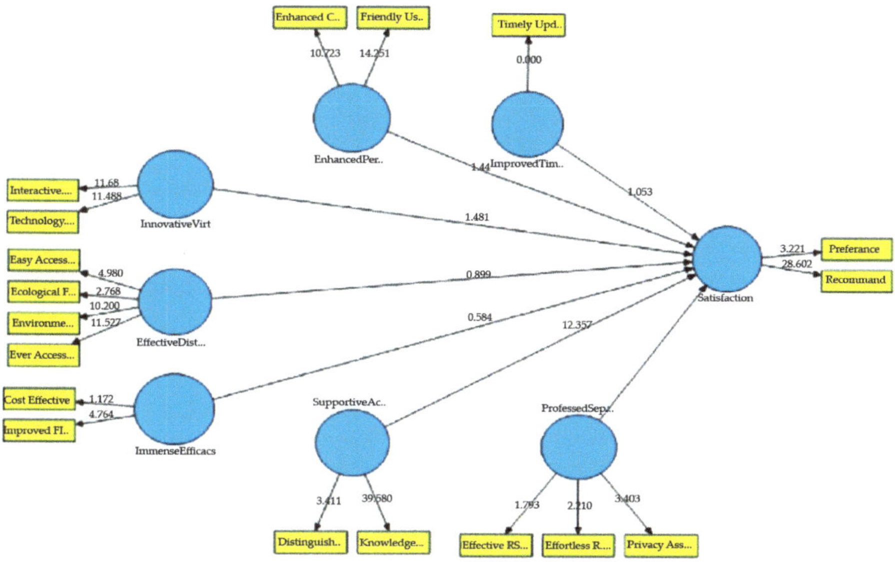

Figure 4: Boot strapping procedure on the final proposed model.

Finally, the study verified the discriminant validity of the instrument by comparing the average variance extracted (AVE). It is clear from the Table 2 that the square root of the average variance extracted for each construct is greater than the levels of correlations with other constructs. The results of the inter-construct correlations also show that each construct shares larger variance with its own measures than with other measures.

Discriminant validity is also confirmed, when items related to a particular factor have the highest load on that factor and is higher than a difference of 0.2 on the other factor in the cross loadings table. When we look at the cross loadings in Table 3, we find that these conditions holds good (some cases difference is nearly equal to 0.2, which is acceptable).

Table 2: Verification of discriminant validity

	Effective Distinctiveness	Enhanced Personalizaton	Immense Efficacy	Improved Timely Updates	Innovative Virtual Environment	Professed Security	Supportive Access
EffectiveDistinctiveness	**0.7**						
EnhancedPersonalization	0.43	**0.8**					
ImmenseEfficacy	0.4	0.4	**0.7**				
ImprovedTimelyUpdates	0.23	0.5	0.08	1			
InnovativeVirtualnvironment	0.51	0.5	0.42	0.276	**0.787**		
ProfessedSecurity	0.5	0.3	0.18	0.264	0.2674	**0.7**	
SupportiveAccess	0.39	0.3	0.29	0.194	0.4394	0.26	**0.77**

Table 3: Cross loadings table

	Effective Distinctiveness	Enhanced Personalization	Immense Efficacy	Improved Timely Updates	Innovative Virtual Environment	Professed Security	Supportive Access
Cost Effective	0.336989	0.275711	**0.538642**	0.294977	0.358582	0.353261	0.146388
Distinguished Methodology	0.461012	0.381896	0.308025	0.182912	0.248721	0.265623	**0.539511**
Easy Accessibility	**0.652428**	0.27005	0.339927	0.16151	0.319972	0.45703	0.253891
Ecological Friendly	**0.532577**	0.397893	0.036552	0.34409	0.328522	0.329703	0.143276
Effective Risk Measurement	0.446833	0.208741	0.252383	0.238452	0.188217	**0.562223**	0.117993
Effortless Recoverability	0.278932	0.171136	0.124752	0.125794	0.275643	**0.675414**	0.192548
Enhanced Customizations	0.37866	**0.794887**	0.377858	0.396556	0.376919	0.292004	0.276643
Environment Collaboration	**0.784649**	0.24001	0.237869	0.079461	0.416883	0.298894	0.270797
Ever Accessibility	**0.805895**	0.320827	0.425828	0.10167	0.373301	0.34417	0.382911
Friendly User Interface	0.341301	**0.857276**	0.271849	0.376186	0.446248	0.188087	0.29624
Improved Flexibility	0.287511	0.304226	**0.91181**	-0.04134	0.299339	0.035976	0.257776
Interactive Technology	0.486623	0.375193	0.341738	0.225883	**0.786775**	0.275228	0.356593
Knowledge Integration	0.271985	0.25047	0.216246	0.151733	0.410038	0.197535	**0.943605**
Privacy Assurance	0.369033	0.220072	0.06868	0.210606	0.118971	**0.790606**	0.20662
Technology Affable	0.325191	0.417718	0.319294	0.211971	**0.799639**	0.15073	0.340776
ImprovedTimely Updates	0.225943	0.465265	0.084008	1	0.275851	0.264042	0.193517

Table 4: Correlation between dimensions of mobile banking and user satisfaction related to mobile banking

	Original Sample (O)	Sample Mean (M)	Standard Deviation (STDEV)	Standard Error (STERR)	T Statistics (|O/STERR|)
EffectiveDistinctiveness Satisfaction	-0.04763	-0.03923	0.052974	0.052974	0.899187
EnhancedPersonalization Satisfaction	0.115168	0.10632	0.079941	0.079941	1.440659
ImmenseEfficacy Satisfaction	-0.03275	-0.02423	0.058033	0.058033	0.564373
ImprovedTimelyUpdates Satisfaction	0.056612	0.0548	0.053739	0.053739	1.053457
InnovativeVirtualEnvironment Satisfaction	0.083925	0.084684	0.057437	0.057437	1.461162
ProfessedSecurity Satisfaction	-0.03444	-0.0188	0.040367	0.040367	0.853076
Supportive Access Satisfaction	0.876938	0.870258	0.070968	0.070968	12.356767

The PLS modeling approach involved two steps-validating the measurement model and then fitting the structural model. The former is accomplished primarily by reliability and validity tests of the measurement model, followed by a test of the explanatory power of the overall model by assessing its explained variance, and the testing of the individual hypotheses (structural model). The model shows that the explanatory power for user performance is 88.6%, which is considered excellent for the studies of this nature. For testing the individual hypotheses, a bootstrap re-sampling procedure was conducted and coefficients were estimated (Figure 4 and Table 4).

The results revealed that hypothesis H04 stands rejected at 5% level of significance because the calculated value of t is more than tabulated value (1.645). Thus, supportive Access is an important factor which is directly associated with User Satisfaction related to mobile banking.

CONCLUSIONS, SUGGESTIONS AND LIMITATIONS

The results of the study revealed that Effective Distinctiveness, Professed Security, Immense Efficacy, Innovative Virtual Environment, Enhanced Personalization and Improved Timely Updates were not associated with satisfaction related to mobile banking while Supportive Access is an important factor which is directly associated with User Satisfaction related to mobile banking. This seems to be true since user did not find the importance of those features which are common to e-banking while the distinctive features of mobile banking were always given a priority. Supportive Access constituted of 2 factors knowledge integration and distinguished methodology. User did rightly gave a importance to these features because distinguished methodology helped the user to outweigh traditional banking features and the knowledge integration feature of mobile banking is the parameter which helps the user to give more priority to mobile banking. However, other features seem to be important to mobile banking but are common with e-banking. The explanatory power of the model was 88.6% which was very good. This suggest that the features constituted in the model did had a significant contribution in assessing the satisfaction related to mobile banking.

An extensive study of research papers clearly depicts that in order to fulfill the expectations of the consumers and to increase the mobile banking users, mobile banking service provider needs to increase the awareness about the mobile banking services. Banks and the mobile service providers need to come together to bring a revolution in the field of mobile banking. Mobile device manufactures need to make efforts so that penetration of mobile banking reaches from high-end to low-end users and from metros to the middle towns and rural areas. It is well recognized that mobile phones have immense potential of conducting financial transactions thus leading the financial growth with lot of convenience and much reduced cost. The mobile manufacturing company must work together with operating system and network provider companies that make a most reliable and user trust security system.

Our study provided bank managers, a clear view of the relative performance of the various factors of the enterprise, which can be used to identify needed improvements and take advantage accordingly. Managers could periodically evaluate the factors in the study, benchmark the results with the expected satisfaction levels and diagnose which factors are problematic and need further consideration. The future designs will thereby form a clear understanding of business requirements, gain more vision and acquire ability to expand knowledge and skills to better assimilate and utilize mobile banking, and therefore minimize the risks associated. Taking into account the most important needs of the implementation; the architecture should be established well before the deployment. To ease the process; rigorous and sophisticated software testing should be performed.

Since the research was conducted in India with a unique culture, the results might not hold true in other countries. Hence, the result cannot be generalized and therefore variation in the user's perception can be checked by conducting the same research at different locations. This opens the scope of comparative research in the mobile banking; since users belonging to different countries will have different exposure and perception related to mobile banking.

The study has given emphasis on the perception of mobile banking users. While the technology comfort length, level of experience, amount of usage and frequency of assessing mobile banking could be considered in order to segregate the user into early adopter, late adopter or laggard. Hence, it opens a scope of further research in special context of mobile banking users. This study was based on a selfadministered exploratory survey, where only closed ended questions were used in the response sheet. This restricted the ability of researcher to ask open-ended questions, which may have assisted in offering a better understanding.

REFERENCES

1. Laukkanen T, Kiviniemi V (2010)The role of information in mobile banking resistance. International Journal of Bank Marketing 28: 372-388.
2. Chung N, Kwon SJ (2009)The effect of customers' mobile experience and technical support on the intention to use mobile banking. Cyber Psychology and Behavior 12: 539-543.
3. Yu TK, Fang K (2009) Measuring the post-adoption customer perception of mobile banking services. Cyber Psychology and Behavior 12: 33-35.
4. Palani A, Yasodha (2012) A Study On Customer Perception Towards Mobile Banking In Indian Overseas Bank Chennai. IJMT 2: 2249-1058.
5. Edgar, Dunn and Company and Mobile Payments World Magazine (2008) 2008 mobile financial services.
6. Wang YS, Lin HH, Luarn P (2006) Predicting consumer intention to use mobile service. Information Systems Journal 16: 157-79.
7. Kleijnen M, Wetzels M,Ruyter KD (2004) Consumer acceptance of wireless finance. Journal of Financial Services Marketing 8: 206-17.
8. Laukkanen T, Pasanen M (2008) Mobile banking innovators and early adopters: How they differ from other online users? Journal of Financial Services Marketing 13: 86-94.
9. Amin H, Muhammad MZ, Hamid MRA, Lada S (2006) Explaining intention to use SMS banking among Bank Islam Malaysia Berhad (BIMB) customers: Is gender a good indicator? Proceeding of IBBC 2: 92-101.
10. Luarn P, Lin H (2005)Toward an understanding of the behavioral intention to use mobile banking. Computers in Human Behavior 21: 873-91.
11. Mattila M (2004) Factors affecting the adoption of mobile banking services. Journal of Internet Banking and Commerce.

12. Uppal RK, Kaur R (2007) Indian Banking Industry: Comparative Performance Evaluation in the Liberalized and Globalized Era. Gyan Management 2: 3-24.
13. Kwiatkowski A (2010) Can mobile bankingfulfil its potential?Telecoms.
14. The World Bank (2009)The infinite potential of mobile banking.Private sector development.
15. Wilcox H (2009) Banking on the mobile white paper. Juniper Research, Basingstoke.
16. Donner J, Tellez CA (2008) Mobile banking and economic development: Linking adoption, impact and use. Asian Journal of Communication 18: 318-32.
17. Goyal V, Pandey US, Batra S (2012) Mobile Banking in India: Practices, Challenges and Security Issues. International Journal of Advanced Trends in Computer Science and Engineering 1: 56-66.
18. Shastri RV (2000) Perspectives Banking Technology in India. Bank Economists Conferences pp110.
19. Kohli K (2004) SMS in banking. Paladion Knowledge Series.
20. LeeMSY, GoldrickPF, Keeling KA, Doherty J (2003) Using ZMET to explore barriers to the adoption of 3G mobile banking services. International Journal of Retail and Distribution Management 31: 340-348.
21. Suoranta M, Mattila M (2004) Mobile banking and consumer behaviour: new insights into the diffusion pattern. Journal of Financial Services Marketing 8: 354-366.
22. Eurostat (2009) Europe in Figures - Eurostat Yearbook 2009. Eurostat Statistical Books, Luxembourg.
23. Sharma A (2011) Mobile Banking as Technology Adoption and Challenges. Zenith International Journal of Multidisciplinary Research 2: 1-4.
24. Ewe SY, Yap SF (2012) Exploring Motivations and Barriers for Mobile Banking Adoption: A Qualitative Approach. World Journal of Social Sciences 2: 184-194.
25. Suoranta M (2003) Adoption of mobile banking in Finland. Studies in Business and Economics, Finland.
26. Laukkanen T (2007) Internet vs mobile banking: comparing customer value perceptions. Business Process Management Journal 13: 788-797.
27. Yang K (2005) Exploring factors affecting the adoption of mobile commerce in Singapore. Telematics and Informatics 22: 257-277.
28. Wang YS, Wang YM, Lin HH, Tang TI (2003) Determinants of user acceptance of internet banking: An empirical study. International Journal of Service Industry Management 14: 501-519.
29. Kim D, Benbasat I (2003) Trust-related arguments in Internet stores: A framework for evaluation. Journal of Electronic Commerce Research 4: 49-64.
30. Lee YK, Park JH, Chung NH (2009)An exploratory study on factors affecting usage intention toward mobile banking: a unified perspective using structural equation modeling. Society for Marketing Advances Proceedings pp: 347.

31. Lewis NK, Palmer A, Moll A (2010) Predicting young consumersÃ¢ÂÂ take up of mobile banking services. International Journal of Bank Marketing 28: 410-432.
32. Liden SB, Skalen P (2003)The effect of service guarantees on service recovery. International Journal of Service Industry Management 14: 36-58.
33. Irwin B, Cajee Z, Douglas D, Stroebel S (2003) Cell phone banking: Predictors of adoption in South Africa-an exploratory study. International Journal of Information Management 23: 381-394.
34. Ramdhony D, Munien S (2013)An Investigation on Mobile Banking Adoption and Usage:A Case Study of Mauritius. World Journal of Social Sciences 3: 1-21.
35. Skeldon P (2011) Growing consumer demand for mobile prompts massive investment in new multichannel platforms as retailers look to integrate everything. The strategy and innovation report.
36. Laforet S, Li X (2005) Consumer attitudes towards Online and Mobile Banking in China. International Journal of Bank Marketing 23: 362-380.
37. Nayak N, Nath V, Goel N (2014) A Study of Adoption Behaviour of Mobile Banking Services by Indian Consumers. International Journal of Research in Engineering and Technology 2: 209-222.
38. Vinayagamoorthy A, Sankar C (2012) Mobile Banking Ã¢ÂÂAn Overview. Advances in Management 5: 24-29.
39. Dahlberg T, Mallat N, Ondrus J, Zmijewska A (2008) Past, present and future of mobile payments research: A literature review. Electronic Commerce Research and Applications 7: 165-181.
40. Mallat N (2007) Exploring consumer adoption of mobile payments-A qualitative study. The Journal of Strategic Information Systems 16: 413-432.
41. Shih KH (2010) The perceived valuation factors for mobile trading services. International Journal of Mobile Communications.
42. Shih KH, Hung HF, Lin B (2010) Assessing user experiences and usage intentions of M-banking service. International Journal of Mobile Communications 8: 257-277.
43. Laukkanen T, Lauronen J (2005) Consumer value creation in mobile banking services. International Journal of Mobile Communications 3: 325-338.
44. Kahandawa K, Wijayanayake J (2014) Impact of Mobile Banking Services on Customer Satisfaction:A Study on Sri Lankan State Commercial Bank. International Journal of Computer and Information Technology 3: 546-552.
45. Zhihong Li, XueBai (2010) Influences of Perceived Risk and System Usability on the Adoption of Mobile Banking Service. Third International Symposium on Computer Science and Computational Technology, PR China.
46. Zhou T (2011)An empirical examination of initial trust in mobile banking. Internet Research 21: 527-540.
47. Au YA, Kauffman RJ (2008)The economics of mobile payments: Understanding stakeholder issues for an emerging financial technology application. Electronic Commerce Research and Applications 7: 141-164.

48. Ondrus J,Pigneur Y (2006)Towards a holistic analysis of mobile payments: A multiple perspectives approach. Electronic Commerce Research and Applications 5: 246-257.

49. Jayawardhena C, and Foley P (2000) Changes in the banking sector - the case of Internet banking in the UK. Internet Research: Electronic Networking Applications and Policy 10: 19-30.

50. Sathye M (1999) Adoption of Internet banking by Australian consumers: an empirical investigation. International Journal of Bank Marketing 17: 324-333.

51. Tan M, Teo TSH (2000) Factors influencing the adoption of Internet banking. Journal of the Association for Information System 1: 1-42.

52. Polatoglu VN, Ekin S (2001)An empirical investigation of the Turkish consumers' acceptance of Internet banking services. International Journal of Bank Marketing 19: 156-165.

53. Howcroft B, Hamilton R, Hewer P (2002) Consumer attitude and the usage and adoption of home-banking in the United Kingdom. International Journal of Bank Marketing 20: 111-121.

54. Wolfinbarger M, Gilly MC (2003)eTailQ: dimensionalizing, measuring and predictingRetail quality. Journal of Retailing 79: 183-98.

55. Crosman P (2011) Banks Have Yet to Create the Killer App for Mobile Banking. Bank Systems and Technology.

56. Harrison T (2000) Financial Services Marketing. Wiltshire: Prentice Hall.

57. Kim G, Shin B, Lee HG (2007) Understanding dynamics between initial trust and usage intentions of mobile banking. Information Systems Journal pp: 283-311.

58. Majali MA, Mat NK (2011)Modeling the antecedents of internet banking service adoption (IBSA) in Jordan: A Structural Equation Modeling (SEM) approach. Journal of Internet Banking and Commerce pp: 1-16.

59. Liza FY (2014) Factors Influencing the Adoption of Mobile Banking: Perspective Bangladesh. Global Disclosure of Economics and Business 3: 92-112.

60. Adewoye JO (2013) Impact of Mobile Banking on Service Delivery in the Nigerian Commercial Banks. International Review of Management and Business Research 2: 333-344.

61. Alter S (2002) Information System: The Foundation of E-Business. New Jersey: Prentice Hall.

62. Ibrahim M, Jabri A, Sohail MS (2012) Mobile Banking Adoption: Application Of Diffusion Of Innovation Theory. Journal of Electronic Commerce Research 13: 379.

63. Vrechoupoulos A, Constantiou I, Sideris G,Mylonopoulos N (2003)The critical role of consumer behaviour research in mobile commerce. International Journal of Mobile Communications 1: 239-340.

64. Islam S (2014) Systematic Literature Review: Security Challenges of Mobile Banking and Payments System. International Journal of u- and e- Service, Science and Technology7: 107-116.

65. Sadi A, Noordin MF (2011) Factors influencing the adoption of M-commerce: An exploratory Analysis. International Conference on Industrial Engineering and Operations Management, Malaysia.
66. Chaipoopirutana S, Combs H, Chatchawanwan Y, Vij V (2009) Diffusion of innovation in Asia: A study of Internet banking in Thailand and India. Innovative Marketing pp: 27-31.
67. Lee I, Kim J, Kim J (2005) Use contexts for the mobile internet: a longitudinal study monitoring actual use of mobile internet services. International Journal of Human-Computer Interaction 18: 269-92.
68. Coelho F, Easingwood C (2003) Multiple channel structures in financial services: A framework. Journal of Financial Services Marketing 8: 22-34.
69. Suoranta M, Mattila M, Munnukka J (2005) Technology-based services: A study on the drivers and inhibitors of mobile banking. International Journal of Management and Decision Making 6: 33-46.
70. Wold H (1982) Soft Modeling: The Basic Design and Some Extensions. Systems Under Indirect Observation: Causality, Structure, Prediction, North-Holland Publishing Company, Amsterdam.
71. Chin WW (1998) Issues and Opinion on Structural Equation Modelling. MIS Quarterly 22: 7-16.
72. Chin WW (1998) The Partial Least Squares Approach to Structural Equation Modelling. Modern Methods for Business Research pp: 295-336.
73. Chin WW, Newsted PR (1999) Structural Equation Modelling Analysis with Small Samples Using Partial Least Squares. Statistical Strategies for Small Sample Research pp: 307-341.
74. Chin WW, GopalA (1995) Adoption intention in GSS: Relative importance of beliefs. Database Advances 26: 42-64.

13
CHAPTER

A MOBILE BANKING ADOPTION MODEL: AN INTEGRATION OF TAM WITH PERCEIVED RISKS AND PERCEIVED BENEFITS

Khasawneh MHA

Keywords: Mobile banking, TAM, Perceived risks, Perceived benefits, adoption of m-banking

INTRODUCTION

Mobile phones have become a tool for everyday use, which creates an opportunity for the evolution of banking services to reach the population through mobile banking (m-banking). The use of m-banking can make basic financial services more accessible to people, minimizing time and distance to the nearest retail bank branches [1]. This newly emerging tool for providing financial services via mobile devices has generated the foundation of m-banking, which can be applied through such technological means as downloadable applications, mobile browsers, text messaging, and preloaded applications [2].

Rapid growth of m-banking enabled people to settle their banking transactions easily while saving time as every step of the procedure was at their fingertips. M-banking has evolved into a prominent system because of such features related to mobile technologies such as ubiquity, convenience and interactivity [3]. Particularly, m-banking is considered as an emerging facet of electronic banking [4], a new retail self-service delivery channel for banks [5] and is a pivotal topic of growth strategies for both banks and mobile provider services industries [6], that enables banks to offer information and provides services to their customers more easily, quickly and conveniently with the use of mobile devices [7,8]. M-banking is defined as a form of

Citation: Khasawneh MHA, (2015), A Mobile Banking Adoption Model: An Integration of TAM with Perceived Risks and Perceived Benefits. J Internet Bank Commer 20:128.

banking transaction via a mobile phone or Personal Digital Assistant (PDA) devices [9]. Taking this point further, m-banking allows customers to check their account balances, transfer funds, reload on phone airtime, perform credit card transactions as well as receive information alerts on the latest transactions in their debit and credit accounts.

However, despite the fact that m-banking enables customers to conduct banking services at anyplace and at any time [7], the usage and adoption of m-banking has not spread as was expected [9-11], and is still in early stage in comparison to other services provided by the banking sector due to uncertainty and security concerns [6-8,12,13]. More specifically, m-banking related literature proposed perceived risk as a salient obstacle to consumer acceptance of e-banking as well as m-banking mainly due to high risk concerns [6,12]. Although consumer perceptions of the risks of adopting e-banking have been studied by many researchers [14-16], the perceived risk variable has only been examined as a single construct, which fails to reveal the actual attributes of perceived risk and clarify why consumers refuse to use such banking services. In order to provide a more comprehensive clarification of the perceived risks of adopting m-banking in Jordan, a more in-depth study of the characteristics of the perceived risks was conducted. Perceived risk was divided into five categories: performance, financial, time, social and security/privacy risks, as theorized by Jacoby and Kaplan [17], in order to explain which risk facets are more imperative in this arena.

In order to provide a concrete theoretical foundation for investigating the adoption of m-banking services, the current research is derived based on thoughts regarding the nomological structure of the technology acceptance model (TAM) [18]. As TAM has been applied in numerous studies to investigate and clarify customers' perceptions of system use and the possibility of adopting an online system [19-21], it is considered as the most suitable model for understanding m-banking adoption.

The current research is designed to integrate the five dimensions of perceived risk mentioned above with the TAM in order to present a more comprehensive model of m-banking acceptance and adoption in Jordan. Furthermore, the current study extends the scope of the adoption choice to obviously comprise both negative (perceived risk) and positive factors (perceived benefits) concurrently. In particular, the study makes a strong contribution to the current m-banking literature by extending TAM to include perceived benefits and the five facets of perceived risk. That is, previous TAM studies in the context of m-banking [22-24] did not include the importance and influence of perceived benefits and perceived risk; as a consequence, they may have omitted crucial factors that influence consumer adoption of m-banking. As a result, the present study may be of great benefit to practitioners by providing them with an increased understanding of how users interact with innovative technology so that providers can assess and cultivate benefits and reduce risk perception toward the eventual adoption. The current study will offer instrumental insights to traditional brick and mortar and web based banks before they shift towards the new m-commerce model. Theoretically, this study can contribute to the existing literature relating to benefits, risk, and emerging IT m-banking acceptance.

The rest of this paper is presented as follows. In the next section, the significance of the current research is presented. Then, a review of the related research is conducted in order to identify the theoretical framework for this study. Then, we present the methodology employed to conduct the study. The following section describes the statistical analysis and results. Finally, we conclude with a discussion, the study's limitations, implications, and calls for future research.

Significance of the Study

While the use of branch based retail banking is still very popular, banks have other ways of providing customers with financial management services and one of them is m-banking [25]. The use of m-banking can make basic financial services more accessible, minimizing time and distance to the nearest retail bank branches [1]. The outstanding growth of mobile sector worldwide has created a unique opportunity to provide social and financial services over the mobile network. With over four billion mobile phone subscriptions worldwide, mobile network has the ability to immediately offer m-banking to 61% of the world population [26]. According to the International Telecommunication Union (ITU) report, there is significant growth in the use of mobile phones, with over 90% of the population in Jordan using them [27]. However, with all the benefits of m-banking, the usage and adoption of m-banking is still low among banks customers in Jordan [25]. Though many of such people argue that internet and other technology based transaction is not safe, not practical and would lead to fraud, a lot of people think it safer, flexible in time and can be done anywhere and anytime [28]. Hence, it is necessary to investigate the factors that lead customers to adopting or rejecting m-banking services. Although prior studies on m-banking adoption have provided background information on the adoption behavior with regard to m-banking, studies that focus on the risk and benefits perceptions factors that influence consumers to adopt m-banking services are limited. Thus, understanding such factors will play a critical role in reducing the challenges associated with the use of m-banking. For example, risk and privacy issues have been identified as major contributing factors for the slow uptake of m-banking [29]. However, Rammile and Nel [25] revealed that consumers do not consider m-banking to be prone to risk. Risk and privacy are related to trust in the banking industry – which is especially important when banks are trying to increase their customer base and improve their services by introducing technological innovations [29]. However, previous studies still have many limitations and have recommended further research in this field. Among these limitations is the restricted geographical spread of study areas, as most of the previous m-banking studies have been conducted in the United States, Canada, and other developed countries.

Research questions and objectives of the study

The study seeks to investigate the influencing factors of m-banking in Jordan. Thus, it addresses the following questions to be answered.

Question 1: What are the main factors influencing customers to accept and adopt using of m-banking services?

Question 2: How does the user in Jordan perceive risk with regards to m-banking?

Question 3: What is the perception of m-banking users in Jordan about the benefits of using m-banking services?

Hence the specific objectives of the study can be summarized as follows:

i. To examine whether perceived usefulness and perceived ease of use have any role to play in adoption of m-banking in Jordan.
ii. To examine whether perceived risk and benefit significantly influence customers' attitude and behavioral intention to adopt m-banking.
iii. To assess the effect of five components of perceived risk (performance risk, security/privacy risk, time risk, social risk and financial risk) with regards to the customers' attitudes and adoption of m-banking in Jordan.
iv. To explore the role of perceived benefits in customers' attitude towards and behavioral intention to adopting m-banking in Jordan.
v. To understand which factors are more influential in impacting the decision to use m-banking.
vi. To assess whether the TAM provide a solid theoretical basis for examining the adoption of m-banking.

LITERATURE REVIEW

To provide a comprehensive foundation for the current study, the literature related to e-commerce, M-commerce, Internet banking, m-banking, and consumer adoption of new technology were reviewed with a particular focus on identifying the variables affecting customers' attitude and intention to adopt m-banking.

M-BANKING DEFINITION

M-banking has received a considerable attention in academic research and thus several conceptualization of m-banking currently exists. As the conceptual agreement is essential requirement for comprehensive discussion regarding the phenomenon [30], literature on m-banking was referred for establishing commonly accepted definitions.

M-banking (m-banking) is defined as is an emerging facet of electronic banking [31], a wireless service delivery channel [32], an application of m-commerce [10], an innovative method for accessing banking services [33] that offers additional value for customers by providing "anytime, anywhere" access to banking service [32]. In particular, Kim et al. [10] and Luakkanen and Passanen [34] viewed m-banking as a potential platform for automated banking and other financial services which enables customers to access bank accounts through mobile devices or personal digital assistant to conduct and complete bank-related transactions such as balancing cheques, checking account statuses, transferring money and selling stocks. For the current study, this definition was considered as it represents the m-banking scenario in the best possible mode.

Goswami and Raghavendran [5] debate the general goal of m-banking is to ensure the presence of a financial institution on a mobile phone. This view was further supported by Crosman [35] who stated that m-banking facilitates for users to have a bank branch in their pocket at any convenient time and place. Indeed, as asserted by Coelho and Easingwood [36], some consumers are less willing to visit traditional branches and are more receptive to bank virtually through new electronic channels such as m-banking. More importantly, m-banking is enabling consumers to conduct a variety of financial functions including micropayments to merchants, bill payments to utilities, person to person (P2P) transfers, business to business (B2B) transfers, business to person (B2P) transfers and long distance settlements [2].

RELEVANT LITERATURE

As an aim of the current research is to investigate the factors that influence consumer's acceptance and adoption of m-banking services in Jordan, the literature related to electronic banking and m-banking was reviewed. However, much of this literature is largely focused on Internet banking, whereas research focusing on m-banking in Jordan is relatively limited and receives underrated attention [37,38]. Indeed, there has been limited research conducted from Jordanian users' perspectives for enhancing the adoption and acceptance of mobile based technologies [39-41]. For example, a literature review carried out by Jaradat and Faqih [41] on the adoption and acceptance of m-technology services in Jordan, demonstrating that even though this specific technology has lately received a large scale of attention from marketers, businesses and research community, the individual acceptance and adoption of m-technology have not progressed and proliferated as expected in both developed and developing countries. Therefore, it seems that there is a gap in the existing related literature regarding the most important factors responsible for motivating and/or deterring potential consumers from adopting and using m-technology services. Consequently, this research endeavours to fill this gap in literature by identifying the m-technology adoption in the context of banking.

Although differences exist in customers' perception of their value, the literature regarding Internet banking may provide significant understandings into innovative m-banking adoption as a result of the resemblance in terms of human users facing e-commerce systems. For example, Internet banking research, such as studies conducted by Nor and Pearson [42] as well as Kim et al. [43] have examined the fundamental constructs leading to the acceptance of Internet banking and concluded that risk and the multidimensionality of trust play a vital role. In addition, they asserted that such major constructs as social norms, perceived usefulness, perceived ease-of-use, attitude, and self-efficacy, can also be applied to the Internet banking field. In another study conducted by Tan and Teo [15], which had combined the diffusion of innovation theory and TPB to explain intention to adopt Internet banking, revealed that relative advantage, compatibility, trialability, perceived risk, perceived self-efficacy, and government support of Internet commerce are significant determinants.

Moving into the m-banking context, several studies have examined the attitude and/or intention to adopt m-banking services in different countries, apart from Jordan [7,13,32,44-46]. In the extended domain of m-banking, previous studies have attempted to identify the major set of variable related to the consumer as well as the m-banking system that are influencing users' intention to adopt m-banking. In earlier studies in this regard, different results have been provided such as Brown et al. [47] who have applied the innovation diffusion theory and added additional factors such as banking needs, perceived risk , Internet experience, subjective norms and self-efficacy in order to investigate their influence on the adoption of m-banking in South Africa. They found that relative advantage, trial periods, perceived risk and consumer banking needs are negatively related to the adoption of m-banking. In another study conducted on middle class populations by Wu and Wang [21], it was found that cost had minimal significant impact on the adoption of m-banking while perceived risk, compatibility and perceived usefulness have significant influences.

Other researchers have examined the applicability of the technology acceptance model (TAM) in m-banking context and recommended that new additional constructs should be used to examine the adoption of m-banking. For example, Lauren and Lin [44] added perceived credibility, perceived self-efficacy and perceived financial cost to the TAM and demonstrated that the extended TAM had a higher capability to predict and describe users' behavioral intention to use m-banking. In the same vein, Amin et al. [48] in a study based on TAM, found that credibility, amount of information and normative pressures significantly influence the adoption of m-banking. A more recent research, conducted by Dasgupta et al. [49], affirmed the previous view regarding the applicability of TAM, found that in addition to perceived usefulness and perceived ease of use, image, value, self-efficacy and credibility significantly affect intention towards m-banking usage, thereby providing more impetus for using TAM in the current research.

The relevant m-banking literature discussed the importance of perceived risk on adoption behavior [43,50]. For example, Lee et al. [43] found Jacoby and Kaplan's six risk dimensions [17] relevant to adoption behavior in the m-banking context. In order to better predict adoption behavior, Brown et al. [47] applied Tan and Teo's Internet banking adoption framework to the m-banking context. Brown et al. [47] found perceived risk to be significant factors affecting m-banking adoption. However, the risk construct in their study is limited to information risk and security concerns.

Lee et al. [43] also included a perceived risk construct under the umbrella of TAM to study its impact on m-banking adoption. Different risk dimensions were examined. Their results indicate that both trust and perceived usefulness have a significant, direct impact on adoption behavior while the impact of perceived risk is only mediated by trust. According to Akturan and Tezcan [12] attitudes of students towards adopting m-banking is the most important factor that influences them to adopt m-banking. Moreover, they discovered that these attitudes are affected by the perceived benefits of using m-banking, risks associated with performance and social factors.

Based on recent research in m-banking which has confirmed perceived risk and perceived benefits as important factors influencing adoption behavior, this research extends the study of these two factors by examining different dimensions of perceived risk, perceived benefits, and their influence on customers attitude and behavioral intention. Since much of literatures are not found related to m-banking in Jordan, this paper is an endeavor to fill the research gap in this regard. Thus on the basis of the above literatures, the paper aims to examine the adoption intention of m-banking by integrating TAM with perceived benefits and perceived risks.

TECHNOLOGY ACCEPTANCE MODEL (TAM)

IT acceptance has been the subject of much research in the past two decades. Several theories have emerged that offer new insights into acceptance and use, at both the individual and organizational levels, including the theory of reasoned action (TRA) [51], the Technology Acceptance Model (TAM) by Davis [52], the extended technology of acceptance model (TAM2) [53], the Theory of Planned Behavior (TPB) [54], the innovation diffusion theory [55], and the Unified Technology Acceptance User Technology (UTAUT) by Venkatesh, Morris, Davis, and Davis [56]. One of the most salient models is the Technology Acceptance Model (TAM), when it comes to investigating the factors that influence the adoption of information systems, which is proposed by Davis [52] and is mainly developed from Fishbein and Ajzen's existing Theory of Reasoned Action (TRA). In particular, previous literature indicated that TAM consistently accounts for 40% of variance in usage intention and behaviors [53]. TAM has been widely examined and validated and is an extensively accepted model in a variety of academic disciplines. In particular, TAM has been validated by investigating different sorts of technologies related to user and organization acceptance and adoption such as the World Wide Web [57,58] Intranet [59], E-commerce [60,61] online shopping [62,63], M-commerce [64], Internet Banking [65,66].

In addition, the widespread acceptance of TAM is justified by the explicit approach it uses to address factors that influence consumers' reasons of using particular information systems [67]. One benefit that comes from using TAM or extended TAM is that these models have broadly been tested and validated which lead to their widespread acceptance. Another advantage is that these models can easily be modified and/or extended by using other theories or constructs [44,53].

According to original TAM suggested by Davis [52], two primary constructs were included namely, perceived usefulness and perceived ease of use. Perceived usefulness (PU) represents the extent to which an individual perceives that using a certain system would enhance their performance. Whereas perceived ease of use (PEOU) refers to the degree to which a person perceives that using a particular system would be free of mental and physical efforts [52]. A more recent study by Chung and Kown [68] revealed that PU and PEOU have a significant positive influence on consumers' intention to adopt m-banking services. Although TAM has been extensively validated, Mathison [67] argued that it is inappropriate to depend only on these two variables of PU and PEOU in examining individual's technology acceptance tendencies. Consistent with this view, TAM theory can be modified or extended using other theories or incorporating other constructs [21,44,69,70]. Singh et al. [71] propose that perceived usefulness and perceived ease of use are the main components of new technology acceptance even though they cannot explicitly explain consumers' attitude and behavior when it comes to m-banking. Taking this point further, several previous studies suggested that there are other potential factors that might be incorporated within the TAM and which would influence users' adoption of m-banking such as perceived risk [33,34,68,72] as well as perceived benefits [12]. Consistent with this view, Chong et al. [73] asserted that it is better to use TAM as a base model and extend by including additional constructs based on the research being conducted. For example, Aldas-Manzano et al. [65] have extended the TAM by incorporating perceived risk in order to investigate online banking adoption. In the same Vein, Akturan and Tezcan [12] have integrated perceived risks and perceived benefits to examine m-banking adoption among nonusers and university students in an emerging country which was considered as the main limitation for their study. In view of this, the current study has extended the TAM by incorporating perceived risks and perceived benefits to the original TAM.

CONCLUSION FOR THE LITERATURE

The scope of this study is to cover the main constructs derived from Technology Acceptance Model (TAM) [18] including attitude and intention to adopt m-banking services, perceived usefulness, and perceived ease of use. After critically reviewing the literature that pertains the developments in Jordan m-banking situation, some important information we gathered, which is the context of this study. The variables perceived risk and perceived benefits are added to TAM in order to develop a research model to probe variables affecting adoption of m-banking in Jordan.

RESEARCH FRAMEWORK AND HYPOTHESES DEVELOPMENT

This section presents a theoretical model that conceptualizes the relationships amongst the focal constructs, that is, the impact of perceived usefulness, perceived ease of use, perceived benefits and perceived risk on consumers' attitude towards and behavioral intention to adopt m-banking in Jordan as shown in Figure 1.

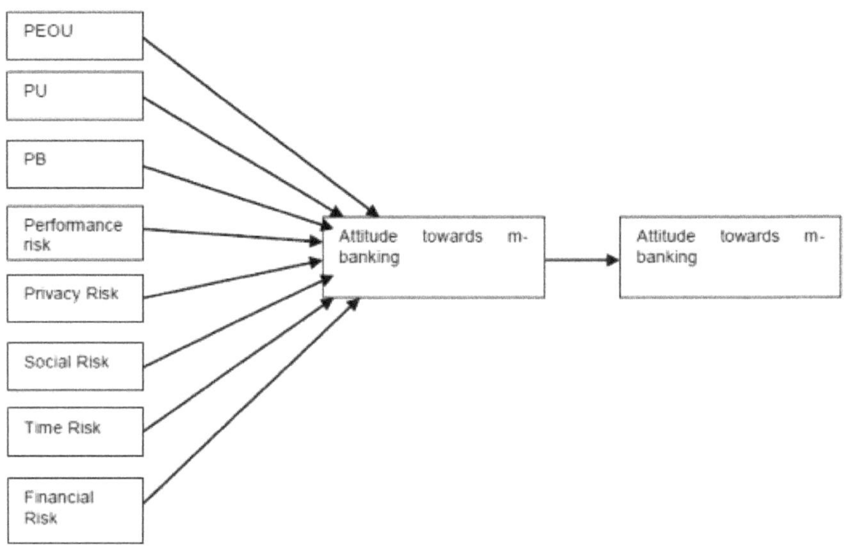

Figure 1: Proposed Research Model

Perceived ease of use

Perceived Ease of Use (PEOU) is one of the fundamental elements in TAM and is viewed as the degree of ease associated with the use of a system [74] and that using a particular system would be free of physical and mental effort [52]. In the context of m-banking, PEOU represents the degree to which a person associates freedom of difficulty with the use of banking services through mobile technology [75]. Most of the previous behavioral decision making literature contended that individuals endeavor to reduce efforts in their behavior. In addition, extensive previous studies demonstrated that perceived ease of use had a direct and a positive significant effect on usage intention [24,65,71,76,77] users' attitude towards using a particular system [2,78] and technology adoption behavior [43,44,52,53,68,69]. Based on these studies, the following hypothesis is proposed:

H1: PEOU has a significant positive influence on customers' attitudes to adopt m-banking.

Perceived usefulness

Perceived usefulness is a critical construct in TAM in which it is defined as "the degree to which a person believes that using a particular system would enhance his or her job performance" [52]. Within the context of m-banking, perceived usefulness can be described as users' perceptions that m-banking will enhance their means of getting the bank services. According to Kim et al. [79], a person generally assesses the consequences of his/her behavior and accordingly makes a choice based on the perceived usefulness. This argument is also supported by Luarn and Lin [44] who proposes that perceived usefulness significantly affects the development of initial willingness to use m-banking. This view has been widely confirmed by many researchers by asserting that perceived usefulness is the primary antecedent of the behavioral intention to use a new technology [48,80-85]. In addition, other researchers found that perceived usefulness has a direct positive influence on consumers' attitudes towards m-banking, and that attitude was the key precursor of m-banking adoption [12]. Moreover, many previous studies have found that perceived usefulness has an influence on m-banking adoption [86,87]. Accordingly; it is hypothesized that:

H2: Perceived usefulness has a significant positive influence on customers' attitudes to adopt m-banking.

Perceived benefits

Perceived benefits refers to the degree to which an innovation provides more benefits than its precursor [10,20,79,88]. In general, Wright [89] stated that consumers tend to engage in a cost-benefit analysis when going through a decision making procedure. Taking this point further, customers when are faced with buying situations, they search for particular benefits from the product and perceive products as a bundle of attributes delivering benefits. Peter and Lawrence [90] noted that perceived risk and perceived benefits are the fundamental aspects of consumer decision-making in purchasing behaviors. Perceived benefit was found as an imperative indicator of online banking adoption. For example, Lee [91] concluded that perceived benefit is mainly and positively related to the intention to use online banking. In the same vein, Laforet and Lin [11] figured out that the inability of comprehending these benefits was considered as an important barrier to the adoption behavior.

Moving to the m-banking context, Kim et al. [43] suggested that customers viewed perceived benefits as a cognitive and affective evaluation of utilitarian and hedonistic benefits. As m-banking is considered a technological innovation, it allows consumers to access banking transactions without restrictions of time and place via mobile devices [9]. In the current study, perceived benefits refer to a consumer's subjective perceptions about the potential positive values from the usage and transaction with m-banking service [79]. In general, when consumers recognize the benefits provided as a result of using m-banking service, they tend to have a positive attitude toward adopting (or continuing to use) and trusting m-banking [4,20,92-95]. Perceived benefits were found also to have a positive influence on behavioral intention [96]. This point was previously supported with a number of previous m-banking studies [79,97]. For example, Lu et al. [96] concluded that perceived benefit has the strongest effect on behavioral intention of m-banking usage. In addition, they found that consumers' perceived benefits of m-banking provide a major incentive for acceptance [96]. Based on the above discussion, it is suggested that:

H3: Perceived benefits have a significant positive influence on customers' attitude to adopt m-banking.

Perceived risk

Perceived risk, in the context of offline and online consumer behavior, has received a considerable attention within the literature. More importantly, a rich stream of consumer behavior literature supports the usage of perceived risk in understanding consumer evaluative and purchasing of products and services [98-100]. Previous related literature have defined perceived risk as a multi-dimensional construct [90] which is related to consumers' perceptions of subjective expected loss [90], uncertainty and potential adverse consequences of buying a product or service [101], seriousness of judgment regarding the outcomes involved [102] and the degree of risk inherent in an innovation [99,103]. Within the context of the current study, perceived risk is viewed as the users' subjective judgment of suffering a loss in pursuit of a desired outcome [61]. Taking this point further, despite the great benefits of m-banking services, concerns of risks regarding privacy, security, performance and financial issues are still vital to consumers.

There is a general agreement in the relevant literature that perceived risk is a strong influential factor influencing users behavioral intention to accept and adopt a new technology particularly, in the context of Internet banking [15,21,104] as well as m-banking [4,47,78]. For example, a study by Tan and Teo [15] on the adoption of Internet banking, found that perceived risk is a significant determinant. Brown et al. [47] applied Tan and Teo's [15] framework to the m-banking context and determined that perceived risk was a significant factor affecting m-banking adoption.

A considerable amount of literature viewed users' perception of risk as a crucial drive to determine m-banking acceptance in different nations and settings [4,78,86,105]. For example, they found that perceived risk is a significant factor influencing consumers' intention to adopt m-banking services in many countries including Singapore [78], Australia [4], South Korea [43], South Africa [47], Brazil [95], and Germany [83]. Most of the previous mentioned studies have found that perceived risk negatively affect the users' behavioral intention to adopt m-banking technology. However, one limitation of the previous studies is that perceived risk has only been examined as a single construct which may not accurately reflect the characteristics of the risk factor [91].

Other studies have examined the influence of perceived risk in the context of Internet banking by viewing risk from into five different facets (performance risk, social risk, financial risk, time risk and privacy/security risk), which provided a more in-depth understanding of the characteristics of risks regarding Internet banking [91]. As m-banking may be considered an extension of Internet banking, but with its own unique characteristics given that a smartphone is used rather than a web browser on a PC [47], a similar set of risk factors can be derived for m-banking by using the five risk facets as used by [91], in the context of Internet banking, as a basis: performance risk, social risk, financial risk, time risk and privacy/security risk. As defined by Lee [91], these five risks can be described for m-banking as follows:

a. Performance risk: It represents the losses incurred by deficiencies or malfunctions of m-banking servers [91].

b. Privacy/security risk: It is defined as a potential loss due to fraud or a hacker compromising the security of m-banking user.

c. Time/convenience risk: It is viewed as a loss of time and any inconvenience incurred due to the delays of receiving payments or the difficulty of navigation (finding appropriate services and relevant commands) [91].

d. Social risk: It refers to the possibility that using m-banking may result in disapproval by one's friends/family/work group [91].

e. Financial risk: It is defined as the potential for monetary loss due to transaction errors or bank account misuse [91].

Previous literature revealed that all five dimensions of perceived risks were found to have a negative impact on users' behavioral intention to adopt online banking [43,91]. Consistent with this view, earlier studies have argued that perceived financial cost [44], security issues [11,44,47], performance risks [97] are the vital constructs in affecting the adoption of m-banking services. On that basis, it is hypothesized that:

H4: Perceived performance risk has a negative influence on customers' attitudes to adopt m-banking services.

H5: Perceived privacy/security risk has a negative influence on customers' attitudes to adopt m-banking services.

H6: Perceived social risk has a negative influence on customers' attitudes to adopt m-banking services.

H7: Perceived time risk has a negative influence on customers' attitudes to adopt m-banking services.

H8: Perceived financial risk has a negative influence on customers' attitudes to adopt m-banking services.

Attitude toward M-banking and Behavioural Intention

Attitude toward m-banking has received considerable attention within the consumer behavior literature. The concept of attitude appears to play an important role in predicting and understanding consumer intention and behavior [106-110]. Indeed, consumer attitudes towards m-banking are an important indicator of customer intention to use m-banking services. Behavioural intention refers to an individual's willingness to perform [107] a specific future behaviour [111]. It has been considered an important predictor of an individual's behaviour [106,112]. Also, customer's intention toward using m-banking significantly affects the adoption of m-banking. This is line with Ajzen [54], as within the framework of the Theory of Planned Behaviour (TPB), customer's intention toward behaviour is largely influenced by consumers' attitudes. Therefore, in this study, it is proposed that customer's attitude towards m-banking will significantly affects their intention towards m-banking. Accordingly, the following hypothesis is posited:

H9: customer's attitude toward m-banking has a significant positive influence on customers' behavioural intention to adopt m-banking.

RESEARCH METHODOLOGY

Sample

The current study was designed to assess the factors affecting m-banking adoption among Jordanian consumers. Thus, the target population of this study was the entire Jordanian population. The target population included people living in Jordan of different age groups, income levels, education levels, ethnic backgrounds, and marital status.

Data collection

A quantitative approach was used in this research. In order to empirically test the hypotheses developed in the previous section, data were collected using a convenience sampling approach via an online self-administered survey. The first reason for using this sampling technique is because it offers an easy way to collect the raw data for further analysis. Secondly, it saves time and costs as the respondents are randomly selected. M-banking was described to participants as a mobile commerce application that gives the user the opportunity to make the everyday bank transactions (such as balance inquiries, check book requests, make money transfers, etc.), mobile brokerage (trading financial instruments), and financial inquiries (bank balance, statement requests, ATM locations, foreign exchange rates, etc.) using a mobile phone or other portable devices. The participation in the study was voluntary. To increase content validity, it was indicated that the survey should be filled out by a respondent who is familiar with m-banking concept. In addition, the questionnaire was created in English and reviewed for content validity. Since it was administered to the Jordanian general population, the English version of the instrument was then translated to Arabic. Following the recommendation of Brislin [113], a professional translator reviewed the instrument for content validity. To encourage participation and reduce self-reporting bias, all participants were given the opportunity to receive the findings of the study. To test the instrument, a pilot study was conducted among a group of 50 college students who were not included in the main survey. Consequently, the wording of some questions was modified. Preliminary evidence showed that the scales were reliable and valid.

Following the pretest, the survey was sent to a user base of people with one or more mobile phones at Jordan. The survey was mainly promoted and hosted online by survey monkey website; a provider of web based survey solutions (Surveymonkey.com). Respondents were invited to take the questionnaire by sending them the link of the survey webpage on their email addresses, Facebook pages, and via a popular mobile-device application called Whatsapp. A total of 835 e-mails were sent using personal hyperlinks that could be used only once, thus preventing repeated responses. A follow-up reminder was sent to nonrespondents after four weeks. To encourage participation; respondents were given an incentive of a 3D photo shoot as a luck draw prize. A total of 432 responses were collected. Twenty eight responses were discarded due duplicate submissions or incompletion, a net sample of 404 usable questionnaires remained. The common method bias was examined using Harman's one-factor test [93]. No significant common method bias was found in the dataset.

Measurement and scaling

A typical seven-point Likert scale was used to measure the constructs presented in the proposed model (scores were ranged from 1=Ã¢ÂÂ strongly agree Ã¢ÂÂ to 7=Ã¢ÂÂ strongly disagree Ã¢ÂÂ with neutral Ã¢ÂÂ score= 4). The conceptualization and development of the questionnaire was based on the existing literature, resulted in total of 35 items. The questionnaire instrument was developed based on the constructs of perceived usefulness, perceived ease of use, perceived benefits, perceived social risk, perceived financial risk, perceived performance risk, perceived time risk, perceived privacy/security risk, attitude to use m-banking and intention to use m-banking. Perceived usefulness, perceived ease of use, attitude to use m-banking, and perceived benefits were adapted from the measurements used by Lee [91], containing three items for the first construct and four items for the remaining constructs.

Intention to use m-banking was adapted from Kim et al. [114] and included three items. Perceived social risk, perceived financial risk, perceived performance risk, and perceived time risk were adapted from Stone and Gronhaug [115], containing three, two, five and three items respectively. Perceived privacy/security risk were adapted from Pikkarainen et al. [116], containing six items. Additional four items were included for capturing demographic information (gender, age, educational level, and marital status).

Demographic profile of the respondents

Data were gathered from a convenience sample of 404 respondents via an online survey. The data relating to respondents' profiles were tabulated to obtain a better feel of the data, as recommended by Sekaran [117]. Therefore, the respondents' demographic profiles were tabulated for gender, age, education level and marital status (Table 1).

Table 1: Demographic Profile of the Sample

Variable	Category	Response Information N=404
Gender	Male	63%
	Female	37%
Age	Less than 20	27%
	21-29	47%
	30-30	13%
	40-49	10%
	50-59	2%
	Above 60	1%
Education	High School	5%
	University Degree	82%
	Higher Education	13%
Marital Status	Single	54%
	Married	44%
	Divorced	2%

As shown in Table 1, male respondents accounted for the majority of the sample (63%) and the majority of the respondents' ages were less than 29 (74%). In relation to educational level, 13% of the respondents reported completing higher education, while 82% reported achieving a university degree. For marital status, single respondents accounted for the majority of the sample (54%).

RESEARCH RESULTS

To test the model, a two-step method was used, beginning with the measurement model to examine the reliability and validity of the instrument and then analyzing the structural model [118]. Since the research is an early stage assessment of m-banking situation in Jordan, the partial least squares (PLS) is the most appropriate method for this study [119,120]. PLS estimation requires ten times the largest number of structural paths directed at a particular construct in the model [121,122]. The sample in our study met the necessary conditions for using PLS.

Measurement model

Tables 2 and 3 present the measurement model results. Composite reliability (CR) is above 0.70 (minimum CR is 0.90) indicating that the scales have internal consistency

(Table 2). To evaluate the indicator reliability, we opted to consider the loadings above 0.70. Hence two items, SR2 and FR1, were eliminated. As seen in Table 2, the instrument presents good indicator reliability as the loadings are above 0.70. Average variance extracted (AVE) was used to test convergent validity. AVE should be higher than 0.50 so that the latent variables explain more than half of the variance of its indicators [120,123]. As seen in Table 2, all constructs meet these criteria. The AVE, CR, and Alpha values are higher than the recommended thresholds of 0.500, 0.700, and 0.770 respectively [122,124,125]. This demonstrates convergent validity and validity indicating that the constructs can be used to test the conceptual model.

Table 2: Individual Item Reliability and Construct Validity

Construct	Factor	Loadings	AVE	Composite Reliability	Cronbach's Alpha
Perceived Ease of Use	PEOU01 PEOU02 PEOU03	.826 .851 .873	.723	.887	.809
Perceived Usefulness	PU01 PU02 PU03 PU04	.867 .885 .903 .776	.738	.919	.882
Perceived Benefits	PB01 PB02 PB03	.747 .817 .833	.640	.841	.717
Perceived Performance Risk	PR1 PR2	.948 .947	.897	.946	.886
Privacy/Security Risk	PRIV1 PRIV2 PRVI3 SEC1 SEC2 SEC3	.909 .910 .828 .839 .754 .727	.690	.929	.910
Social Risk	SR1 SR3	.707 .970	.559	.779	.750
Time Risk	TR1 TR2 TR3	.855 .958 .76	.742	.86	.839
Financial Risk	FR2 FR3 FR4	.872 .921 .912	.634	.864	.871
Consumer Attitude Towards M-Banking	ATT01 ATT02 ATT03 ATT04	.888 .852 .926 .875	.784	.936	.908
Intention to Adopt M-Banking	INT01 INT02 INT03	.905 .839 .902	.779	.914	.858

Finally, discriminant validity was tested based on the square root of AVE for each construct should be greater than the correlations with all constructs [123,126]. In Table 3, we can see that the square root of AVE (in bold) is higher than the correlation between constructs.

Table 3: Latent Variable Correlations

PEOU	**.850**									
PU	.679	**.859**								
PB	.705	.718	**.800**							
Per Risk	.102	-.109	-.021	**.947**						
Privacy	.046	.302	.462	-.06	**.830**					
Social	.047	.113	.240	-.033	.410	**.747**				
Time	-.237	-.17	-.271	.645	-.166	.147	**.861**			
Fin Risk	-.175	-.116	-.187	.502	-.448	.0147	.650	**.798**		
Attitude	.544	.57	.665	-.091	.577	.344	-.232	-.263	**.885**	
Intention	.475	.41	.458	-.296	.48	.293	-.355	-.373	.713	**.882**

The measurement model results indicate that the model has good internal consistency, indicator reliability, convergent validity and discriminant validity. Hence, the constructs from our model are statistically distinct and can be used to test the structural model.

Structural model

The PLS results, as shown in Table 4, indicate that perceived ease of use of m-banking has a significant positive effect on users (consumers) attitude towards m-banking adoption ($ß = 0.143$, $t = 2.557$, $p < 0.01$), indicating that users who perceived m-banking as easy to use, tend to have positive attitude towards using m-banking, thereby, supporting H1. As proposed in H2, a significant positive relationship between perceived usefulness and consumer attitude towards m-banking was found ($ß = 0.171$, $t = 2.465$, $p < 0.01$), suggesting that those consumers who perceive m-banking as useful are more likely to have positive attitude towards m-banking. This finding supports H2. Consistent with H3, perceived benefits of m-banking has a significant positive effect on consumers' attitude towards m-banking ($ß = 0.245$, $t = 3.032$, $p < 0.01$), implying the greater the benefits of m-banking the more positive the attitude toward m-banking, thereby supporting H3. Further, privacy/security risk ($ß = - 0.305$, $t= 3.811$, $p < 0.01$) and social risk ($ß = - 0.146$, $t = 3.055$, $p < 0.01$) are statistically significant in explaining consumer attitude towards m-Banking, thus, supporting H5 and H7. Whereas, performance risk, time risk, and financial risk are not statistically significant in explaining consumer attitude towards m-Banking. Consequently, H4, H6, and H8 are not confirmed. The results also indicate that privacy/security risk and perceived benefits are the most important constructs in explain consumer attitude towards m-Banking. Consistent with H9, attitude toward m-banking has a significant positive effect on intention to adopt m-banking ($ß = 0.713$, $t = 19.461$, $p < 0.01$) implying that the more positive the attitude toward m-banking the greater the intention to adopt m-banking supporting H9. Overall, within the nine hypotheses formulated, only six are confirmed by the data. Table 4 summarizes the empirical results of the research hypotheses.

Table 4: Partial Least Squares Results for the Theoretical Model

Predicted Variable	Predictor Variable	Hypotheses	Path	R Squared	T-statistics
Attitude towards M-Banking	Perceived Ease of Use Perceived Usefulness Perceived Benefits Performance Risk Privacy/Security Risk Social Risk Time Risk Financial Risk	H1 H2 H3 H4 H5 H6 H7 H8	.143 .171 .245 -.002 -.305 -0.146 -0.084 .018	.58	2.557 2.465 3.032 0.036 3.81 3.055 1.174 0.222
Intention to adopt M-Banking	Attitude Towards M-Banking	H9	.713	.51	19.461

As shown in Table 4, the average variance accounted (AVA) for in the endogenous variable by the exogenous variables was 0.53 (53%). In addition, the data indicates that 58% of the variance in consumer attitude towards m-banking is explained by perceived ease of use of m-banking, perceived usefulness of m-banking, perceived benefits of m-banking, perceived social risk and perceived privacy/security of m-banking. Additionally, attitude towards m-banking accounts for 51% of the variance in intention to adopt m-banking.

DISCUSSION AND IMPLICATIONS

The results of this study provided support for the research model and for most of the hypotheses regarding the relationship among the model's variables. In particular, the research model presented in this paper is unique in that it synergistically combines the TAM variables along with perceived benefits, the various dimensions of perceived risks, attitude and behavioral intention in evaluating the decision to adopt m-banking. The interpretation of the results based on the empirical findings is discussed below.

The study demonstrates the applicability of the TAM to a mobile setting, and the empirical results strongly supports the extended TAM in predicting individual's attitudes and intentions to adopt m-banking. Particularly, the overall explanatory power of the current research model had an R-square of 52% for consumer intention to use m-banking and an R-square of 58% for attitude towards using m-banking, implying that the extended model had the capability of explaining a relatively high percentage of variation of consumer attitude towards and intention to adopt m-banking in Jordan. In addition, the current study found that consumer attitude towards using m-banking was significantly impacted by privacy/security risk, perceived benefits, perceived usefulness, social risk, and perceived ease of use, in their order of influencing strength. Whereas, performance risk, time risk and financial risk did not play a salient role in affecting consumer attitude towards using m-banking. Consumer intention to adopt m-banking was significantly impacted by consumer attitude towards using m-banking.

Privacy and social risks have emerged as negative factors influencing consumers attitude towards m-banking and consequently their overall intention to adopt m-banking.

First, the empirical evidence of the current research indicates that the privacy/security risk is the most important and powerful factor in negatively influencing customers' attitudes towards using m-banking, implying that those consumers who perceive m-banking as insecure platform and who have concerns about fraud and identity theft were more likely to have negative attitude towards using m-banking. For this reason, the first priority for Jordanian banks is to provide encryption and ensure strong authentication in order to avert fraud and identity theft.

Second, social risk was found to have a significant negative impact on consumer attitude towards using m-banking and was the third powerful inhibitor to the adoption of such services. This indicates that Jordanian consumers care about social pressure from their reference groups with regards to m-banking acceptance. This implies that m-banking is not very popular among the Jordanian community and most respondents have family or friends or work colleagues who have unfavorable perceptions towards such service.

Third, the results indicate that the influence of performance, time, and financial risks on attitude towards using m-banking were insignificant. The insignificant impact of performance risk on attitude implies that consumers do not care about the risk of mobile platform malfunctioning. Moving into time risk, it appears that m-banking users have no worries about delays in conducting mobile transactions and they may be not concerned about the waiting time required for the mobile platform to operate. Therefore, it can be said that the probability of delays of payment and waiting time are not vital issues to be considered by m-banking providers. This result is inconsistent with previous research conducted by Lee [127] in the Internet banking context. Financial risk was found to have insignificant influence on attitude, implying that most respondents did not find financial transactions as an inhibitor factor to the adoption of such services, which is inconsistent with the findings of Lee [127]. This emphasizes the fact that m-banking users are not concerned about potential monetary loss due to transaction errors or bank account misuses. This may be due to the fact that the banks' staff provided assurance about the efficiency of m-banking transactions in Jordan.

The findings of the study also indicate that consumer attitude to use m-banking is strongly and positively affected by perceived benefits suggesting that perceived benefit is the most significant positive predictor of consumer attitude towards using m-banking, which is consistent with Featherman and Fuller [97] and Lee [127]. Taking this point further, consumers seem to be more likely to form a positive attitude and intention to use m-banking service when they perceive such service to save time, offers a wide range of service and can save the transaction handling fees.

Regarding perceived ease of use, the empirical evidence in the current study is consistent with many previous studies including Kim et al. [79], Taylor and Todd [69], Chitungo and Munongo [2], and Riquelme and Rios [78], Moon and Kim [77], Wu and Chen [70] and Yu et al. [86] which concluded that ease of use had a direct effect on attitude toward use. That is, the current study supports that perceived ease of use plays a determinant role in influencing consumer attitude towards using m-banking, which in turn leading to greater acceptance of m-banking. However, this finding contradicts prior research that considers perceived ease of use as a basic requirement for system design and should not have an influence on attitude in the later stages of adoption [52,128-130]. Based on the research findings, such perceived ease of browsing, identifying information and performing transactions should facilitate favorable and persuasive individual experience.

The data analysis also indicated that perceived usefulness of m-banking has a significant positive influence on consumer attitude towards m-banking. That is, respondents of the current study contended that the nature of the information provided through m-banking is considered as valuable motivations that lead them to react favourably and positively towards such services. When m-banking is perceived as useful, consumers' attitudes towards m-banking will be more favourable. This finding is consistent with previous studies within the m-banking context [6,8,19,76,78,114,131]. Based on the research findings, m-banking should be informative about new products and must demonstrate usefulness for consumers.

Moreover, consumer attitude towards m-banking was found to have a strong positive influence on consumer intention to use and adopt m-banking in Jordan. This conclusion has been confirmed by many previous studies stating that there is a direct relationship between consumer attitudes and consumer behavior within various contexts [126,132,133]. Moreover, attitude is predicted jointly by perceived ease of use, perceived usefulness, perceived benefits, perceived privacy/ security risk and perceived social risk suggested that the inclusion of attitude in the research model is meaningful and significant.

Theoretical implications

The current study contributes to theory within the areas of m-banking and consumer adoption behavior. From a theoretical perspective, the results of the study provide new information related to consumer attitude towards and intention to adopt m-banking that have not been previously examined, to a large extent, in the existing related literature. Thus, the study adds to and expands our knowledge of the most important factors influencing consumer attitude and behavioral intention towards adopting m-banking services. In doing so, the current research has applied proven theory and constructs in traditional banking, online banking and m-banking research, and has extended and validated the theoretical relationships between the focal constructs in the research model. In particular, this model has extended our understanding of the most important predictors of consumer adoption of m-banking in Jordan by synthesizing theories from the m-banking literature.

The study has also extended existing theory via the specification of the research model in relation to PLS causal modelling research, through the conceptualisation of the relationship among the focal constructs. In determining the appropriate epistemic relationships between the constructs and their measures, the proposed model identified all focal constructs, in a reflective mode. In addition, PLS enabled the simultaneous testing of the focal constructs including perceived ease of use, perceived usefulness, perceived benefits, perceived performance risk, perceived privacy/security risk, perceived social risk, perceived time risk, attitude toward m-banking, and intention to adopt m-banking, as well as their underlying measures within their nomological network.

In examining the simultaneous relationships among the set of variables within the research Model, a more accurate representation of the topic being investigated has been obtained. Moreover, the study has provided a further confirmation of the relationships discussed in previous online banking and consumer behaviour literature via an examination within the m-banking context. Such relationships include a direct link between perceived usefulness and attitude towards m-banking [12], the positive influence of perceived ease of use on attitude [2,78], the (positive) relationship between perceived benefits and attitude [92], the negative association between social risk and attitude [12], and the positive relationship between attitude and behavioural intention [106,107,110].

In addition, the study makes a strong contribution to the current m-banking literature by extending TAM to include perceived benefits and the five facets of perceived risk. That is, previous TAM studies in the context of m-banking [22-24] did not include the importance and influence of perceived benefits and perceived risk; as a consequence, they may have omitted crucial factors that influence consumer adoption of m-banking. More specifically, most of previous m-banking studies have modelled perceived risk variable as a single construct, which according to Lee [91], may fail to reveal the actual characteristics of perceived risk. Taking this point into consideration, the inclusion of the five facets of perceived risk in the research model may provide a greater understanding of the perceived risks of adopting m-banking and assist in exploring which risk dimensions are more important in this domain.

Also derived from the examination of the role of perceived benefits and the five facets of perceived risks, from a consumer perspective, was the theoretical implication related to contribution made to the current m-banking knowledge; namely, the first empirical evidence that perceived benefits and two perceived risks facets including privacy/ security and social risks all have significant effects on consumer attitude towards m-banking adoption.

Practical implications

The value of research in the area of marketing lies in its ability to be applied in practice. In this sense, the value of this research is that it expands our understanding of m-banking by identifying and synthesising the most important factors influencing customer adoption of m-banking services in Jordan. The practical implications of these findings are that they add to the understanding of m-banking from a consumer's behaviour perspective and, therefore, act as a valuable base for banks.

Specifically, the findings highlight the need for practitioners to understand that customer attitude towards m-banking represents an important aspect of the consumer acceptance and adoption of such service. That is, when consumers perceive that using m-banking is pleasant and a good idea, wise to use and find it desirable, they will be more likely to adopt m-banking services. Moreover, the findings suggest that particular factors (perceived ease of use, perceived usefulness, perceived benefits, perceived privacy/security risk, and perceived social risk) will determine customer attitude towards m-banking which in turn will influence their behavioural intention to adopt m-banking services. Therefore, perceived ease of browsing, identifying information and performing transactions should facilitate favourable and persuasive individual experience. In addition, m-banking services should be informative about new products and must demonstrate usefulness for consumers. Also, banks should attempt to enhance consumers' perceptions of the beneficial features and nature of m-banking. Marketing activities should focus on the tangible and immediate benefits of using m-banking services including quicker financial transaction speed, broader varieties of financial services, and enhanced financial transparency. Concurrently, social and privacy/ security risks related to the new innovation should be strongly minimized. Thus, banks should search for risk-reducing strategies that might contribute in arousing high confidence in prospecting customers. Taking this point further, it is suggested to focus on the prevention of intrusion, fraud and identity theft through the development of trust-building mechanisms to attract customers. Such mechanisms include long-term customer service, statement of guarantee for every transaction and digital receipts and enhancing security control when designing and updating banking apps.

CONCLUSION

This study is considered valuable to the Jordanian banking sector as it provides a unique and significant managerial and practical contributions as it has focused on the customers' perceptions factors as the major important factors influencing attitude and adoption of m-banking services. This study proposed a model which extended TAM along with risk and benefit perceptions to explain and predict customers' attitudes towards m-banking and behavioural intention with regard to such service. A more comprehensive investigation was added to the current research model by incorporating the five facets of perceived risks along with perceived benefit construct to explore the positive and negative aspects of m-banking. The findings of the current study demonstrate that the proposed model has good explanatory power and approves its robustness in predicting consumers' behavioural intention to adopt m-banking.

Notwithstanding the above findings, this research has some limitations which should be dealt with in future studies. As the current research is applying the survey-based method, it could be argued that this method is prone to the inherent limitation of measurement errors. However, the measurement errors were reduced, as indicated by the study's good reliability and validity results reported in Tables 2 and 3. The current study emphasised on examining consumers' intentions and perceptions rather than their actual behavior. The results by no means are conclusive towards users' actual behavior for adopting m-banking services. Research findings can be substantiated to a rational extent using the causal relationship that exists between intentions and behavior [69]. Nonetheless, more accurate outcomes may be obtained by assessing the actual behavior of m-banking uses.

In future research, it is necessary to verify the results through investigations in other developed and developing countries in order to be able to generalize the findings. This is because the adoption and usage of m-banking are highly varied across countries with different adoption levels and perceptions. In addition, the current study used cross-sectional survey to examine customers' adoption of m-banking where the data were collected at the same point of time. It was indicated that customers' perceptions may change over time when consumers have gained more experience [67]. Thus, future research is needed to replicate and validate the findings using a longitudinal research which would allow for further examination of m-banking adoption at multiple points of time, thus, allowing for tracking customer decision adoption process which may change and fluctuate over time. Another opportunity for future research is to extend the model to include other variables such as culture, facilitating conditions, and perceived cost in order to examine their impact on customer adoption of m-banking.

REFERENCES

1. CGAP (2006) Mobile phone banking and low-income customers. Evidence from South Africa.
2. Chitungo SK, Munongo S (2013) Extending the technology acceptance model to mobile banking adoption in rural Zimbabwe. Journal of Business Administration and Education 3: 51-79.
3. Turban E, King D, Viehland D, Lee J (2006) Electronic commerce 2006: A managerial perspective. New Jersey: Pearson Education.
4. Wessels L, Drennan J (2010) An investigation of consumer acceptance of M-banking. International Journal of Bank Marketing28: 547-568.
5. Goswami D, Raghavendran S (2009) Mobile banking: can elephants and hippos tango. Journal of Business Strategy 30: 14-20.
6. Dineshwar R, Steven M (2013) An investigation on mobile banking adoption and usage: A case study of Mauritius. Proceedings of the 3rd Asia-Pacific Business Research Conference, Malaysia.
7. Gu J, Lee S, Suh Y (2009) Determinants of behavioral intention to mobile banking. Expert Systems with Applications 36: 11605-11616.
8. Safeena R, Date H, Kammani A, Hundewale N (2012) Technology adoption and Indian consumers: Study on mobile banking. International Journal of Computer Theory and Engineering 4: 1020-1024.
9. Laukkanen T (2007) Measuring mobile banking customers' channel attributes preferences in service consumption. International Journal of Mobile Communications 5: 123-138.
10. Kim G, Shin BS, Lee HG (2009) Understanding dynamics between initial trust and usage intentions of mobile banking. Info Systems J 19: 283-311.
11. Laforet S, Lin X (2005) Consumers' attitudes towards online and mobile banking in China. International Journal of Bank Marketing 23: 362-380.
12. Akturan U, Tezcan N (2012) Mobile banking adoption of the youth market: Perceptions and Intentions. Marketing Intelligence and Planning 30: 444-459.
13. Yu C (2012) Factors affecting individuals to adopt mobile banking: Empirical evidence from the UTAUT model. Journal of Electronic Commerce Research 13: 104-121.

14. Liao S, Shao YP, Wang H, Chen A (1999) The adoption of virtual banking: An empirical study. International Journal of Information Management 19: 63-74.
15. Tan M, Teo TSH (2000) Factors influencing the adoption of Internet banking. Journal of the Association for information Systems 1: 1-42.
16. Yousafzai SY, Pallister JG, Foxall GR (2003) A Proposed Model of E-Trust for Electronic Banking. Technovation 23: 847-860.
17. Jacoby J, Leon Kaplan B. (1972) The Components of Perceived Risk. Advances in Consumer Research, Association of Consumer Research Proceedings 1: 382-393.
18. Davis FD, Bagozzi RP, Warshaw PR (1989) User acceptance of computer technology: A comparison of two theoretical models. Management Science 35: 982-1003.
19. Gefen D, Karahanna E, Straub DW (2003) Trust and TAM in Online Shopping: An Integrated Model. MIS Quarterly27: 51-90.
20. Hsu C, Wang C, Lin JC (2011) Investigating customer adoption behaviors in mobile financial services. International Journal of Mobile Communications 9: 477- 494.
21. WuJH, Wang SC (2005)Whatdrivesmobile commerce? Anevaluationempirical of the revised technology acceptance model. Information and Management 42: 719-29.
22. Alsheikh L, Bojei J (2012) Customer's perceived value to use mobile banking services. International Conference on Management, Behavioral Sciences and Economics Issues.
23. Daud MN, Kassim NEM, Said WSRM, Noor MM (2011) Determining critical success factors of mobile banking adoption in Malaysia. Australian Journal of Basic and Applied Sciences 5: 252-265.
24. Lule I, Omwansa T, Waema T (2012) Application of Technology Acceptance Model (TAM) in M-Banking Adoption in Kenya. International Journal of Computing and ICT Research 6: 31-43.
25. Ranimile N, Nel J (2012) Understanding resistance to cell phone banking adoption through the application of the technology model. African journal of Business management 6: 86-97.
26. Sultana R (2009) Mobile Banking: Overview of Regulatory Frame Work in Emerging Market. World Journal of Information Technology 4: 124-131.
27. International Telecommunications Union (2009) World Telecommunication/ICT Indicators Database.
28. Chowdhury S, Ahmmad N (2011) Factors Affecting Consumer Participation in Online Shopping in Malaysia: The Case study of University Students. European Journal of Business and Economics 5: 49-53.
29. Dupas P, Green S, Keats A, Robinson J (2012) Challenges in banking the rural poor: Evidence from Kenya's Western Province. Mimeo, Stanford University.

30. Sinisalo J, Salo J, Karjaluoto H, Leppaniemi M (2006) Managing customer relationships through mobile medium-underlying issues and opportunities. Proceedings of the 39th Annual Hawaii International Conference on System Sciences 6.

31. Tiwari R, Buse S (2007) The Mobile Commerce Prospects: A Strategic Analysis of Opportunities in the Banking Sector. Hamburg University Press, Germany.

32. Lee KC, Chung N (2009) Understanding Factors Affecting Trust in and Satisfaction with Mobile Banking in Korea: A Modified DeLone and McLean's Model Perspective. Interacting with Computers 21: 85-392.

33. Luo X, Li H, Zhang J, Shim JP (2010) Examining multi-dimensional trust and multi-faceted risk in initial acceptance of emerging technologies: an empirical study of mobile banking services. Decision Support Systems 49: 222-234.

34. Laukkanen T, Pasanen M (2008) Mobile banking innovators and early adopters: How they differ from other online users? Journal of Financial Services Marketing 13: 86-94.

35. Crosman P (2011) Banks Have Yet to Create the Killer App for Mobile Banking. Bank Systems and Technology.

36. Coelho F, Easingwood C (2003) Multiple channel structures in financial services: A framework. Journal of Financial Services Marketing 8: 22-34.

37. Al Mashagba F, Nassar M (2014) Modified UTAUT Model to Study the Factors Affecting the Adoption of Mobile Banking in Jordan. International Journal of Sciences: Basic and Applied Research 6: 83-94.

38. Shammot MM, Al-Shaikh MS (2008) Adoption of mobile banking services in Jordan. Scientific Journal of King Faisal Univeristy 9: 253-267.

39. Faqih KMS, Jaradat MRM (2015) Mobile healthcare adoption among patients in a developing country environment: Exploring the influence of age and gender differences. International Business Research 8: 142-174.

40. Faqih KMS, Jaradat MRM (2015) Assessing the moderating effect of gender differences and individualism collectivism at individual level on the adoption of mobile commerce technology: TAM 3 perspectives. Journal of Retailing and Consumer Services 22: 37-52.

41. Jaradat MRM, Faqih KMS (2014) Investigating the moderating effects of gender and self-efficacy in the context of mobile payment adoption: A developing country perspective. International Journal of Business and Management 9: 147-169.

42. Nor MK, Pearson JM (2007) The Influence of Trust on Internet Banking Acceptance. Journal of Internet Banking and Commerce 12.

43. Lee KS, Lee HS, Kim SY (2007) Factors influencing the adoption behavior of mobile banking: a South Korean perspective. Journal of Internet Banking and Commerce 12.

44. Luarn P, Lin H (2005) Toward an understanding of the behavioural intention to use mobile banking. Computers in Human Behavior 21: 873-91.

45. Ratten V, Ratten H (2007) Technological Innovations and m-commerce Applications. International Journal of Innovation and Technology Management 4: 1-14.

46. Zhou T, Lu Y, Wang B (2010) Integrating TTF and UTAUT to explain mobile banking user adoption. Computers in Human Behavior 26: 760-767.

47. Brown I, Zaheeda C, Douglas D, Stroebel S (2003) Cell phone banking: predictors of adoption in South Africa – an exploratory study. International Journal of Information Management 23: 381-394.

48. Amin HM, Lada S, Anis Z (2008) The adoption of mobile banking in Malaysia: the case of Bank Islam Malaysia Berhad (BIMB). International Journal of Business and Society 9: 43-53.

49. Dasgupta S, Paul R, Fuloria S (2011) Factors affecting behavioral intentions towards mobile banking usage: Empirical evidence from India. Romanian Journal of Marketing 3: 6-28.

50. Mattila M (2003) Factors affecting the adoption of mobile banking services. Journal of Internet Banking and Commerce 8.

51. Fishbein M, Ajzen I (1975) Belief, attitude, intention and behavior: An introduction to theory and research. Addison-Wesley.

52. Davis FD (1989) Perceived usefulness, perceived ease of use, and user acceptance of Information Technology. MIS Quarterly 13: 319-340.

53. Venkatesh V, Davis FD (2000) A theoretical extension of the technology acceptance model: Four longitudinal field studies. Management Science 46: 186-204.

54. Ajzen I (1991) The Theory of Planned Behavior. Organizational Behavior and Human Decision Processes 50: 179-211.

55. Rogers EM (1995) Diffusion of innovations. 4th Edition, New York.

56. Venkatesh V, Morris MG, Davis GB, Davis FD (2003) User acceptance of information technology: Toward a unified view. MIS Quarterly 27: 425-478.

57. Lederer AL, Donna, Mark PS, Youlong Z (2000) The technology acceptance model and the World Wide Web. Decision Support System 29: 269-282.

58. Van der Heijden H, Verhagen T (2004) Online store image: conceptual foundations and empirical measurement. Information and Management 41: 947-959.

59. Horton RP, Buck P, Waterson PE, Clegg CW (2001) Explaining intranet use with the technology acceptance model. Journal of Information Technology 16: 237-249.

60. Olson JR, Boyer KK (2003) Factors influencing the utilization of internet purchasing in small organizations. Journal of Operations Management 21: 225-245.

61. Pavlou PA (2003) Consumer acceptance of electronic commerce: Integrating trust and risk with the Technology Acceptance Model. International Journal of Electronic Commerce 7: 101-134.

62. Gefen D (2003) TAM or just plain habit: A look at experienced online shoppers. Journal of End User Computing 15:1-13.

63. Cass A, Fenench T (2003) Web retailing adoption: Exploring the nature of internet users Web retailing behaviour. Journal of Retailing and Consumer Services 10: 81- 94.

64. Yang KCC (2005) Exploring factors affecting the adoption of mobile commerce in Singapore. Telematics and Informatics 22: 257-277.

65. Aldas-Manzano J, Lassala-Navarre C, Ruiz-Mafe C, Sanz-Blas S (2009) The role of consumer innovativeness and perceived risk in online banking usage. International Journal of Bank Marketing 27: 53-75.

66. Lai VS, Li H (2005) Technology acceptance model for Internet banking: an invariance analysis. Informational Management 42: 373-386.

67. Mathieson K (1991) Predicting user intentions: Comparing the technology acceptance model with the theory of planned behavior. Information Systems Research 2: 173-191.

68. Chung N, Kwon S (2009) The effects customers' mobile experience and technical support on the intention to use mobile banking. Cyber Psychology and Behavior 12: 539-543.

69. Taylor S, Todd PA (1995) Understanding information technology usage: a test of competing models. Information Systems Research 6: 144-176.

70. Yen DC, Wu C, Cheng F, Huang Yu (2010) Determinants of users' intention to adopt wireless technology: An empirical study of integrating TTF with TAM. Computers in Human Behavior 26: 906-915.

71. Singh S, Srivastava V, Srivastava RK (2010) Customer acceptance of mobile banking: A conceptual framework. SIES Journal of Management 7: 55-64.

72. Donner J, Tellez CA (2008) Mobile banking and economic development: Linking adoption impact and use. Asian Journal of Communication 18: 318-332.

73. Chong A, Ooi K, Lin B, Tan B (2010) Online banking adoption: an empirical analysis. International Journal of Bank Marketing 28: 267-287.

74. Dholakia RR, Dholakia N (2004) Mobility and markets: Emerging outlines for m-commerce. Journal of Business Research 57: 1391-1396.

75. Knutsen L, Constantiou ID, Damsgaard J (2005) Acceptance and perceptions of advanced mobile services: alterations during a field study. Proceedings International Conference on Mobile Business, Australia.

76. Amin H (2009) An analysis of online banking usage intentions: an extension of the technology acceptance model. International Journal Business and Society 10: 27-40.

77. Moon JM, Kim YG (2001) Extending the TAM for a World-Wide-Web context. Information and Management 38: 217-230.

78. Riquelme H, Rios R (2010) The moderating effect of gender in the adoption of mobile banking. International Journal of bank marketing 28: 328-341.

79. Kim DJ, Ferrin DL, Rao HR (2008) A trust-based consumer decision-making model in electronic commerce; the role of trust, perceived risk, and their antecedents. Decision Support Systems 44: 544-564.

80. Alsamydai MJ, Yousif RO, Al Khasawneh MH (2012) The Factors Influencing Consumers' Satisfaction and Continuity to Deal with E-Banking Services in Jordan. Global Journal of Management And Business Research.

81. Cheong J, Park M (2005) Mobile internet acceptance in Korea. Electronic Networking Applications and Policy 15: 125-140.

82. Curran JM, Meuter ML (2005) Self-Service Technology Adoption: Comparing Three Technologies. Journal of Services Marketing 19: 103-113.

83. Koenig-Lewis N, Palmer A, Moll A (2010) Predicting young consumers take up of mobile banking services. International Journal of bank marketing 28: 410-432.

84. Nysveen H, Pedersen PE, Thorbjornsen H (2005) Explaining Intention to Use Mobile Chat Services: Moderating Effects of Gender. Journal of Consumer Marketing 33: 247-256.

85. Yu-Bin Chiu, Chieh-Peng Lin, Ling-Lang Tang (2005) Gender differs: assessing a model of online purchase intentions in e-tail service. International Journal of Service Industry Management 16: 416- 435.

86. Kazi AK, Mannan MA (2013) Factors affecting adoption of mobile banking in Pakistan: Empirical Evidence. International Journal of Research in Business and Social Science 2: 54-61.

87. Aboelmaged M, Gebba R (2013) Mobile Banking Adoption: An Examination of Technology Acceptance Model and Theory of Planned Behavior. International Journal of Business Research and Development 2: 35-50.

88. Lin H (2011) An empirical investigation of mobile banking adoption: The effect of innovation attributes and knowledge-based trust. International Journal of Information Management 31: 252-260.

89. Wright P (1975) Consumer choice strategies: Simplifying vs. optimizing. Journal of Marketing Research 12: 60-67.

90. Peter J, Lawrence X, Tarpey (1975) A Comparative Analysis of Three Consumer Decision Strategies. Journal of Consumer Research 2: 29-37.

91. Lee MC (2009) Factors influencing the adoption of internet banking: an integration of TAM and TPB with perceived risk and perceived benefit. Electronic Commerce Research and Applications 8: 130-141.

92. Yang YT (2009) A study of purchase intention behavior to consumers on innovation technology smart phone in technology acceptance model and theory of reason action. Unpublished master thesis, Nan Hua University, Taiwan.

93. Podsakoff PM, MacKenzie SB, Lee JY, Podsakoff NP (2003) Common Method Biases in Behavioral Research: A Critical Review of the Literature and Recommended Remedies. Journal of Applied Psychology 88: 879-903.

94. Chu S, Yao-bin L (2009) Trust Transference in Mobile Banking: An Investigation of the Initial Trust. Services Science, Management and Engineering 1: 204-208.

95. Puschel J, Mazzon JA, Hernandez JMC (2010) Mobile banking: Proposition of an integrated adoption intention framework. International Journal of Bank Marketing 28: 389-409.

96. Lu Y, Cao Y, Wang B, Yang S (2011) A study on factors that affect users' behavioral intention to transfer usage from the offline to the online channel. Computers in Human Behavior 27: 355-364.

97. Featherman MS, Pavlou PA (2003) Predicting e-services adoption: a perceived risk facets perspective. International Journal of Human Computer Studies 59: 451-474.

98. Cunningham SM (1967) The Major Dimensions of Perceived Risk. Risk Taking and Information Handling in Consumer Behavior 1:82-111.

99. Gerrand P, Cunningham JB (2003) The diffusion of Internet banking among Singapore consumers. International Journal of Bank Marketing 21: 16-28.

100. Mitchell VW (1999) Consumer perceived risk: conceptualisations and models. European Journal of Marketing 33: 163-195.

101. Dale L, Demetris M (2006) Consumer Perceptions of Risk and Uncertainty and The Implications for Behavior towards Innovative Retail Services: The Case Of Internet Banking. Journal of Retailing and Consumer services 13: 431-443.

102. Glover S, Benbasat I (2011) A comprehensive model of perceived risk of e-commerce transactions. International Journal of Electronic Commerce 15: 2: 47-78.

103. Ram S, Sheth JN (1989) Consumer resistance to innovations: The marketing problem and its solutions. Journal of Consumer Marketing 6: 5-14.

104. Im I, Kim Y, Han HJ (2008) The effects of perceived risk and technology type on users' acceptance of technologies. Information and Management 45: 1-9.

105. Ghalandari K, Ghahremanpour J, Hasanluei HN (2013) The Effect of Considerable Risks and Benefits on Consumers' Mobile Banking Acceptation in the Background of the Technology Approval Model in Iran. Journal of Basic and Applied Scientific Research 3:63-69.

106. Ajzen I (2005) Attitudes, Personality and Behavior. (2ndedn), Open University Press.

107. Ajzen I (2002) Perceived behavioral control, self-efficacy, locus of control, and the theory of planned behavior. Journal of Applied Social Psychology 32: 665-683.

108. Al Khasawneh M, Shuhaiber AA (2013) Comprehensive model of factors influencing consumer attitude towards and acceptance of SMS advertising: An empirical investigation in Jordan.

109. Alsamydai MJ, Khasawneh MH (2013) Antecedents and consequences of E-Jordanian consumer behavior regarding Facebook advertising. International Journal of Business Management Research 3: 41-59.

110. Smith J, Terry D, Manstead A, Louis W, Kotterman D, et al. (2008) The attitude

behaviour relationship in consumer conduct: The role of norms, past behaviour, and self-identity. The Journal of Social Psychology 148: 311-333.

111. Konerding U (1999) Formal models for predicting behavioral intentions in dichotomous choice situations. Methods of Psychological Research4: 1-32.

112. Castañeda JA, Muñoz-Leiva F, Luque T (2007) Web Acceptance Model (WAM): Moderating effects of user experience. Information and Management 44: 384-396.

113. Brislin RW (1970) Back Translation for CrossCultural Research. Journal of Cross Cultural Psychology 1: 185-216.

114. Kim H, Chan H, Gupta S (2007) Value-based adoption of mobile internet: an empirical investigation. Decision Support Systems 43: 111-126.

115. Stone RN, Gronhaug K (1993) Perceived Risk: Further Considerations for the Marketing Discipline. European Journal of Marketing 27: 39-50.

116. Pikkarainen T, Pikkarainen K, Karjaluoto H, Pahnila S (2004) Consumer acceptance of online banking: an extension of the technology acceptance model. Internet Research 14: 224-235.

117. Sekaran U (2003) Research methods for business: A skill building approach. John Wiley and Sons, New York.

118. Anderson JC, Gerbing DW (1988) Structural Equation Modeling in Practice: A Review and Recommended Two - Step Approach. Psychological Bulletin 103: 411-423.

119. Al Khasawneh MH (2012) A development and empirical validation of the consumer response towards Sponsored Search Advertising (SSA) model. Global Journal of Management and Business Research 12: 41-53.

120. Henseler J, Ringle CM, Sinkovics RR (2009) The Use of Partial Least Squares Path Modeling in International Marketing. Advances in International Marketing 20: 277-320.

121. Chin WW (1998) The partial least squares approach to structural equation modeling. Modern methods for Business Research 295-336.

122. Gefen D, Straub DW, Boudreau MC (2000) Structural equation modeling techniques and regression: Guidelines for research practice. Communications of AIS 7: 1-78.

123. Fornell C, Larcker D (1981) Structural equation models with unobservable variables and measurement error. Journal of Marketing Research 18: 39-50.

124. Bagozzi RP, Yi Y (1988) On the evaluation of structural equation models. Journal of Academy and Marketing Science 16: 74-94.

125. Nunnally JC (1979) Psychometric Theory. McGraw-Hill, New York.

126. Boudreau MC, Gefen D, Straub DW (2001) Validation in Information Systems Research: A State-of-the-Art Assessment. MIS Quarterly 25: 1-16.

127. Lee MC (2008) Predicting behavioral intention to use online banking. Proceedings of 978 the 19th international conference on information management. Taiwan.

128. Agarwal R, Prasad J (1997) The Role of Innovation Characteristics and Perceived Voluntariness in the Acceptance of Information Technologies. Decision Sciences 28: 557-582.

129. Chau P, Hu P (2002) Examining a Model of Information Technology Acceptance by Individual Professionals: An Exploratory Study. Journal of Management Information Systems 18: 191-229.

130. Karahanna E, Straub DW, Chervany NL (1999) Information Technology Adoption Across Time: A Cross-Sectional Comparison of Pre-Adoption and Post-Adoption Beliefs. MS Quarterly 23: 183-213.

131. Bhatti T (2007) Exploring Factors Influencing the Adoption of Mobile Co mmerce. Journal of Internet Banking and Commerce12: 1-13.

132. Haghirian P, Madlberger M, Tanuskova A (2005) Increasing Advertising Value of Mobile Marketing- An Empirical Study of Antecedents. 38th Annual Hawaii International Conference on System Sciences.

133. Tsang MM, Ho SC, Liang TP (2004) Consumer attitude toward mobile advertising: An empirical study. International Journal of Electronic Commerce 8: 65-78.

14
CHAPTER

E-BANKING: OPPORTUNITY AND CHALLENGES

Chai Lee Goi

INTRODUCTION

E-banking is defined as the automated delivery of new and traditional banking products and services directly to customers through electronic, interactive communication channels. ECbanking includes the systems that enable financial institution customers, individuals or businesses, to access accounts, transact business, or obtain information on financial products and services through a public or private network, including the Internet. Customers access e-banking services using an intelligent electronic device, such as a personal computer (PC), personal digital assistant (PDA), automated teller machine (ATM), kiosk, or Touch Tone telephone (Federal Financial Institutions Examination Council, n.d). The first virtual bank was the ATM (Kass, 1994; Wan, Luk and Chow, 2005). Other forms of virtual banking include telephone banking and home banking (Mahoney, 1994; Straeel, 1995; Talmor, 1995; Wan, Luk and Chow, 2005). E-banking services are typically classified based on the type of customer they support. Table 1 lists some of the common retail and wholesale ECbanking services offered by financial institutions.

Table 1: Common E-Banking Services

Account management	Account management
Bill payment and presentment	Cash management
New account opening	Small business loan appliations. app advances
Consumer wire transfers	
Investment/Brokerage services	Commercial wire transfers
Loan application and approval	Business-to -business payment

Citation: Chai Lee Goi, 2005, e-Banking: Opportunity and Challenges, journal of internet banking, http://www.icommercecentral.com/open-access/ebanking-in-malaysia-opportunity-and-challenges.php?aid=38622.

E-banking systems can vary significantly in their configuration depending on a number of factors. Financial institutions should choose their e-banking system configuration, including outsourcing relationships, based on four factors, therefore strategic objectives for ECBanking; scope, scale, and complexity of equipment, systems, and activities; technology expertise; and security and internal control requirements. Financial institutions may choose to support their e-banking services internally. Alternatively, financial institutions can outsource any aspect of their e-banking systems to third parties. Few entities could provide or host, therefore allow applications to reside on their servers E-bankingrelated services for financial institutions, which covers another financial institution, Internet service provider, Internet banking software vendor or processor, core banking vendor or processor, managed security service provider, bill payment provider, credit bureau, and credit scoring company. At the same time, E-banking systems rely on a number of common components or processes, therefore Website design and hosting, firewall configuration and management, intrusion detection system or IDS (network and host-based), network administration, security management, Internet banking server, E-commerce applications (e.g., bill payment, lending, brokerage), Internal network servers, core processing system, programming support, and automated decision support systems. All these components work together to deliver E-banking services (Federal Financial Institutions Examination Council, n.d).

E-BANKING IN MALAYSIA

The financial services industry has been subject to dramatic changes over the past decades, as a result of advances in IT, deregulation, and globalisation. These changes have reduced margins in traditional banking activities, leading banks to merge with other banks as well as with non-bank financial institutions. The forces of consolidation are also having a profound impact on the operation of securities exchanges, as well as the brokerage and asset management industries (International Monetary Fund, 2001). The merger programme of the banking institutions has resulted in the consolidation of 51 banking institutions into 10 banking groups. The mergers, which involved the consolidation of 96% of the total assets of the banking institutions was achieved with minimum disruption and dislocation to the system. This has been a major accomplishment by the domestic banking industry. The domestic banking groups are now in a position to reap greater benefits from economies of scale, through greater investment in technology and the more substantive pool of skilled staff. This will allow the banking institutions to make further gains on efficiency and competitiveness with each banking institution having attained the minimum of shareholders funds of RM2 billion and total assets of RM25 billion. The completion of the legal and operational mergers will place the Malaysian banking institutions in a better position to respond to the forces of change, in particular, to advances in technology and the greater demands for more customised and differentiated products and services by consumers and businesses. It will allow the banking institutions to be less vulnerable and more resilient to external developments and thus be in a better position to contribute to the economic growth process and the development of the nation (Bank Negara Malaysia, 2001a).

Under the Bank Negara Malaysia guidelines, all licensed banking institutions in Malaysia are allowed to establish informational Web sites. For more advanced Internet banking services, only domestic banking institutions are allowed to establish communicative or transactional Web sites with effect from June 1 2000. Locally incorporated foreign banks, however, are only allowed to incorporate communicative Web sites from Jan 1 2001 and transactional Web sites from Jan 1 2002 (Low, 2000). Only banking institutions licensed under the Banking and Financial Institutions Act 1989 and the Islamic Banking Act 1983 are allowed to offer Internet Banking services in Malaysia (BankInfo, 2005).

There are 12 banks offering Internet banking facilities while five have introduced mobile banking. The adoption of chip technology now also offers new forms of payment choices and higher security to the public. The introduction of the Bankcard to replace the magnetic stripe ATM cards and efforts towards migrating to EMV compliant credit cards before end-2004 is indeed an important step forward. A further development has been the introduction of the MEPS Cash, the national e-purse scheme as an alternative electronic payment mode to using cash for making retail payments. The ATM machines of the participating banks and terminals at retail outlets are being upgraded to facilitate MEPS Cash transactions. The number of interbank Giro payments has more than quadrupled in 2002, while electronic funds transfer and bill payments conducted through Internet banking has been on an increasing trend. More customers are likely to be drawn to Internet banking, which is gaining acceptance in Malaysia with now over 1 million subscribers (Bank Negara Malaysia, 2003).

The trend of the Web site adoption especially for business purpose in Malaysia consists of three layer stages, therefore promotion, provision and processing. This is similar to the classification applied by the business process of Ho (1997) model. These three stages hopefully can support the Internet marketing activities, therefore communication, transaction and distribution (Peterson, Balasubramanian and Bronnenberg, 1997). Refer to Malaysia banks Web site, it shows that banks Web site designed at least for promotion purpose and provide the communication activity to the customer. Few banks in Malaysia, example Maybank (http://www.maybank2u.com.my) provides quite completely of online business process stages and Internet marketing activities. Table 2 lists the commercial banks, as well as banks which offering the Internet banking in Malaysia. The provision of E-banking services in Malaysia mainly via electronic devices especially automated teller machine (ATM), telephone, personal computer or the Internet.

Table 2: Commercial Banks in Malaysia

Commercial Banks	Ownership	Web site
Affin Bank Berhad	Local	http://www.affinbank.com.my
Alliance Bank Malaysia Berhad	Local	AllianceOnline, http://www.alliancebank.com.my
AmBank (M) Berhad	Local	AMDIRECT, http://www.ambg.com.my
Bumiputra-Commerce Bank Berhad	Local	http://www.bcb.com.my
		Channel-e, http://www.channel-e.com.my
EON Bank Berhad	Local	http://www.eonbank.com.my
Hong Leong Bank Berhad	Local	http://http://www.hlb.com.my
		Hong Leong Online, http://http://www.hlb.com.my/inban.html
Malayan Banking Berhad	Local	Maybank2U, http://www.maybank2u.com.my
Public Bank Berhad	Local	http://www.publicbank.com.my
		PBeBank.com, http://www.pbebank.com
RHB Bank Berhad	Local	RHB Internet Banking Service, http://www.rhb.com.my
Southern Bank Berhad	Local	http://www.sbb.com.my
		SBB Direct, http://www.sbbdirect.com.my

ABN AMRO Bank Berhad	Foreign	http://www.abnamromalaysia.com
Bangkok Bank Berhad	Foreign	-
Bank of America Malaysia Berhad	Foreign	http://www.bankamerica.com.my
Bank of China (Malaysia) Berhad	Foreign	-
Bank of Tokyo-Mitsubishi (Malaysia) Berhad	Foreign	-
Citibank Berhad	Foreign	CitiDirect, http://www.citibank.com.my
Deutsche Bank (Malaysia) Berhad	Foreign	db-direct Internet, http://db-direct.my.db.com
HSBC Bank Malaysia Berhad	Foreign	online@hsbc, http://www.hsbc.com.my
J.P. Morgan Chase Bank Berhad	Foreign	-
OCBC Bank (Malaysia) Berhad	Foreign	http://www.ocbc.com.my
		eCafe, http://ecafe.ocbc.com.my
Standard Chartered Bank Malaysia Berhad	Foreign	http://www.standardchartered.com.my
The Bank of Nova Scotia Berhad	Foreign	http;//www.scotiabank.com.my
United Overseas Bank	Foreign	UOB Internet Banking, http://www.uob.com.my

The central banks Minimum Guidelines on the Provision of Internet Banking Services, which was issued in May 2000, requires banking institutions to have face-to-face interaction with customers prior to the opening of accounts or the extension of credit. Banking institutions are also required to establish appropriate measures to identify customers reached over third party websites and the customer verification process as stringent as that for face-to-face customers. In providing Internet banking services, banking institutions are also required to implement monitoring and reporting mechanisms to identify potential money laundering activities. This enables the Central

Bank to ensure that the banking industry, while keeping abreast with developments in ICT, that is, information, communications and technology, would maintain the integrity of the financial system and prevent it from being abused by the money launderers (Bank Negara Malaysia, 2001b).

The Internet wave has caught on in Malaysia, especially through the MSC initiatives undertaken. In the first wave of the Internet, it is extensively being used for communications, messaging and the posting of static information. Businesses use it as a form of online brochure, publicising their corporations (Ganesarajah, 2000a). The most important role in phase one of the Internet revolutions has been played by the telecommunications and Internet service providers. It is because of them that a large number of Malaysians can now access the Internet (Ganesarajah, 2000b). Through the Phase 2 of MSC project (2003 C 2010), a Web of similar corridors will be established in Malaysia and a global framework of cyberlaws will be passed; furthermore at least four of five intelligent cities will be linked to other global cities worldwide (Multimedia Super Corridor, 2005). Phase two is where the Government and banks come in, with the latter playing the fundamental role of enabler for E-Commerce, laying out the foundation where transactions can be made securely and effectively (Ganesarajah, 2000b).

OPPORTUNITY

The development of ICT in Malaysia has moved very fast especially through the introduction of MSC in 1996. Financial institutions also perceived the advantages from MSC activities and at the same time provide more benefits and opportunities especially in E-banking services. Few studies have been done related to the development of ICT in Malaysia.

Based on the Networked Readiness Index (NRI) framework 2002C2003 shows that Malaysia is ranked 32 with the score of 4.28 (see Figure 1).

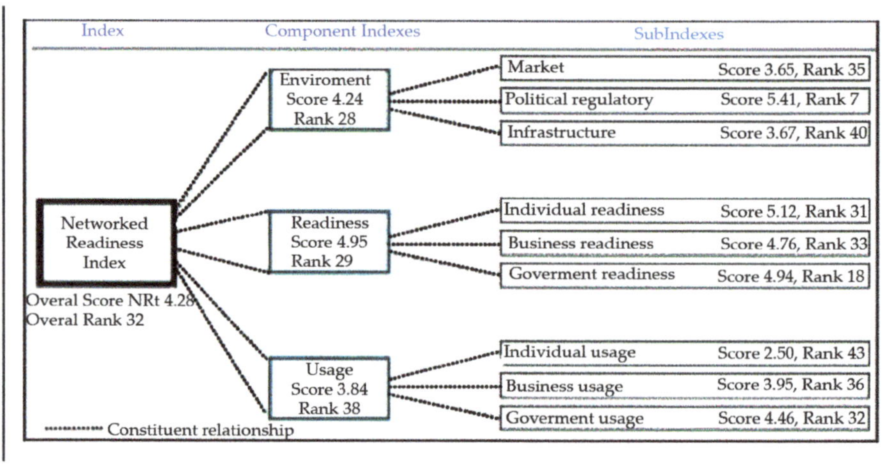

Figure 1: The networked Readiness Index of Malaysia

A result of study in April 2001 by using Framework for characterising the state of the Internet (The Mosaic Group, 1998) as the research methodology based on six dimensions are pervasiveness, geographic dispersion, sectoral absorption, connectivity infrastructure, organisational infrastructure and sophistication (see Figure 2) shows that pervasiveness is rated at level 4 that is Pervasive. Geographic dispersion is rated at level 3.5, that between highly dispersed and nationwide. Sectoral absorption is rated at level 2.5 that is between moderate and common. The connectivity infrastructure is rated at level 2.5 that is between expanded and broad. International connectivity is over 350 Mbps and it offers a domestic backbone of 155 Mbps. High-speed local accesses is limited with leased line and ISDN being the main access method. The organisational infrastructure is at level 3.5, that between competitive and robust. The two leading ISPs, JARING and TMnet dominate the Internet services. Finally, sophistication of use is at level 2.5 that is between conventional and transforming. The Malaysian government has equipped core areas in the MSC with high-capacity global telecommunications and logistics networks (Minges, Gray and Firth, 2002).

Dimension	Value
Pervasiveness	4
Geographic Dispersion	3.5
Sectoral Absorption	2.5
Connectivity Infrastructure	2.5
Organisational Infrastructure	3.5
Sophistication of Use	2.5
TOTAL	**18.5**

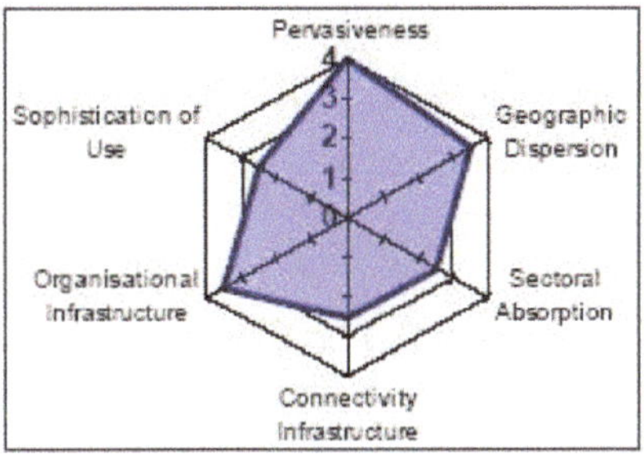

Note: The higher the value, the better, 0 = Lowest, 4 = highest
Source: ITU

Figure 2: The state of the internet in Malaysia

Another study based on E-Readiness (The Economist Intelligence Unit, 2003), or the extent to which a market is conducive to Internet-based opportunities, takes into account a wide range of factors, from the quality of IT infrastructure to the ambition of government initiatives and the degree to which the Internet is creating real commercial efficiencies. Nearly 100 quantitative and qualitative criteria, organised into six distinct categories, feed into the E-Readiness rankings. Below is the E-Readiness for Malaysia (see Table 3).

Table 3: EIU 2003 E-Readiness for Malaysia

Ranking (of 60 countries)	Overall score (score of 10)	Connectivity (score of 10)	Business environment (score of 10)	Consumer and business (score of 10)	Legal and policy adoption (score of 10)	Social and cultural (score of 10)	Supporting E-services (score of 10)
33	5.6	4.3	7.2	5.5	5.9	5.5	4.8

As the Internet and Web revolution moves into full swing, commercial banks not only stand only on bricks-and-mortar services, but also clicks-and mortar activities. E-banking is another medium to achieve the marketing objective, especially to reach more customers. A study by Sulaiman, Lim and Wee (2005) shows that the E-banking adopters' perceptions of E-banking appear to be very favourable. On the whole, it can be seen that the adopters perceived E-banking to be useful, easy and better way to conduct banking transactions than more conventional means. Table 4 shows the full list of perceptions of E-banking. Another result based on Likert scale of 1-5 also shows that among the Ebanking products and services, account balances inquiry was rated most useful by E-banking adopters. The other factors are saving account, current account, transaction summary report, e-payments, fund transfer, credit card services, cheque services and fixed deposit. Table 5 lists the usefulness of banking product/ services with mean scores. Based on these two results, acceptance and perception of customers on clicks-and-mortar is high.

Table 4: Perceptions of E-Banking

Items	Mean Scores
Easy to conduct banking transactions	5.35
Convenient way to manage finance	5.20
Able to manage finances more effectively and efficiently	5.15
Compatible with my lifestyle	5.08
Greater control over finances	4.99
Fits well with the way to manage finance	4.98
Useful for managing financial resources	4.97
Fits into working style	4.95
Faster internet access speed	4.81
Concern information will be known to others	4.57
Confident over security aspect	4.39
Can be frustrating	4.30
Requires mental effort	4.14

Table 5: Usefulness of banking product/ services

Products/Services	Mean Scores
Balance inquiry	3.07
Saving account	3.06
Current account	2.99
Summary report of transaction	2.98
Electronic bill payments	2.97
Funds transfer	2.93
Credit card	2.87
Cheque services	2.78
Fix deposit	2.70
Online insurance	2.58
Stock information	2.57
Market information	2.56
Car/house loan	2.53
Financial planning and analysis	2.51
Personal investment	2.46
Housing mortgage	2.45
Personal loan	2.44
Unit trust	2.40

Rapid advances in ICT has also significantly revolutionised the banking business, transforming processes as well as the strategic focus of banking institutions. It has fully opened the doors for new business opportunities as well as offering new methods of delivery of banking products and services, such as through the Internet. Under the new environment, competitiveness will not depend only on physical presence as in traditional markets, but rather on the ability to capitalise the technology strategies so as to deliver efficient and effective services. Successful banking institutions will be the ones that are able to leverage most from the ICT revolution as greater recognition is accorded to ICT as a driver of change. The 21st century will also see changes to the regulatory philosophies and framework following the development of an increasingly more complex and competitive market. The new regulatory philosophy allows for a greater role for market discipline. This approach emphasises on high standards of corporate governance, transparency and accountability. In adapting, banking institutions would need to reassess their internal practices as well as the overall corporate culture to be consistent with the new rules and regulation (Bank Negara Malaysia, 2001a).

To improve the financial industry in Malaysia, the banking system policy has evolved from financial sector restructuring during the late 1990s to institutional development and capacity building, and the development of supporting infrastructure to enhance efficiency and the strengthening of prudential regulation to enhance resilience and preserve stability. In terms of the development of the financial infrastructure, efforts were intensified towards evolving a more diversified financial infrastructure to facilitate the economic transformation into a more diversified economic structure. This has involved the development of a more diversified financial structure anchored by a more efficient and resilient banking system, to support economic transformation and growth. The blue print for the development of the financial sector in Malaysia is outlined in Financial Sector Masterplan that was released March 2001. Positive results have been achieved on several fronts related to the adoption of the ICT to the Ebanking system. First, domestic banking institutions have embraced a higher level of technology and improved business processes. Second, new delivery channels through innovative technology-based mechanisms such as internet and mobile banking have enhanced the delivery of products and services as well as widened access to banking services (Bank Negara Malaysia, 2004a).

In 2004, Financial Process Exchange was launched, which is multi-bank Internet payment platform marks another step forward in enhancing the financial infrastructure of the Malaysian financial system. In the quest for efficiency in the payment systems of the nation, an essential task for the banking industry is thus to strengthen the focus on meeting the specific demands of the consumers, and at the same time, forging alliances in common infrastructure building. The FPX is a right step forward in this direction. The efficiency of the financial system will be further enhanced with the FPX that reduces transaction costs and contributes to the overall functioning of the economy. This advancement forward can only be successfully achieved when there is active participation by the banking institutions, individuals as well as businesses, in utilising and promoting the system nation-wide. The payment system landscape is continuing to evolve - shaped for the most part by the availability of various electronic payment infrastructures and the consumers' adoption pattern. It is noted, however, that while a vast array of electronic payment systems and instruments have been introduced against a background of more flexible regulatory policies and advancements in technology, the use of cheques remains pervasive in Malaysia. More than 90% of the non-cash retail payments in Malaysia are made by way of issuing cheques, albeit at a slower average annual growth rate of 2% in the recent two years, compared to the use of the Inter-Bank Giro, which has increased at the rate of 197% (Bank Negara Malaysia, 2004b).

CHALLENGES

As online transaction risks are many and varied, risk management must take into account the state of technology, the banking industry, the non-bank competitors for payment business and adoption rate of new technology by the consumer. Bank Negara Malaysia a regulatory and supervisory approach to technology risks, which include three aspects. The first is research and collaboration among organisations such as banks, other central banks, vendors of technology and multi- lateral organisations like the Southeast Asian Central Banks (SEACEN) or the Bank for International Settlement (BIS). The second aspect is the issuance of minimum guidelines and standards for banking practices including the management of technology risks. Bank Negara Malaysia issued a guideline in relation to Internet banking that compels all banking institutions, which offer Internet banking services to adopt a rigorous risk management structure and system. This includes many online defensive mechanisms such as virus detection, intrusion management and authentication tools. The third aspect relates to the monitoring of risks and actual compliance to the standards issued. This involves a combination of off-site supervision, based on reports submitted by the banking institutions, as well as on- site examinations by examiners. Fundamental to all three aspects is the ability to understand and manage the complexity of technology risks, whether in relation to online transactions or otherwise (Sani, 2000).

Many of the businesses that are piling onto the Internet may totally misunderstand what this medium is all about (Willcocks, Graeser and Lester, 1998). Marketer cannot succeed in exploiting Internet and ICT unless the right IT infrastructure and development are in place to meet the demands of the users. In the ICT area significant importance has been placed on perceived usefulness as a significant contributor to attitudes and thus adoption of new technology (Fenech and OCass, 2001). If a firm adopts ICT-based innovations without a clear understanding of the scope and implications of that adoption, then not enough attention may be paid to realigning business strategy. As a result, business resources needed to achieve competitive advantage from the ICT investment may not be made available and the investment in innovation may in the end be wasted, or even be detrimental to the firms pre-adoption competitive position (Pires and Aisbett, 2002).

Customer satisfaction may increase based on the want and need, times, power of buying, and status. Todays companies have moved from a product and sales philosophy to a new marketing philosophy. Customer-centred companies have emphasised a better understanding of customers needs and wants and then translated them into the capability to give customers what they really need and want. The technology of E-Commerce determines what can be offered to customers, but only customers determine which of those technologies will be accepted. The key to success for E-Commerce lies in knowing customers (Lin, 2003).

CONCLUSION

Malaysia still has not reached a critical mass to ensure a sustained momentum, which can only be achieved if the nervousness of trading via the Internet is overcomed. Technologies are already here; it is the desire and willingness that needs to be converted into action (Sangaran, 2001). Malaysian banks will have to develop appropriate E-banking strategies to successfully compete both in the local and global marketplace. Proper understanding and planning is required to deploy the strategy or service effectively and safely.

REFERENCES

1. Bank Negara Malaysia (2001a), Governor Dato' Dr. Zeti's Interview with The Star, 3 May, Available at:http://www.bnm.gov.my/index.php?ch=9&pg=15&ac=24
2. Bank Negara Malaysia (2001b), Governor's Welcoming Remarks at the 4th Annual Meeting of theAsia/Pacific Group on Money Laundering, Speech by Governor of Bank Negara Malaysia, Tan Sri Dato'Sri Dr. ZetiAkhtar Aziz at Mandarin Oriental Hotel, Kuala Lumpur, 22 May, Available at:http://www.bnm.gov.my/index.php?ch=9&pg=15&ac=2.
3. Bank Negara Malaysia (2003), Governor's Speech at the Promotion of Electronic Banking & PaymentsLaunching Ceremony, Electronic Banking: The Way Forward, Speech by Governor of Bank Negara Malaysia, Tan Sri ZetiAkhtar Aziz at Nusantara III, Sheraton Imperial Hotel, 8 May, Available at:http://www.bnm.gov.my/index.php?ch=9&pg=15&ac=131
4. Bank Negara Malaysia (2004a), Governor's Keynote Address at the Malaysian Banking Summit 2004 :Towards World-Class Banking - Efficient, Effective and Resilient Banking System, Speech by Governor of Bank Negara Malaysia, Tan Sri Dato' Sri Dr. ZetiAkhtar Aziz at Nikko Hotel Kuala Lumpur, 14 May,Available at http://www.bnm.gov.my/index.php?ch=9&pg=15&ac=136
5. Bank Negara Malaysia (2004b), Governor's Speech at the Official Launch of The Financial ProcessExchange (FPX), Speech by Governor of Bank Negara Malaysia, Tan Sri Dato' Sri Dr. ZetiAkhtar Azizat kutiara Hotel, Kuala Lumpur, 28 October, Available at: http://www.bnm.gov.my/index.php? ch=9&pg=15&ac=159.
6. BankInfo (2005), Available at: http://www.bankinginfo.com.my.Federal Financial Institutions Examination Council (n.d), Booklet: E-Banking, Section: Introduction, Available at: http://www.ffiec.gov/ffiecinfobase/booklets/e_banking/ebanking_00_intro_def.html
7. Fenech, T.; and OCass, A. (2001), Internet Users Adoption of Web Retailing: User and ProductDimensions, Journal of Product & Brand Management, Vol. 10, No. 6, pp. 361 C 381.
8. Ganesarajah, P. (2000a), Killer Applications for ECBanking?, Business Times, Jul 6.
9. Ganesarajah, P. (2000b), Banks Set to Play E-Commerce Enabler, Business Times, Jul 20.
10. Hawkins, J. (2002), E-Finance and Development: Policy Issues, E-Finance for Development: NationalPractices and Prospects for Future, E-Finance for Development, UN International Conference on Financing for Development, 19 March, Monterrey, Mexico, Available at:http://r0.unctad.org/ecommerce/event_docs/monterey/hawkins-bis-EFfD.pdf
11. Ho, J. (1997), Evaluating the World Wide Web: A Global Study of Commercial Sites, Journal ofComputer-Mediated Communication Vol. 3, Issue 1, June, Available at:http://www.ascusc.org/jcmc/vol3/issue1/ho.html

12. International Monetary Fund (2001), IMF International Capital Markets, Chapter 5 of 6 Financial SectorConsolidation in Emerging Markets, August 22, p. 120, Available at: http://www.imf.org/external/pubs/ft/icm/2001/01/eng/pdf/chap5.pdf.JIBCfile:////omics accounts/...C%20HTML%20TO%20PDF/2006-10-3/E-banking%20in%20Malaysia%20Opportunity%20and%20Challen es. html[13-02-2015 12:19:24]

13. Kolodinsky, J.M.; Hogarth, J.M.; and Hilgert, M.A. (2004), The Adoption of Electronic BankingTechnologies by US Consumers, International Journal of Bank Marketing, Vol. 22, No. 4, pp. 238-59.

14. Low, I.M. (2000), Internet Banking Offers Convenience to Consumers, Computimes, December 28.Lin, C.C. (2003), A Critical Appraisal of Customer Satisfaction and E-Commerce, Managerial AuditingJournal, Vol. 18, No. 3, pp. 202 C 212.

15. Minges, M.; Gray, V.; and Firth, L. (2002), Multimedia Malaysia: Internet Case Study, InternationalTelecommunication Union, March, Available at: http://www.itu.int/ITUD/ict/cs/malaysia/material/MYS%20CS.pdf.

16. Multimedia Super Corridor (2005), Available at: http://www.msc.com.my.Peterson, R.A.; Balasubramanian, S.; and Bronnenberg B.J. (1997), Exploring the Implications of the

17. Pires, G.D.; and Aisbett, J. (2002), The Relationship between Technology Adoption in Business-to-Business Markets C The Case of E-Commerce, Industrial Marketing Management, Vol. 32, Issue 4, pp.291 C 300.

18. Sangaran, S. (2001), Room for Growth in Local B2B Marketplace, Computimes, Aug 27.

19. Sani, R. (2000), Internet Banking Needs Better Risk Management, Computimes, Jun 16.

20. Sulaiman, A.; Lim, C.H.; and Wee, A. (2005), Prospects and Challenges of E-Banking in Malaysia, TheElectronic Journal of Information Systems in Developing Countries, September, Vol. 22, Available at:http://new.ejisdc.org/ojs/include/getdoc.php?id=167&article=184&mode=pdf

21. The Economist Intelligence Unit (2003), The 2003 E-Readiness Rankings, The Economist IntelligenceUnit Limited and IBM Corporation, Available at: http://graphics.eiu.com/files/ad_pdfs/eReady_2003.pdf.

22. Wan, W.W.N.; Luk, C.L.; and Chow, C.W.C. (2005), Customers Adoption of Banking Channels in HongKong, International Journal of Bank Marketing, Vol. 23, No. 3, pp. 255-272.

23. World Economic Forum (2003), Global Information Technology Report 2002-2003 - Readiness for theNetworked World, Available at: http://www.weforum.org

24. Willcocks, L.; Graeser, V.; and Lester, S. (1998), Cybernomics and IT Productivity: Not Business atUsual?, European Management Journal, Vol. 16, No. 3, pp. 272 C 283

15
CHAPTER

FACTORS INFLUENCING THE ADOPTION OF INTERNET BANKING IN MALAYSIA

Ahmed EM, Phin GS

Keywords: Competencies, IT-solutions; Crowdsourcing, Platforms, Open innovations, Key competencies management

INTRODUCTION

Digital innovation has been rapidly grow and increased in the banking industry to promote and help to increase the competition ability from current competitors, new potential entrants, rapidly increase in terms of costs and the increasing demands and needs by banks to fulfil the mass consumer real time demands. Internet banking is the new innovative and creative ideas that occurred in the banking industry as the digital distribution channel [1]. Moreover, Karin [2] and Elham [3] stated that the internet banking represents a means of revolutionize and modernise the formal traditional banking environment. According to Suganthi [4] sooner and soonest internet banking will become a critical part of the transformation. In this study aims to offer the helpful and valuable information of the existing market for internet banking in Malaysia and the factors determining it, this includes demographic factors and social influences towards internet banking. The objective of this study is to investigate and examines the factors influencing the adoption of internet banking in Malaysia. There are few previous studies conducted in Singapore show that an understanding on the users' acceptance level of internet banking services and this could help bank managers to implement and improve the internet banking service. In fact, Malaysia has the same trails as other developed and developing countries in the rate of adoption of internet banking. Therefore, it indicates that there is a request to have this study on this field based study of this nature.

Citation: Ahmed EM, Phin GS (2016) Factors Influencing the Adoption of Internet Banking in Malaysia. J Internet Bank Commer 21: 164.

Theoretical Perspective and Review of Literature

According Agarwal et al. [5] Information and communications technology (ICT) services are considered as the main key driver for the changes taking place around the world. Recently, internet banking is the most innovative and effective service and it is also become the new trend among some of the new customers to perform their transaction via internet banking instead of over the banking branches. The movement and switch from the formal traditional banking environment to internet banking has been a 'leap' change. This study it will help to identify the determinants of the factors that influence the consumer's adoption of internet banking in Malaysia. Besides, it will also help to investigate the influence of perceived usefulness of internet banking, perceived ease of usage of internet banking and perceived risk on usage of internet banking by the customers. It is a necessary part of a bank's strategy of transformation process in an emerging economy to ensure the sustainability of the bank in the banking industry of Malaysia. In this study, data was collected via the survey approach that was based on questionnaire.

In this respect, Technology Acceptance Model (TAM) was founded by Davis [6] to introduce the acceptance point of Bodoni font entropy applied science and indirectly it may be adopted to forecast the adoption of cyberspace banking. TAM is a faultless model to feature shows acknowledgement level of exploiter and connected science .TAM additionally finds that the utilization and embracing of an early engineering is undaunted by his demeanour to use it. In any case, the fundamental antigenic causal variable of medication utilizes appropriation evaluation are the two principles which are seen handiness (PU) and saw simplicity of profit (PEOU). Both of this unremarkable will be characterized in the edge opus of this request. As can be optically recognized that gives a considered the segment that influence the customer air to increase the use of beginning connected science. Utilizing TAM ideas within forecasting customers' demeanour of selection of the internet keeping money were sustained the case that of as per the front matter circle done by Chen et al. [7].

Meanwhile, Qureshi [8] communicated about the believability element which is focus on the investigation of e-keeping money in a solid style and asserted that Atomic number 94, testament and mystery are the principles key constituent to acknowledge web managing an account convenience. PU and PEOU are immediate determinants of customer position towards using web banking as per the determination predictable with the 3 faculties of finding of Celik [9] who participates in the same variables. In course, order nation the trust-based human relationship between responder solace soul level, feel of security measure and their postures towards e-managing an account. From his meditation, he found that there is a coefficient of correlativity between these components with the client long time, yearbook compensation, and level of enlightenment. This association was adventitiously described by different analysts excessively, for example, Alda's-Manzano [10] concentrated on the ampleness of variables and surmise that TAM impression and saw danger in state of security, insurance, open presentation and blender have a prompt effect one-dealing with a record gathering. In other Scripture, he considered trust as key apples and oranges variable that lessens saw peril and recognized ten considerable components related to the clients' appropriation of web managing an account Robert William accommodation. Security office and protection were the significant reasons for disatonement. Both of these acumens free rein a principal part in deciding the clients' embrace purpose of web saving money facilities as to diverse division of long time bunch, ordinate transcription level, and wage level. Alternate variables, for example, accessibility, contraption, outline and limit were turned into the reasons for contentment.

In summation, Padachi et al. [11] study essentially get the same close however; talk about how considerable are different components, for example, the cost of electronic machine, web availability, and accommodation of profit. Consequently, also found in Liao et al. [12] subject field .They find that the same three components Atomic number 94, PEOU, and Personal machine have essentially impact on client major connection with net keeping money and that the individuals would circumstance an incredible eagerness on the endorsement of the internet-predicated monetary transactions. They also asserted that the considered parts of Plutonium the indispensable determinants of web dealing with a record getting. The impact shows that those components have an overwhelming and positive substance on clients to acknowledge web keeping money and religious settlement.

One of a useful speculative model in serving to understand and elucidate use direct in the information system utilization which supported by Vincent [13] study is Technology Acceptance Model (TAM). They said that TAM is an immaculate model and has been affirmed the viability in distinctive viewpoint and component. Both analysts were intrigued to direct an examination concentrate on the TAM for web saving money focused around an invariance dissection. In their study, they utilized diverse levels of invariance dissection on the TAM build in the setting of the web saving money acknowledgement. They found that the TAM build was invariant for their example crosswise over diverse in the demographic variables and ICT ability subgroups.

A comparable research by Kent et al [14] is to examine the engineering acknowledgement of web managing an account in Estonia. In this study, they highlighted that web keeping money as a paramount appropriation channel. The finding of their examination recommended that expand the use of web managing an account as client see it compelling and supportive administration. They presumed that the apparent helpfulness of web managing an account is the key develop ought to distinguish by banks and utilization to push the client use of web saving money. They additionally prescribed that the TAM ought to be rebuilt to center all the more on the key driver of the apparent convenience of the administration union and blend in the engineering.

It should be noted that there are few previous studies discussed the relationship between social influences factors and adoption of internet banking by using technology acceptance model (TAM). The pervious study of Amin [15] is targeted to examine the factors influencing the internet banking acceptance in Kota Kinabalu, Northern Borneo, Malaysia. He used technology acceptance model (TAM) as base framework of the study. He found that social norm, perceived usefulness, perceived ease of use, and perceived credibility are statistically significant while perceived enjoyment is statistically insignificant.

Pervious study done by Hakkak [16] is to discover the influencing factors that promote customer to use internet banking in Khorramabad. They were using technology acceptance model (TAM) and incorporates some additional critical control variables. From the study, they concluded that the social influence, internet connection quality, the internet banking awareness and its advantages, and computer self-efficacy have significant impact on the perceived usefulness (PU), and perceived ease of use (PEOU) of internet banking acceptance and adoption. They also mentioned that trust and resistance to change also have the significant impact on the attitude toward the acceptance and adoption of internet banking.

Not only that, Leng et al [17] studies also had emphasised to tackle a study need for extending the technology acceptance model (TAM) by adding contextual factors for internet banking case. They found that the social influences factors such as perceived usefulness and computer self-efficacy were the main factors influencing internet banking acceptance and usage. They also recommended to banks managers to focus and take more initiative on social influences factors such as advertising about internet banking benefits and advantages, and sales and marketing activities so that banks promotion of customer acceptance and adoption of internet banking.

CONCEPTUAL FRAMEWORK

This stud aims to identify the demographic and social influence factors that incfluencing the adoption of internet banking in Malaysia. This study used quantitative research approach and collected the primary data based on the nature of quantitative approach. The vaildation is used in this study to ensure the quality of the questionnaire in its development in order to obtain the information required. The data was collected by using the finalised version of the questionnaire. Meanwhile, cross-sectional research is the most frequently approach that is adopted in the descriptive design in the marketing research. Moreover, cross-sectional research also involved in the information collection only once from any given sample of population factors, therefore, this study used single cross-sectional design.

In this study, the developed research framework and measurements are based on the findings of the previous studies. It has determined the determinants and hypotheses from other studies based on the problem statement, research questions and research objectives determined by this study. For each determinant in the study, it proposed the relevant hypotheses and all the hypotheses were tested based on data collected. In this respect, this study examined the impact and influence between demographic factors and social influences factors towards internet banking and the adoption of internet banking in Malaysia (Figure 1)

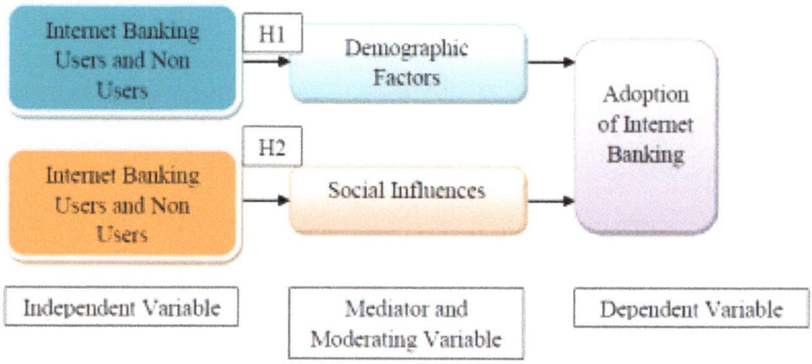

Figure 1: The Study Framework.

Due to the difficulties to identify the elements in advance as the list of the required factors and random sampling were unavailable, therefore non-probability sampling was adopted. In sampling the population, the judgmental sampling was used in this study to filter and select the sampling units to discover the following two aspects.

H1: There is a difference between users and non-users with their demographic factors influences with internet banking adoption. H2: There is a difference between users and non-users with their perceptions of social influences with internet banking adoption.

SOURCES OF DATA

In this study aims to identify and examine the impact and influence between demographic factors and social influences factors towards the adoption of internet banking. In order to achieve and complete this study, the survey questionnaire has been distributed to all the relevant party and respondents. The questionnaire has been distributed to 300 respondents at each of three departments in the bank which are EBusiness, Group Information System, and Group Communication and Marketing. However, in this study, there are only 120 respondents who answered and gave feedback to the survey questionnaires distributed that used in this study as the complete and clean. Sampling units E-Business, Group Information System, and Group Communication and Marketing are the three departments in three different specialize which were filtered and chosen via the method of judgmental sampling that is mentioned in previous section. The selection is based on variables categories that measure perception using nominal and ordinal scales.

Convenience sampling also called haphazard or accidental sampling is considered as one of the sampling method in conducting the research. It refers to the sampling by obtaining units or group who are most conveniently available and familiarizes with the field of the study. It is the method of choosing items arbitrarily and in an unstructured manner from the frame. For instance, in this study, it may be convenient and economical to collect the data from the population of sample in local and multi-national banking industries in Malaysia. By using convenience samples, it can obtain a large number of completed questionnaire quickly and economically.

In this study, the respondents of the questionnaires consist of all positions of employees working in local and multi-national banking industries in Malaysia which include department manager, senior ICT consultant, associate ICT consultant, customer help desk consultant and so on. Besides that, there is no limit and selective on age, gender, and years of experience as long as they are employed for local and multi-national banking industries in Malaysia.

This study is conducted by using Malaysia as sample and the sample saize is 120 respondents from local and mulit-national banking industries in Malaysia. The data was collected via questionnaire. Due to considering the reliability and validity of the data collection, therefore the survey questionnaire is distributed to 300 respondents at each of three departments in the bank which is E-Business, Group Information System, and Group Communication and Marketing. After that the respondents' feedback that filtered and selected based on variables categories that measure perception using nominal and ordinal scales.

In this study, the questionnaire created based on the literature review done in earlier section. However, the source of the questions being indicated and following authors are stated on the right row of the table below. All the questions have been modified to better suit of this study and the interview approaches will following with and after the questionnaire have been distributed out to the respondents.

The questionnaire of this study consisted of five sections as shown in Appendix A1. Section 1 of the questionnaire is focus on the question related to the internet usage. In this section, it tested on the frequency and the usage of the internet and the respondents adopt the internet for what purpose. In section1, it also used to explain and as the indicators for respondents express the frequency and usage of the internet. However, section 2 of the questionnaire acquired the feedback about the respondents' practice in the internet banking in Malaysia. In this section, it were highlighted and tested the frequency and the usage of the internet banking and the purpose of using internet banking was used. Next, section 3 of the questionnaire seek to explore and understand the cognition and manner of respondents about using the internet banking service. Then, in section 4 of the questionnaire acquired demographic information of respondents and at the same time it also ensure that the respondents' identity as anonymity which is the respondents' names were not required. This is to ensure the accuracy and reliability of the honest opinions and answers obtained from respondents. Lastly, section 5 of the questionnaire was an open-discussed question which is given to the respondents an opportunity to add in the clarify on some issues or highlighted and expressed any concerns and ideas in their mind which they considered applicable with their own words.

RESULTS AND ANALYSIS

In this study, the respondents of the questionnaire consist of all positions of employee working in local and multi-national banking industries in Malaysia which include department manager, senior ICT consultant, associate ICT consultant, customer help desk consultant and so on. Besides that, there is no limit and selective on age, gender, and years of experience as long as they are employed for local and multi-national banking industries in Malaysia. This study is conducted by using Malaysia as sample and the sample saize is 120 respondents from local and mulit-national banking industries in Malaysia.

The data was collected via questionnaire. Due to considering the reliability and validity of the data collection, therefore the survey questionnaire is distributed to 300 respondents at each of three departments in the bank which is E-Business, Group Information System, and Group Communication and Marketing. After that the respondents' answer and feedback that filtered and selected based on variables catogories that measures perception using nominal and ordinal scales.

Response rate Total of 300 questionnaires were mailed to the targeted survey respondents. 130 questionnaires (43.33%) were returned at the end of the data collection period after one reminder letter and one follow up email were sent. Out of the 130 questionnaires received, 120 questionnaires were completely answered while 10 were not. Thus, the overall response rate received in this study is 40% as summarized in Table 1.

Table 1: Response Rate of the Survey

Item	Number of Respondents	Percentage (%)
Total questionnaire sent to respondents	300	-
Overall response rate	130	43.33
Unusable questionnaire (Partially completed)	10	3.33
Overall usable response rate	120	40

Factor Analysis

Factor analyses has been used to examine the degree of responses on measured variables are being influenced by the underlying constructs. There have two main types of factor analysis which is exploratory and confirmatory. Exploratory factors analysis (EFA) is adopted in identifying the possibilities of underlying factor structure of a set of observed variables without expressing a pre-assumed structure on the outcome. However, confirmatory factor analysis (CFA) is adopted in verifying the factors structure of a set of observed variable. Factor analysis being used in this study is to test validity of all variables. Factor with Eigen values greater than 1 will be used and retained for further analysis but factor with Eigen values less than 1 will be categorized as insignificant and removed from the study.

Reliability and validity

According to Malhotra [18] the scale of validity can be explained as the degree to which the divergence in observed scale scores highlighted the real differences between the objects on the characteristics being measured rather than systematic or stochastic errors. However, according to Malhotra et al. [19] reliability defined as the degree to which the extent to which a scope yields for the consistent results if the measurements are used again and again.

In this study, the interview approaches was adopted to increase the reliability and validity for the survey instrument which is the questionnaire. To ensure the quality of the questionnaire, so an interview approaches have did together and after the questionnaire have been finalised and distributed out to the respondents. On the other hand, this study used to ask the comment from the professional bank staff with expertise on internet banking in a local bank and multi-national banking to assess the reliability and validity of the questionnaire and it is also used to ensure that it have included the best factors influencing the usage of the internet banking service. Reliability is concerned with estimates of the extent to which a measure is free of random error. In this study, adding similar questions to the data-collecting instrument will expand the sample of measurement questions. Cronbach's Alpha is one of the approaches adopted to evaluate the reliability and validity of the instrument.

Correlation analysis

In this study, correlation analysis is adopted to test all the possible relationship between the dependent and independent variables. The correlation coefficient (r) value must between positive value of 1.0 and negative value of 1.0. It used to indicating the strength of the relationship between the dependent and independent variables. When r more than zero, it indicates there is a positive relationship. When r less than zero, it indicates there is a negative relationship. When r equal to zero, it indicates there is no relationship. On the other hand, if r equal to positive value of 1.0, it indicates that is a perfect positive correlation. However, if r equal to negative value of 1.0, it indicates that is a perfect negative correlation. The value of coefficient closer to 1 then it indicates that the stronger strength of the relationship between variables.

Demographic factors

Age: There are about 40% of the respondents fall in the 21 to 29 age group. 30% of the respondents fall in the 30 to 39 age group, 23.33% of the respondents fall in the 40 to 49 age group and 6.67% of the respondents fall in the over 50 age group (Figure 2). Figure 3 shows that internet users are relatively young about 47.1% of the respondents fall in the 21 to 29 age group, while non-internet banking users are likely older. This result shows that age is an important factor that impact on internet banking usage. The result implies that younger users are the dominant users of internet banking.

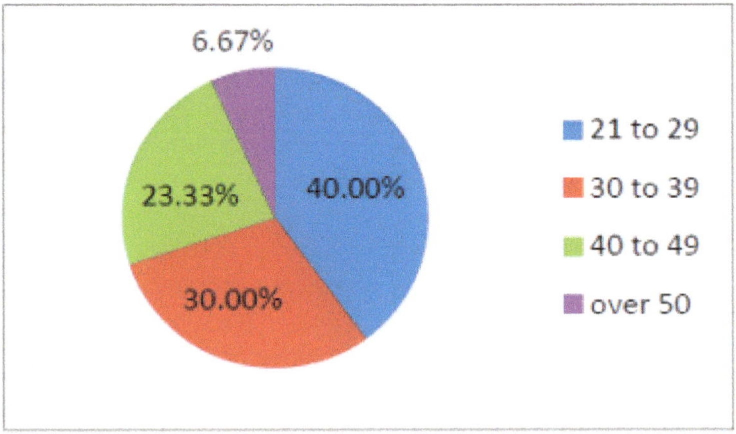

Figure 2: Age.

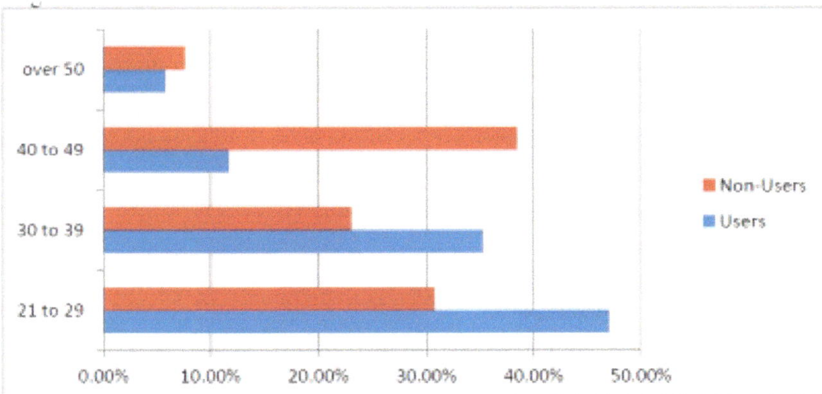

Figure 3: Users and Non-Users by Age.

Internet usage: The respondents' internet usage patterns were discussed in this section and how often they use the Internet.

- What respondents use the internet?

There are 87.8% of respondents will use internet for email usage so that they are keep up to date with any news available. 88.4% of the respondents normally use Internet for entertainment usage, 38.1% of the respondents use Internet for study purpose and 44.67% of the respondents do their banking on the internet.

- Frequency of internet usage

Figure 4 indicates that 6% of the respondents use the Internet more than 2 times a week; 15% use the internet once a week; 73% use the Internet daily and 5% use the Internet once a month.

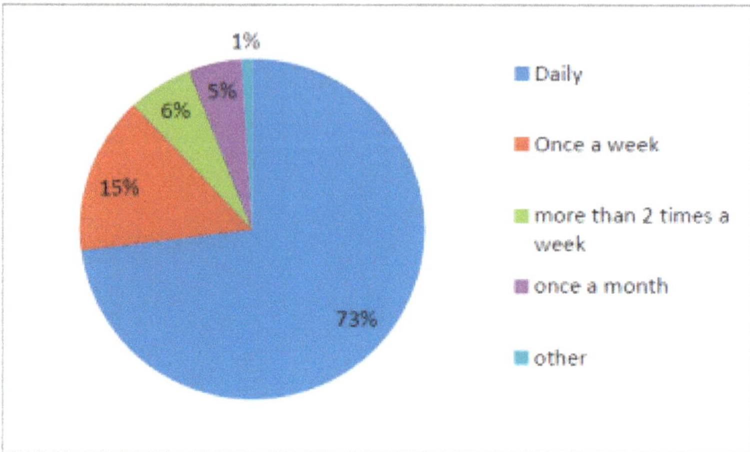

Figure 4: Frequency of Internet Usage.

Internet banking (IB): This section depicts the findings about internet banking (IB) user's habit in Malaysia where why they use IB and what is the usage of IB to them.

- Internet banking (IB) users as illustrated in Figure 5, there is 57% of the respondents use internet banking (IB) while 43% of the respondents do not use IB.
- Factors impeding the Use of Internet Banking (IB)

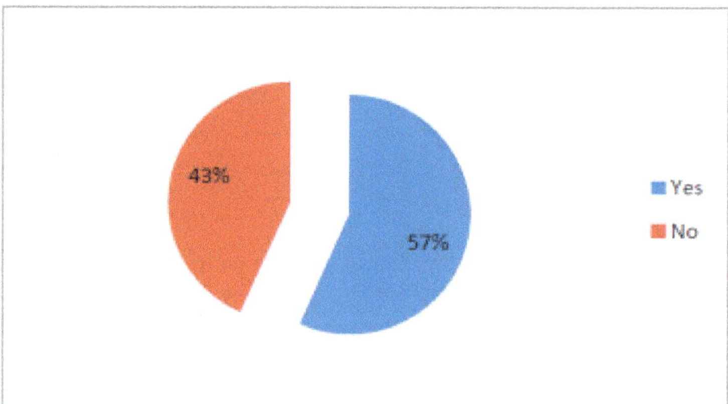

Figure 5: Internet Banking (IB) Users.

Referring to Appendix A1) Descriptive Statistics, the mean for the use of internet banking for 120 respondents is 1.17 with a standard deviation of 0.374. The trimmed mean value of 1.13is similar to the mean above. Hence, possibly there are no outliners in the data set. The maximum and minimum of use of Internet Banking are 2 (Implicit for answer of no) and 1 (Implicit for answer of yes). The range is 1. The interquartile range, the difference between the first and the third quartiles, is 0. The median of use of Internet Banking is 1, indicating at least 50% of the respondents have been used Internet Banking before (Table 2).

Table 2: Factors Impeding the Use of Internet Banking (IB)

Factors impeding the use of IB	Yes	No	Total
No Internet access	12	40	52
No computer devices	12	40	52
Not good at computer	16	36	52
Not good in using Internet	18	34	52
High Internet access cost	30	22	52
Internet banking is not safe	40	12	52
No need	24	28	52
Not heard about Internet banking	16	36	52
Other	0	52	52

Since the mean and median values are very close to each other, perhaps the data is symmetrical. The skewness value is 1.812, which is within ± 1. Hence, the data can be assumed to be symmetrical. The kurtosis value is 1.303, which is within ± 1. Therefore, the data distribution can be assumed to be mesokurtik. Besides, referring to the extreme values (Appendix A1), Descriptive Statistics, the top five values are 2, 2, 2, 2 and 2a. The bottom five values are 1, 1, 1, 1 and 1b. SPSS provides two methods for testing if data are normally distributed. The Shapiro-Wilk test is useful to test normality when the sample size is small, generally less than 50. The Kolmogorov-Smirnov test can be used when the sample size is large. In both tests, if the p-value is more than 0.05, normality can be assumed. In this study, since the sample size is 120, the Kolmogorov-Smirnov test will be used. The p-value of the test is more than 0.05 which is showing in Tests of Normality table from Appendix B1: Descriptive Statistics. Hence, the data can be assumed to be normally distributed.

In SPSS, normality can also be viewed from the Q-Q (quantile-quantile) plot which is showing in Appendix B1: Descriptive Statistics. This plots the expected normal values against the observed values, where the straight line represents a perfect normal distribution. The dots represent the observed values. When the dots fall very close to the linear line, there is an indication of data normality. When dots fall away from the linear line, there is a departure from normality.

Referring to (Appendix A2), Frequency, Descriptive Statistics it has been showed that of the 120 respondents, 100 (83.3%) respondents mentioned that they have been used internet banking before. And 20 (16.7%) respondents mentioned that they have never use Internet Banking before.

Referring to (Appendix A3), one-Sample T-Test, the sample mean for 120 respondents is 1.17 with a standard deviation 0.374. The standard error, SE, is 0.034.

In this study, the finding of this One-Sample T-Test shown that the mean difference is -118.833 and the standardized difference, t = -3478.388. The two tailed p-value of the test is 0.000, which is less than 0.05. The 95% confidence interval for mean difference is [-118.90, - 118.77], which does not contain 0. The 95% confidence interval for population mean is [(-118.90 + 120), (-118.77 + 120)] = [1.1, 1.23]. In short, the 95% confidence interval for mean difference does not contain the tested value of 0 and the p-value of the test is less than 0.05. The effect size is moderate to large and the power of the test is more than 80%. Thus, the mean of use of Internet Banking of the study population is not 120. We are 95% confident that the use of Internet Banking for this population is between 1.1 and 1.23.

Referring to (Appendix A4), Paired Sample Statistics, the mean of use of Internet is 1.00 with a standard deviation of 0.000. The mean of use of Internet Banking is 1.17 with a standard deviation of 0.374. In this study the finding of this Paired Sample Statistics shown that the mean difference is -0.167 with a standard deviation of 0.374. The standardized difference, t = -4.879 and df = 119. The two tailed p-value of the test is 0.000, which is less than 0.05. The confidence interval for mean difference is [-0.234, - 0.099], which does not contain 0. In short, the 95% confidence interval for mean difference does not contain the tested value of 0 and the p-value of the test is less than 005. Thus, there is significant change in the mean use of Internet Banking. Thus, the special differentiation use of Internet and Internet Banking is effective influenced the use of Internet Banking.

Referring to Appendix A5: One-Way ANOVA, the sample mean for use of Internet Banking is -1.00 (Implicit for answer of no) is 2.00 with a standard deviation of 0.000. The samples mean for 0.00 (Implicit for answer of yes) is 1.00 with a standard deviation of 0.000. In this study, the finding shown that the p-value for Levene's test for equality of variance is 0, which is less than 0.05. Thus, equality of variance is not assumed. The Fvalue is 0 and the degrees of freedoms are 1 and 118. The p-value of the test is 0, which is less than 0.05 too. In short, the p-value of the test is less than 0.05. Hence, at least one pair of mean differ significantly. When there is a difference, there is a need to identify the pair(s) that differs significantly. This is done using post hoc tests.

Encouraging factors to use internet banking (IB): The objective of this question was to ascertain some of the encouraging factors to use internet banking (IB). Out of 52 nonusers, 40 non-users discovered that the major factor will be free internet access, 20 respondents stated that if they are being provided with free skills training, then they would adopt to use IB and 3 respondents agreed that they would adopt to use IB if banks provide better security (Table 3).

Bank of preference: Figure 6 showed that foreign bank is preferable by the respondents who use internet banking (IB).

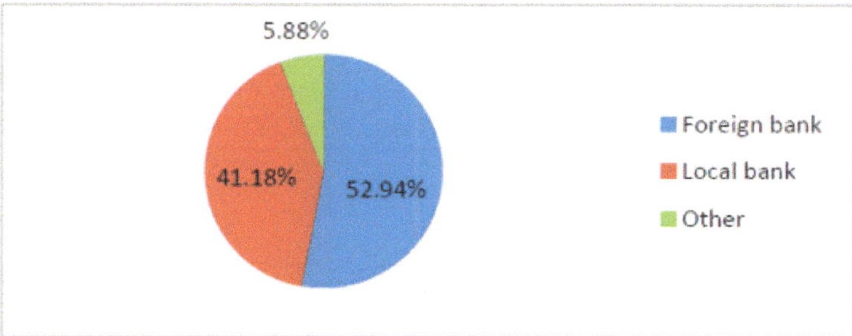

Figure 6: Preference Bank.

Table 3: Encouraging Factors to Use Internet Banking (IB)

Encouraging Factors for use of IB	Yes	No	Total
Free internet access provided	44	8	52
Free skills training provided	20	32	52
More economical banking transactions	36	16	52
Better security features	40	12	52
Other	8	44	52

Uses of internet banking (IB): Table 4 shows that the respondents that use their internet banking (IB) service to perform payments (94.1%), for transferring funds (88.2%), for account statements inquiry (76.5%) and for cheque account balances inquiry (41.2%).

Frequency of using internet banking (IB): Figure 7 illustrates that there are about 47.10% of the respondents using internet banking (IB) weekly, 35.30% of the respondents using IB daily, 11.80% of the respondents using IB monthly, 5.88% of the respondents using IB quarterly, and none of the respondents using IB yearly Appendix A6.

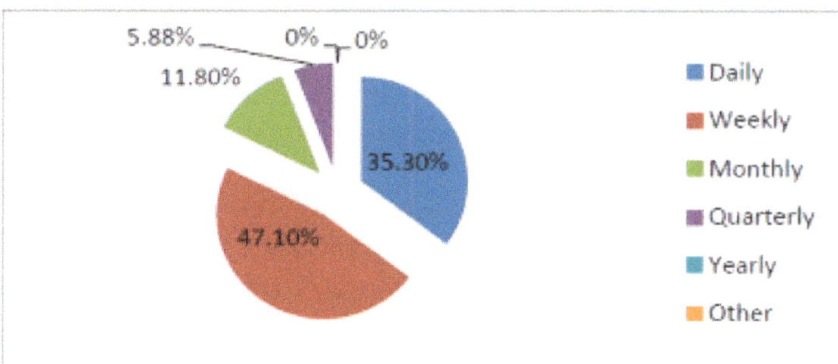

Figure 7: Frequency of Using Internet Banking (IB).

Table 4: Uses of Internet Banking (IB)

Uses of Internet Banking (IB)	Yes	No	Total
Viewing account statements	52	16	68
Viewing cheque account balances	28	40	68
Making payments	64	4	68
Transferring funds	60	8	68
Other	12	56	68

The comparative advantages of internet banking (IB)

Internet banking (IB) promotes greater finance management: As illustrated in Table 5, there are about 56.67% of the respondents agree that internet banking (IB) enables them for greater finance management compare to brick and mortar banking services provided. There is 20% of non IB users agreed that IB allow them to better manage finance.

Table 5: Internet Banking (IB) Enables Better Management of Finances.

Option	Frequency	Percentage	IB users Frequency	IB users Percentage	Non IB users Frequency	Non IB users Percentage
Strongly Disagree	12	10	0	0	12	30
Disagree	40	33.33	20	25	20	50
Neither	0	0	0	0	0	0
Agree	48	40	40	50	8	20
Strongly Agree	20	16.67	20	25	0	0
Total	120	100	80	100	40	100

Internet banking (IB) promotes time savings: 56.67% of the respondents agree that internet banking (IB) promotes time saving as they can manage all the financial transactions done with just at fingertips and not visiting a branch. Besides that, there are 100% of respondents agree IB allows them to perform financial transaction at anytime, anywhere and 7*24 throughout a year. Thus the adoption of IB has eliminates the time and place boundary constraints. Contrary, there are more than half of non-internet banking users (84.61%) disagree that IB can save time (Table 6).

Table 6: Internet Banking (IB) Saves Time

Option	Frequency	Percentage	IB users Frequency	IB users Percentage	Non IB users Frequency	Non IB users Percentage
Strongly Disagree	4	3.33	0	0	4	7.69
Disagree	40	33.33	0	0	40	76.92
Neither	8	6.67	0	0	8	15.39
Agree	20	16.67	20	29.41	0	0
Strongly Agree	48	40	48	70.59	0	0
Total	120	100	68	100	52	100

Internet banking (IB) cause respondents more comfortable communicating with bank: A total of 56.66% of respondents agreed that internet banking (IB) allow them to communicate with the bank more comfortable. From the survey, 83.33% of users agreed that IB makes them to communicate with the bank more comfortable while only 16.67% of non-internet banking users agreed that IB makes them to communicate with the bank more comfortable (Table 7).

Table 7: Internet Banking Causes Respondents More Comfortable Communicating with Bank.

Option	Frequency	Percentage	IB users Frequency	IB users Percentage	Non IB users Frequency	Non IB users Percentage
Strongly Disagree	20	16.67	4	5.56	16	33.33
Disagree	24	20	8	11.11	16	33.33
Neither	8	6.67	0	0	8	16.67
Agree	40	33.33	32	44.44	8	16.67
Strongly Agree	28	23.33	28	38.89	0	0
Total	120	100	72	100	48	100

Internet Banking (IB) Compatibility

Internet banking (IB) suits respondents' life styles: 56.66% of the respondents agree that internet banking (IB) suits their life style. 88.24% of internet banking users concurred that IB suits their life style, whereas just 15.39% of non-internet banking users agreed that IB suits their life style (Table 8).

Table 8: Internet Banking (IB) Suits Respondents' Life Styles

Option	Frequency	Percentage	IB users Frequency	IB users Percentage	Non IB users Frequency	Non IB users Percentage
Strongly Disagree	20	16.67	4	5.88	16	30.76
Disagree	32	26.67	4	5.88	28	53.85
Neither	0	0	0	0	0	0
Agree	40	33.33	32	47.07	8	15.39
Strongly Agree	28	23.33	28	41.17	0	0
Total	120	100	68	100	52	100

Internet banking (IB) suits respondents' work styles: A total of 63.33% of respondents agree internet banking (IB) can accommodate with their working life style. 80%of users agreed whereas 30%of non IB users concurred that IB can lodge with work life Style (Table 9).

Table 9: Internet Banking (IB) Suits Respondents' Work Styles

Option	Frequency	Percentage	IB users Frequency	IB users Percentage	Non IB users Frequency	Non IB users Percentage
Strongly Disagree	32	26.67	12	15	20	50
Disagree	12	10	4	5	8	20
Neither	0	0	0	0	0	0
Agree	48	40	40	50	8	20
Strongly Agree	28	23.33	24	30	4	10
Total	120	100	80	100	40	100

Internet banking (IB) makes life convenient: A total of 86.66% of the respondents agree that internet banking (IB) provide more convenience to them. 100% of users agreed that IB makes their life more convenience while just 50% of non-internet banking users agreed that IB makes their life more convenience (Table 10).

Table 10: Internet Banking (IB) Makes Respondents' Life Convenient.

Option	Frequency	Percentage	IB users Frequency	IB users Percentage	Non IB users Frequency	Non IB users Percentage
Strongly Disagree	8	6.67	0	0	8	25
Disagree	8	6.67	0	0	8	25
Neither	0	0	0	0	0	0
Agree	88	73.33	72	81.82	24	50
Strongly Agree	16	13.33	8	18.18	0	0
Total	120	100	80	100	40	100

Internet banking (IB) complexity

Ease of use of internet banking (IB): 46.67% of the respondents concurred that internet banking (IB) is ease of use. 80% of the users concurred that it is easy to use internet banking but only 13.33% of the non-internet banking respondents concurred that IB is easy to be used (Table 11).

Table 11: The Ease of Conducting Internet Banking (IB)

Option	Frequency	Percentage	IB users Frequency	IB users Percentage	Non IB users Frequency	Non IB users Percentage
Strongly Disagree	32	26.67	4	6.67	28	46.67
Disagree	32	26.67	8	13.33	24	40
Neither	0	0	0	0	0	0
Agree	48	40	40	66.67	8	13.33
Strongly Agree	8	6.66	8	13.33	0	0
Total	120	100	60	100	60	100

Internet banking (IB) complexity: 53.34% of respondents agreed that Internet Banking (IB) is very complex to be used. 100% of non-internet banking users concurred IB is a very complex system to be used (Table 12).

Table 12: The Complexity of Using Internet Banking (IB)

Option	Frequency	Percentage	IB users Frequency	IB users Percentage	Non IB users Frequency	Non IB users Percentage
Strongly Disagree	16	13.33	16	26.67	0	0
Disagree	40	33.33	40	66.67	0	0
Neither	0	0	0	0	0	0
Agree	60	50	4	6.66	56	93.33
Strongly Agree	4	3.34	0	0	4	6.67
Total	120	100	60	100	60	100

The simplicity of the internet banking (IB) process

56.67% of the respondents agree Internet Banking (IB) is simple to be used. 94.12% of users and 7.69% of non-internet banking users agree that IB is simple to be used (Table 13).

Table 13: The Simplicity of the Internet Banking (IB) Process

Option	Frequency	Percentage	IB users Frequency	IB users Percentage	Non IB users Frequency	Non IB users Percentage
Strongly Disagree	8	6.67	0	0	8	15.39
Disagree	40	33.33	4	5.88	36	69.23
Neither	4	3.33	0	0	4	7.69
Agree	64	53.34	60	88.24	4	7.69
Strongly Agree	4	3.33	4	5.88	0	0
Total	120	100	68	100	52	100

The perceived cost of internet banking (IB)

Expensive telecommunication costs: 69.99% of the respondents agree that expensive telecommunication costs have play an important role to determine internet banking adoption. Only 13.34% disagree that the telecommunication costs are expensive. 76.19% of the non-users agree that the telecommunication costs are expensive while

22.22% of the users did not agree that the telecommunication costs are expensive. This finding indicates that perception of cost plays an important part in the consumer decision-making process whether to adopt the usage of internet banking (IB) (Table 14) Appendix A7.

Table 14: Telecommunication Costs are Expensive

Option	Frequency	Percentage	IB users Frequency	IB users Percentage	Non IB users Frequency	Non IB users Percentage
Strongly Disagree	8	6.67	4	11.11	4	4.76
Disagree	8	6.67	4	11.11	4	4.76
Neither	20	16.67	8	22.22	12	14.29
Agree	80	66.66	20	55.56	60	71.43
Strongly Agree	4	3.33	0	0	4	4.76
Total	120	100	36	100	84	100

The Cost of internet installation: 69.99% of the respondents concurred that the internet installations cost are too high and expensive. 22.22% of the respondents don't agree that cost of internet installation is expensive. 76.19% of non-internet banking (IB) users agree that internet installation costs are too high and expensive (Table 15).

Table 15: The Cost of Internet Installation.

Option	Frequency	Percentage	IB users Frequency	IB users Percentage	Non IB users Frequency	Non IB users Percentage
Strongly Disagree	8	6.67	4	11.11	4	4.76
Disagree	8	6.67	4	11.11	4	4.76
Neither	20	16.67	8	22.22	12	14.29
Agree	40	66.66	20	55.56	60	71.43
Strongly Agree	4	3.33	0	0	4	4.76
Total	120	100	36	100	84	100

The Cost-effectiveness of internet banking (IB): A total of 56.67% of the respondents consider internet installation costs to be too expensive. 88.24% of users noticed that internet banking (IB) is cost-effective, but 61.54% of non IB users who don't concurred that IB is cost-effective (Table 16)

Table 16: The Cost-Effectiveness of Internet Banking (IB).

Option	Frequency	Percentage	IB users Frequency	IB users Percentage	Non IB users Frequency	Non IB users Percentage
Strongly Disagree	8	6.67	0	0	8	15.39
Disagree	32	26.67	8	11.76	24	46.15
Neither	12	10	0	0	12	23.08
Agree	48	40	40	58.82	8	15.38
Strongly Agree	20	16.66	20	29.42	0	0
Total	120	100	68	100	52	100

The perceived risk of internet banking (IB)

Banking at branch safety: 18 of the respondents believe that banking at branch is safe. 23.08% of users and 88.24% of non-internet banking users perceive that banking at branch is safe (Table 17).

Table 17: Safety of Banking at the Branch

Option	Frequency	Percentage	IB users Frequency	IB users Percentage	Non IB users Frequency	Non IB users Percentage
Strongly Disagree	8	6.67	8	15.38	0	0
Disagree	40	33.33	32	61.54	8	11.76
Neither	0	0	0	0	0	0
Agree	72	60	12	23.08	60	88.24
Strongly Agree	0	0	0	0	0	0
Total	120	100	52	100	68	100

The internet banking (IB) safety: 56.67 % of the respondents agreed that internet banking (IB) is safe. Most of the users (100%) agree, and 100% of the non IB users consider IB to be safe (Table 18).

Table 18: The Safety of Internet Banking (IB).

Option	Frequency	Percentage	IB users Frequency	IB users Percentage	Non IB users Frequency	Non IB users Percentage
Strongly Disagree	20	16.67	0	0	20	38.46
Disagree	32	26.67	0	0	32	61.54
Neither	0	0	0	0	0	0
Agree	60	50	60	88.24	0	0
Strongly Agree	8	6.66	8	11.76	0	0
Total	120	100	68	100	52	100

Credit card/account details disclosure on digital: 43.33% of respondents are not confident in disclosing their credit card/account details digital. 100% of non-users are not confident to reveal their credit card and account details on the internet, and this is a reluctance that is shared by 100% of the users (Table 19).

Table 19: Credit Card/Account Details Disclosure on the Internet

Option	Frequency	Percentage	IB users Frequency	IB users Percentage	Non IB users Frequency	Non IB users Percentage
Strongly Disagree	40	33.33	0	0	20	38.46
Disagree	12	10	0	0	32	61.54
Neither	0	0	0	0	0	0
Agree	60	50	60	88.24	0	0
Strongly Agree	8	6.67	8	11.76	0	0
Total	120	100	68	100	52	100

Personal information disclosure on digital: About 56.67% of the respondents not are comfortable with disclosing personal information on digital. 100 % of users are confident to disclose their particulars on the internet but the majority of non-internet banking (IB) users (100%) are taciturn. This confirms that negative perceptions concerning the safety of IB abound among consumers (Table 20) Appendix A8.

Table 20: Personal Information Disclosure on the Internet

Option	Frequency	Percentage	IB users Frequency	IB users Percentage	Non IB users Frequency	Non IB users Percentage
Strongly Disagree	20	16.67	0	0	20	38.46
Disagree	32	26.67	0	0	32	61.54
Neither	0	0	0	0	0	0
Agree	60	50	60	88.24	0	0
Strongly Agree	8	6.66	8	11.76	0	0
Total	120	100	68	100	52	100

CONCLUSION AND IMPLICATIONS

The objective of this study is to determine the factors that influenced the adoption of internet banking in an emerging economy: Malaysian consumer's perspective. Besides that, the impact of usefulness of internet banking, ease of use of internet banking and risks of using Internet Banking has also been assessed. From the literatures review of prior studies, several determinants has been identified such as usefulness of internet banking, ease of use of internet banking and risks of internet banking.

In this research, some of the factors that influenced the adoption of internet banking in an emerging economy: Malaysian consumer's perspective have been studied.

This study results show that ease of use of internet banking, usefulness of internet banking and risks of internet banking are the most important factors determining the internet banking adoption. Moreover, the small sample size is one of the setbacks on this study. Internet banking services adoption is the main factors for this study to be conducted to explore the feasibility of the service. In this respect, wider scale of internet banking customers and both local and overseas consumers' cultures is vital for the auxiliary generalization of these findings.

The regression analysis results conducted on the factors indicate that usefulness of internet banking, ease of use of internet banking and risks of internet banking were found to be the most influential factors. The results show that risks of internet banking are negatively related to the adoption of Internet Banking use which supports the hypothesis. Also it shows that usefulness and ease of use have activist relation with Internet Banking use supporting the hypotheses. Consumer use internet banking for the benefits of ease of use while compare to the brick and mortal channels. Customer's intention to adopt internet banking will be great if internet banking services are perceived as useful. When internet banking is easy to use, most of the bank customers will start to adopt it as they would like to anchor their internet banking to the beneficial outcomes and ease of use of the internet banking system. Some of the banks customers are reluctant to adopt internet banking entail that the risk associated with it even though internet banking provides real time flexibility in performing financial transactions which is fast and easy. Security and privacy are the two main elements in the risks of internet banking that has caused some of the consumers not prepared to take the risk of internet banking adoption.

Banking industry should highlights the benefits of using internet banking, enhance internet banking to make it ease of use, and improvise the internet banking security to improve consumer's trust on internet banking adoption. Besides that, awareness and education must be made available to consumers about the details benefits of using internet banking together with the promotional and advertising activities run by the banking industry. Banking industry also plays a vital role in enhancing their internet banking security parameters such as encryption, firewall, security intrusion detection and multi-factor authentication must be embedded. Hence, bank should invest to find out more risk-reducing strategies that may boost the high confidence level of consumers to use internet banking. Besides, this study reveals that banking industry should focus more on intrusion mitigation, fraud attempts, identity theft, and account hi-jacking. Also, this study suggests that banking industry should develop trust-based relationship between the bankers and consumers to entice consumers to perform internet banking with confidence and peace of mind.

There are few limitations in this study that should be taken into considerations in future research. The study focused solely on the local and multinational banking industries in Malaysia. With the mix of local and local multinational against overseas banking industries, we could obtain different results from the research since local and local multinational against overseas banking industries provide different Internet Banking capabilities and securities.

Finally, there are some limitations with the data collection process. We have distributed the questionnaire to 300 respondents and only 130 respondents (43.33%) returned. Out of 130 questionnaires received, 10 are not completed thus the overall response rate for the survey is only 40%. Due to limited time frame, we have to proceed with the data analysis based on the 120 questionnaire returned instead of 300 respondents that we targeted previously.

REFERENCES

1. 1. Nui Polatoglu V, Ekin S (2001) An empirical investigation of the Turkish consumers' acceptance of Internet banking services. International journal of bank marketing 19: 156-165.
2. 2. Karin (2005) Are there still growth opportunities in the Internet Banking market?
3. 3. Elham KM (2013) An Assessment of Users' Acceptance of Internet Banking: An Empirical Case of Egypt. American Academic & Scholarly Research Journal 5: 132-154.

4. 4. Suganthi B (2001) Internet banking patronage: an empirical investigation of Malaysia pp: 20-32.
5. 5. Agarwal R, Prasad J (1998) A conceptual and operational definition of personal innovativeness in the domain of information technology. Information systems research 9: 204-224.
6. 6. Davis FD (1989) Perceived usefulness, perceived ease of use, and user acceptance of information technology. MIS quarterly 13: 319-340.
7. 7. Chen YH, Barnes S (2007) Initial trust and online buyer behaviour. Industrial management & data systems 107: 21-36.
8. 8. Qureshi T, Zafar M, Khan M (2008) Customer Acceptance of Online Banking in Developing Economies. Journal of Internet Banking and Commerce 13: 1-8.
9. 9. Celik H (2008) What determines Turkish customers' acceptance of internet banking. International Journal of Bank Marketing 26: 353-370.
10. 10. Aldas-Manzano J, Lassala-Navarre C, Ruiz-Mafe C, Sanz-Blas S (2009) Key drivers of internet banking services use. Online Information Review 33: 672-695.
11. 11. Padachi K, Rojid S, Seetanah B (2007) Analyzing the factors that influence the adoption of internet banking in Mauritius. Proceedings of the 2007 Computer Science and IT Education Conference pp: 559-574.
12. 12. Liao Z, Cheung M (2002) Internet-based E-Banking and Consumer Attitudes: An Empirical Study. Information & Management 39: 282-295.
13. 13. Vincent SL, Honglei L (2005) Technology acceptance model for internet banking: an invariance analysis. Information & Management 42: 373-386.
14. 14. Kent E, Katri K, Daniel N (2005) Customer acceptance of internet banking in Estonia. International Journal of Bank Marketing 23: 200-216.
15. 15. Amin H (2009) An analysis of online banking usage intentions: an extension of the technology acceptance model. International Journal of Business and Society 10: 27.
16. 16. Hakkak M, Vahdati H, Biranvand V (2013) An extended technology acceptance model for detecting influencing factors: An empirical investigation. Management Science Letters 3: 2795-2804.
17. 17. Leng GS, Lada S, Muhammad MZ, Ibrahim AA, Amboala T (2011) An exploration of social networking sites (SNS) adoption in Malaysia using technology acceptance model (TAM), theory of planned behavior (TPB) and intrinsic motivation. Journal of Internet Banking and Commerce.
18. 18. Malhotra Y, Galletta DF (1999) Extending the technology acceptance model to account for social influence: Theoretical bases and empirical validation. Proceedings of the 32nd annual Hawaii international conference pp: 14.
19. 19. Malhotra P, Singh B (2009) The Impact of Internet Banking on Bank Performance and Risk: The Indian Experience. Eurasian Journal of Business and Economics 2: 43-62.

16

CHAPTER

ANALYZING E-BANKING IN IRAN AND OTHER COUNTRIES

E. Abbasi, H. Ranjbar, S. Ranjbar, M. Shabanpour, S. Alipour

INTRODUCTION

E-Banking is applying electronic devices such as internet, wireless connection networks, ATM, phone and cell phone in banking services. These services are instruments for providing currency and economic system in a country. Nowadays, E-Banking is commonly defined as phone and cell phone bank, internet bank and also ATM. For instance, cell phone banking can be regarded as providing banking services using cell phone. E- Banking provides the clients with the rights and facility of doing banking affairs by sing internet and under the authority of a specific bank. Firstly, E-Banking aimed just to attract clients to a certain bank. B the help of internet in banking industry, banks were starting to broaden their range of applying it, and nowadays, check exchange, accounting, currency exchange, clients' reports, and account criteria are performed immediately using such system. It is not only helpful to both clients and banks, but also decreases costs of banking such as wasting time and long lines. And from the perspective of banks, with the help of E- Banking, the costs of banking services decrease, because there is no need to extra paper, extra employee and investments with other section and other banks. In fact, nowadays, banking services do not act Justin a traditional form but they are act as international ones. Nowadays, banks are facing a very stringent competition with each other in some areas such as investment and they play the roles like providing currency and economic well-fare. In a nut, banks play a very prominent role in economic domains, and without them the economic part of the society will be affected. E- Banking is one aftermath of information and communication revolution. The E- Banking changes paradigm and pattern of banking and provides faster banking services, and also minimizes wasting issues in the best way. E- Banking

Citation: Abbasi, Hojat Ranjbar, Saeed Ranjbar, Marzie Shabanpour, Sara Alipour .Analyzing E-banking in Iran and other Countries Scientific. Journal of Pure and Applied Sciences.2014;3(5)318-329 DOI 10.14196/sjpas.v3i5.140.

is composed of several levels which each one must be defined. In all levels, we can see the presence of computer systems and digital process of information. The higher levels of E- Banking, less manual works, more systematized computers, more networks available, less time restriction, and finally more secure banking system. Services are performed by internet network that takes privilege of a high security. On the other hand, E- Banking is the application of communication in exchanging currency in banking system. In addition, E- Banking could be regarded as a service producer with low costs by the help of electronic channels. These productions and services include account bill, loan, deposit management, Epayment, E-money. E- Banking is utilizing internet or intranet. Definitions such as digital money, E- check, Emoney, E- signature are modern phenomena that their origin refers to E- Banking. Accounting, exchanging, receiving bill, and paying bill are given to the clients a list with time order. E- Banking has a lot of advantages such as increasing clients and reducing bank costs. Furthermore, by using E- Banking it is easy to the bank to do faster and more secure services. They can also attract more shareholders (Meihami, et al, 2013).

METHODOLOGY

For the purpose of this study the descriptive analytical method will be used. Electronic banking advantages: The main advantage of Electronic banking is new a distribution channels, giving improved services to customers and use of electronic commerce strategies. Electronic banking has the view of long term, middle term and short term which is a benefit. For example, short term planning consists, integrated competition & customer attraction (shorter than one year). In middle term view (18 month): channel integration (consolidation), data management, different customers, customer guide and cost decrease. For long term view: decreasing the costs of transaction processing, services to customers, income generation. Electronic banking services in Iran: Automated teller machine (ATM): which is capable of doing a variety of banking activities and eliminating human interferes. Based on statistics related to installing ATM devices ranging from 1998 to 2004 all around the world, they have an improvement rate of 45%. Therefore, the big investment incurred in ATM installing for currency distribution around the globe. The installation rate of ATM devices in developed countries indicates that there must be one ATM device for each 742 persons. Now considering our population, Iran needs to have 95007 ATM to be along with developed countries. However, the number of ATM in Iran is 11065, i.e. 88.3% shortage in this case. To summarize, the ATMs are electronic processers or points installed by banks in specific places which are available round the clock. Using ATMs, clients are capable of doing some functions such as accounts cashing, accounts bill, cashing the check and currency. In addition to the above options, another function of ATMs is paying the bills. An ATM is able to act as a bank branch. Many banking services could be performed by them without human interfere. In addition, the ATM works round the clock and it significantly decrease the bank's costs. Point of sale (POS): A POS is a device that installed in sale centers to remove the need to transfer the physical money and to deduct money from buyer account and to add it to seller account. This activity is done by a POS connected to central computer in the bank. It is provided by the bank for the seller and has modem and printer. Sale center and department stores are where POS is used. POS functions: -Exchanging currency from buyer account to seller account, that is very secure -printing the account on paper -Bill paying availability Phone Banking: The conduction of a little business between bank and clients through phone is called phone banking. Phone banking aspects: -Giving account flow and remaining -Bill payment availability -Currency transferring to other account Internet banking system: (SIBA) at this moment of time, household banking is done through internet and with the help of debit card. The following is a list of economic services: E- check, bill payment, and other services conducted through this way. The combination of home computers and intelligence cards has the availability of sending information to them. The banks may have website to let their clients check their account remaining, account flow, loan applying, and ordering their exchanging through internet. -The availability of transferring currency to private account or other accounts that are member of SHETAB -The availability of seeing bills in accordance with account -The availability bill ordering in chronological order -The awareness of all remaining of accounts -Bill payment availability -The ability to announce the check founds to the bank through the system -The availability of seeing last 30 transactions Cell phone banking: The clients are able to use bank services through installing bank software on their Cell phone. Current Cell phone banking availability: -Enabling to know about account remaining, flow, exchanging of founds among accounts with one ID member, bill payment, buying prepaid Cell phone charge, and seeing pre-paid Cell phone charge remaining information. Card service: Card service is another activity of the banks to makes the clients more comfortable. It is the use of magnetic cards instead of money. These cards are issued through a very secure procedure to let clients use them. The owner of this card is able to use it round the clock and in off days in POS, and with Pin Pad to exchange his/her founds and currency. As the number of Iranian Internet users exceeds 33 million, businesses in Iran are making the transition from traditional methods to Internet methods. This is also true about banks, which are considered as one of the links in the chain of business, that is, order, payment and delivery. In this regard, Iranian users' lack of preference for adopting this electronic method has created a gap which is seen as a major obstacle to the adoption of Internet banking. Currently, banks are faced with a dynamic environment, and all banks, regardless of their size, have set their goals to attract and retain customers to be able to adjust to rapid changes in competitive situations and market conditions (Akbari Moghadam, 2012).

ATMs: In the late 1980s, Iranian banks attempted to automate banking processes and to computerize their banking tasks. First, there was only 7 – 10 ATMs in Tehran and Sepah bank was the first bank which issued electronic cards used for very limited banking tasks in ATMs. Then, Melli bank issued electronic cards with more functionality and soon all banks were issuing cards and installing ATMs in their branches. Unfortunately, the banks were incapable of performing transactions with another one; they were isolated and none of them were integrated with another one. They had created an e-banking system based on a network not connected to other bank networks. Saderat bank had the Sepehr system, Keshavarzi bank created the Mehr system. Melli bank introduced the Siba system and Melat bank featured the Jam network. Banks were encouraging users to use their system and advertising their e-banking systems, where none of them had a significant advantage over the other.

In 2002, a network was introduced to connect Melli bank with Shahrvand superstore POSs; then the idea was generalized and a superhighway of banking transactions was designed. It was called Shetab and was tested with integration of 2 popular specialized banks of Toseésaderat and Keshavarzi and one commercial bank Saderat. In 2003, by joining the network, Saman bank was the first private bank integrated with governmental banks and in 2004 Melli bank as the Iran's biggest bank with the highest number of branches joined the network. Nowadays, a variety of governmental and private banks have joined the network and She tab has been the infrastructure network for electronic banking. Based on the Iran ministry of ICT 14,000 branches out of 15,600 are now connected to national banking network in Iran. In 2007, 8,440 ATMs and 244,000 POS with a total number of 27 million electronic cards were present in the whole country and it is predicted to install 30,000 ATMs and 900,000 POSs and to provide 75 million electronic cards for the customers until 2010 (Elli, 2011).

Internet Banking: Technological advances have created radical shifts in the world. Introducing IT has altered the way in which individuals perform their business affairs. The World Wide Web (WWW) exerts a significant impact, since it facilitates the Internet to both individuals and businesses. The number of World Wide Web users has significantly increased since its emergence in the early 1990s. Based on the numbers published by World Internet Stats, there are approximately 1,596 million users throughout the world but in year 2000 were only 360 million users. The average penetration rate and the users' growth rate are approximately 23.8 and 342.2 percent, respectively. The projected users' growth rate in the Middle East is more significant. In year 2000, there were only 3 million users in the Middle East which this rate increased by approximately 46million users in 2009; therefore, this part of the world has growth rate of 1,296.2 percent. Among the Middle East countries, Iran second to Syria has the highest growth rate. According to the numbers published by World Internet Stats, Iran in year 2000 had only 250,000 internet users where in the year 2009 with a growth rate of 9,100 percent Iran takes privilege of approximately 23 million internet users. 1993 was the first year that Internet introduced in Iran and it was applied for academic use only, since then it has been growing rapidly and now with the penetration rate of 34.9 percent Iran has more than 50% share among Middle East internet users. Such a considerable and rapid increase in the number of internet users, have provided new opportunities for a variety of businesses and has introduced new horizons for many industries (Mishra and Sahoo, 2013).

E-Banking in India: The red-tapism in public sector banking and lesser consumer base are among the reasons for the Indian banks to enter into the online banking this late. The online bank has become a feasible mode of banking in India, due to some reasons such as the rapid development in the technological infrastructure and the more equipment in legal framework. Regulatory framework in India has dramatically progressed, and Information Technology Act 2000 seeks to address a number of e-commerce regulatory issues, to analyze the need of banks to go online and to have security actions to be adopted (since online banking bears some resemblances to ecommerce and having consider cross-border jurisdictions), and with the comprehensive and proactive guidelines brought out by the RBI (Tapas et al, 2010).

E-banking in Malaysia: The Automated Teller Machine (ATM) was the first electronic innovation used by Malaysian banks in 1981. Later, telephone banking service was introduced in 1990s. Then, in 2000, the Central Bank of Malaysia granted permission to local banks to offer Internet banking services to their customers. Maybank is the first bank to offer e-banking in Malaysia through its website www.maybank2u.com. Some of the services include banking enquiry functions, bill payment, credit card payment, fund transfers, account summary and transaction history. Up to 2001, Suganthi et al., (2001) realized that the adoption of e-banking was not widespread initially, due to various factors such as internet accessibility, poor awareness, and security concerns. In 2006, the statistics did not change much. Three distinguished banks in the country, CIMB, Maybank and RHB Bank Berhad had approximately 917,000 e-banking users in 2006 which this figure is only 8 percent of the total number of Internet users in 2006. Thus, the figure is still considered low. However, according to a report by Bank Negara Malaysia and the Malaysian Communications and Multimedia Commission (2009), the average number of the ebanking users had increased higher than doubled from 2006 (3.2 mil) to the third quarter of 2009 (7.5 mil). Therefore, the e-banking adoption is gradually increasing (Jano, et al, 2011).

Electronic Banking in Jordan: Jordanian banking sector have been enhanced through e-banking services. In 2010, study reported ratio of banks total assets to GDP of 176% which was the highest compared to other service sectors. This improvement showed that the adoption of e-banking increases e-banking operational strategies to cope with customer's satisfaction at low-cost. Positive improvement of e-banking practices in Jordan is visible from the increase of credit facilities to different economic sector.

E-banking in in Pakistan: Currently in Pakistan, the listed numbers of banks under governmental documents are 41. The number of three nationalised commercial banks is 3. There are 15 private banks, almost 15 foreign banks. While other 6 comes under specialized banking category. The major portion of population still believes on cash tradition rather than online banking. Utility bills are still sent to houses and people wait in longs queues outside banks to pay those bills. Lack of customer trust keeps them away from adopting electronic service resulting to lack of e-readiness. The major reason for lack of e-readiness is lack of trust, unavailability of proper infrastructure and security, service charges and lack of education. Computer literacy is basic requirement for usage of online banking systems. Computer cost in Pakistan is too high and it's not possible for common man to purchase computer as its cost three times higher than common man salary (Oye, et al, 2008).

E-banking in Egypt: Egypt has a very fragmented banking system, with over 42 licensed banks. The government wants to see a reduction in the number of banks to around 25 by 2010. Banking in this North African nation is dominated by four institutions: National Bank of Egypt, Banque Misr, Banque du Caire and Bank of Alexandria. They represent half of the banking system's assets. Egypt is cash based society and no more than 10 percent of Egyptians have a bank account. However, Egypt's cellular market is experiencing unprecedented growth, a phenomenon that BIS Shrapnel forecasts will result in the number of mobile subscribers in Egypt reaching 21.1 million by the end of 2008. This offers a huge window of opportunity for banks, which have started offering mobile banking services. NSGB was the first bank in Egypt to offer mobile banking options, starting in May 2000. Around 4,000 NSGB customers receive SMS alerts on their account balances, as well as foreign exchange and stock prices. European based ATM provider Euronet and, more recently, local IT conglomerate Raya have entered the mobile banking market, with Euronet operating a similar service for Arab Bank and Egyptian American Bank. Raya works with Commercial International Bank. When MNS started in 1998, it focused on applications for Internet-related banking services. The company shifted its strategy in mid-1999 to cater to a market where mobile penetration far exceeds personal computer use. Egyptian mobile banking has already taken its first steps from mere notification to actual transactions. NBE customers can now pay for their MobiNil bills using their phones – the first time a bank has offered bill payment using SMS. EAB offers a similar service for Vodafone bills. The current number of people using mobile banking in Egypt is estimated at less than 200,000, but bankers believe there is considerable growth potential. The key is to push the use of the technology beyond banking transactions and into everyday retail use. Some banks have reduced their mobile banking overheads by outsourcing their IT hosting requirements. Technology for mobile banks a mobile and e-banking solution enabling convenient, fast, simple, and secure branchless banking, with support for e-payment gateways, is indispensable for banks reaching out to the unbanked. Such a solution can help reduce costs while increasing speed and efficiency through SMSdriven banking services (Banking the Unbanked: Going Mobile in Africa, 2009).

E-banking in USA: In contrast with the rest of the world, mobile banking in the US took some time to take off. One of the primary reasons was the legislative hassle involved. By tying a bank's mobile service to particular telecom service providers, banks lost control over the application's Pan-American availability and its look and feel which were essential to brand identification. Moreover, differing state laws made providing mobile banking to customers across the US a near impossible experience. Mobile banking in its initial stages also suffered from a lack of compelling features and consumer friendliness and limited device support, poor network availability and slow speeds. However, with the network neutrality legislation expected to be passed in the US Congress, the mobile banking experience is set for an overhaul. The long-awaited Broadband Investment and Consumer Choice Act, expected to be passed by the US Congress, will do away many current federal and state rules for the delivery of voice, video and data services. It aims to level the playing field between telephone, cable and satellite companies while opening the door for the delivery of emerging broadband services. It calls for removing state and local franchise requirements for all video providers, including telephone companies. Most significantly, the bill states that consumers may not be denied access to any legal content provided over the facilities used for broadband communications. Broadband services are largely freed from federal and state regulation at both the wholesale and retail levels. Communication services in the US are going to be modernized – finally. And, as legal roadblocks to mobile banking are removed, mobile banking is set to become even more popular. Today, the mobile banking channel in the US is no less important than online banking was in the late 1990s. This growth is attributed to improvements across wireless networks, handsets and applications, and marketing and technology investments being made by top banks to increase consumer awareness. With a mobile subscriber base of 255.4 million subscribers, mobile device penetration at an all-time high of 84.06%, and legal and market dynamics shifting, mobile banking is set for takeoff. It is estimated that mobile penetration in the US will touch 100% by 2013. Even a relatively low-key acceptance of mobile banking services among mobile subscribers can result in impressive numbers. Further, consumers are demanding mobile banking, spurred by the advantages it offers in terms of convenience, control, self-service and immediacy. According to a July 2008 report the demand for internet-enabled services is strong and consumers are looking to access the internet, with the added convenience of mobility. It forecasts that innovation in wireless products is accelerating, and wireless data take-up rates will increase. Mobile banking is likely to see a surge in such a scenario. Surveys have been conducted that show US consumers will respond to mobile banking if they feel banks will support a broad range of devices with good security and a simple user experience. An ever-greater number of consumers are taking to mobile banking in the US and even more are expected to join in over the next couple of years. Survey estimates that up to 30% of online banking users will adopt the mobile channel in the next five years. However, mobile banking is also likely to appeal to a segment of the banking population that accesses services via ATMs, but is not willing to use or is comfortable with online banking. Competitive pressures from banks that have entered the m-banking market, vendor solutions, and demand from corporations will be important drivers. It was estimated that 8 of the top 25 banks will have a solution out in 2008, and 14 of the top 25 would address this channel in one way or another by the end of 2009. Banks will increasingly adopt the mobile banking channel because of the varied advantages it offers in terms of customer satisfaction and retention, cost effectiveness and revenue growth. Bilizing the numbers suggest that mobile banking is set to transform the financial services industry by providing convenient solutions for access to a wide range of financial services while on the move. Once mobile banking becomes popular, it's likely to pave the way for e-wallet transactions where the mobile phone is used to make payments at physical points-of-sale (PoS) terminals. Perhaps the most exciting development will be the use of mobile wallets to allow overseas remittances. This constitutes a significant market in the US. As the market for mobile banking expands, let us look at how banks in the US can leverage it to their advantage (Mobilizing Customers: Mobile Banking in the US. 2013).

Position of E-Banking in Other Countries: In 2012, over 40% of Europeans will use online banking. The figure will probably be 47% in Germany. Growth trends have been mostly stable in Europe within the last few years. Two considerable exceptions are France where online banking adoption jumped 11 pp. in 2010 and the UK where adoption remained flat. Chart 1. Online banking provides highest channel satisfaction. Globally, 83% of banking clients feel satisfaction with online banking (Germany: 80%). This could be regarded as the highest score of all banking channels. Users of online banking are a dynamic group of financial clients who are eager to gather information, compare and evaluate financial products. Such self-directedness develops financial literacy: online banking users are more likely to consider themselves as efficient investors. Chart 2. A considerable number of Germans have downgraded their financial literacy. The number of clients who regard themselves as savvy investors has decreased over the last few years. Consequently, clients may avoid making informed choices. But there is also a responsibility for financial firms to explain the future events. Unlike the trend, an increasing number of DB clients consider themselves in the know–users of online banking. Chart 3 (Meyer, 2012). Online banking grows mostly at the expense of branch visits. Bank customers in Europe significantly increased their use of online banking. However, in France and Italy, they also visited bank branches more often. See chart 4. Security concerns are often a significant barrier to online banking. It could be said that there exists a negative correlation between security concerns and online-banking adoption. French customers are somewhat exceptional because despite they have the most concerns, they show medium adoption rates. See chart 5. Education is the driving factor in online banking adoption. Europeans equipped with higher formal education are inclined to use the internet and to do financial transactions online. More educated people are early adopters and have fewer reservations against such technology. Furthermore, they are confident to protect themselves against security threats. See chart6

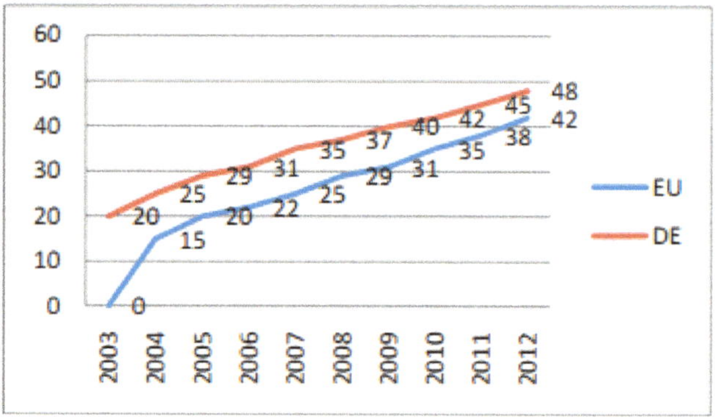

Chart 1: More than 40% of European will bank online by 2012 Online banking adoption, % of all individuals.

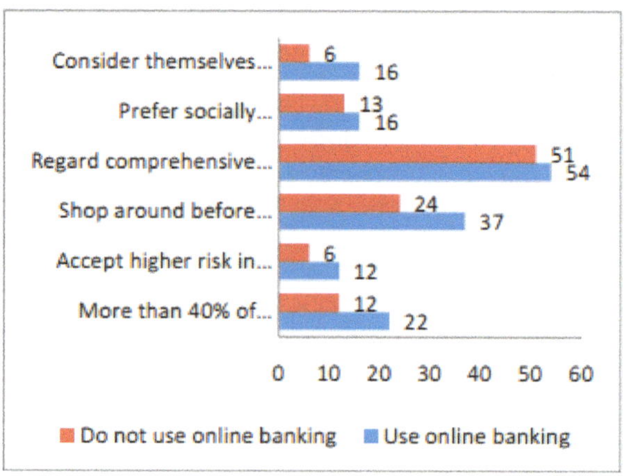

Chart 2: Online banking does crowd out personal consultation. % of German consumers, 2011.

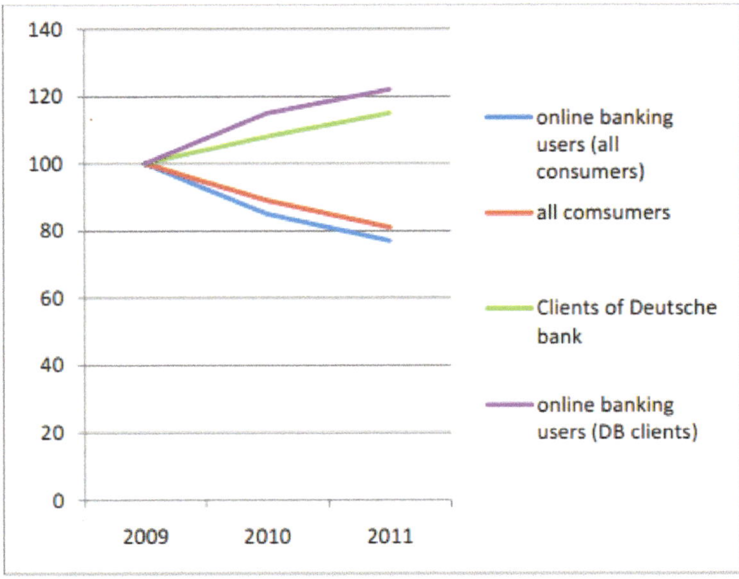

Chart 3. German downgrade their financial competence Share of German consumers considering they savvy investors, rebased 2009=100.

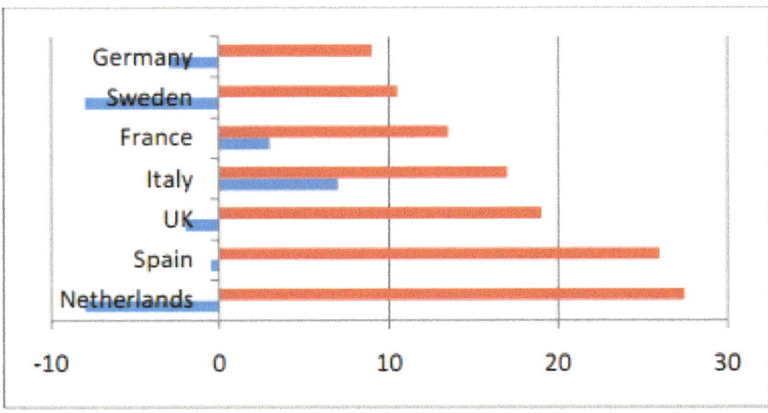

Chart 4: Online banking grows – usually, but not always at the expense of branch visits Q: Which banking channels do you use at least monthly?

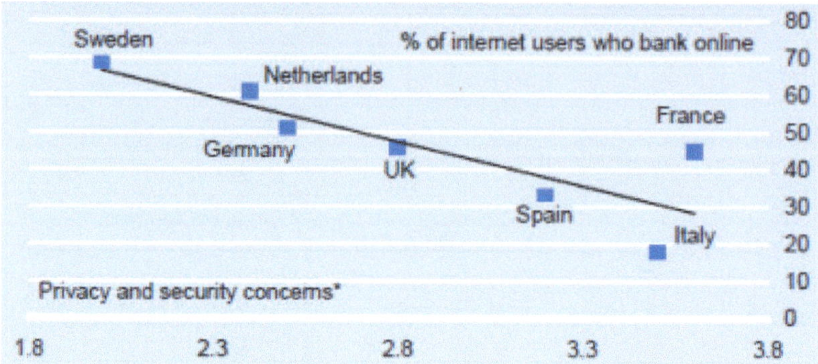

Chart 5: Security concerns correlate with low online banking adoption.

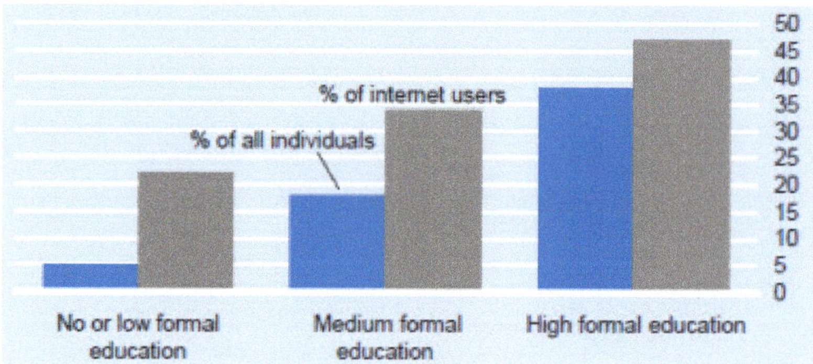

Chart 6: Education boosts online-banking adoption.

METHOD OF PAYMENT IN EUROPEAN COUNTRIES

France - In France credit cards are the dominant online payment method. To a much lesser extent cash-on delivery and alternative payment methods are also used. PayPal ranks second in the top of the most popular online payment systems in France, following Visa, according to ITespresso.fr In 2008, the volume of payments via PayPal reached EUR 1 billion on the French market alone (versus EUR 41 billion in the world). The number of PayPal account holders has reached 8 million in this country. France is the third European country in terms of the number of PayPal accounts, after the UK (21 million) and Germany (10 million). In Europe there are 52 million PayPal account holders.

Germany - German consumers have a clear preference for direct debit payment method ELV. This is followed by payment by credit cards, online bank payment methods such as giropay and so for tuberweisung, and e-wallets. PayPal is gaining popularity across Europe, especially in Germany: in March 2009, PayPal had more than 10 million accounts, as compared to 5 million in February 2007.

Italy - In Italy consumers primary use credit cards to pay online although cash-on-delivery and alternative payment methods are also frequently used.

United Kingdom - Debit and credit cards are most frequently used for online purchasing, with Maestro representing around 10% of all transactions. Other methods such as e-wallets and pre-paid cards are used to a lesser extent. Factors that contribute to success of online banking based Internet payments.

There are several variables that influence the level of success:

- Guaranteed payment. Buyers are not able to reverse a completed payment one-sided (charge back), because they authenticated the transaction personally through their online banking. For merchants and banks this eliminates fraud and therefore costly losses and back office processes.
- Price model. Some schemes have a transaction pricing and others use a percentage pricing model. With a rising e-commerce average transaction value, a fixed fee per transaction is more advantageous for merchants. When a percentage based pricing model is used there is little price differentiation with credit cards. The differences in success between the different countries of this payment method category can largely be attributed to the different pricing models. Where a percentage based pricing model is used merchants have little incentive to widely promote this alternative payment method.
- Acceptance by the consumer community. People like to stick to their habits, also in the process of doing a payment. When a payment strongly resembles an online banking transaction, the change of habit is minimal.
- Level of commitment and push from the merchant communities. In countries with successfully introduced payment methods the merchant community plays an important role in the adoption of the payment method.
- Amount of cooperation between the participating banks. In some markets the scheme is rolled out by the inter-bank organization, in others the banks themselves take the lead. This depends on the specific market structure. In Germany almost 2000 banks are active on the retail market, whereas in the Netherlands only 4 banks represent more than 97% of the account holders. Some of the schemes are offered by one bank only, such as Nordau's Solo (Nordic) and ING's Home 'Pay (Belgium). For these payment methods the market development will be slow, and the reach will always stay limited. -Level of adoption of online banking in a particular country. The adoption rate of online banking is different per country but in general it is growing in each market.

Online banking reach in Europe in 2009

Despite the big differences between countries, we strongly believe that online banking based Internet payments are a compelling proposition to Internet merchants, if the surrounding conditions (pricing, marketing, market attitude etc.) are optimised. The main value drivers for merchants are elimination of fraud and reduction of cost. Cost reduction is a direct consequence of the fraud reduction and instant payment confirmation, but also a low processing cost per transaction contributes to this. The main value driver for buyers is the ease of use and increased trust when doing a transaction. More standardization is needed on a European level. At present, online banking based e-payments (OBePs) are mostly a local affair, with the mono- and multi-bank solutions restricted to their domestic market. Through the ICPNO attempts are made to make these local services interoperable while through the European Payments Council efforts have been made to create a European standard for these payment methods. The intermediary services, on the other hand, are not limited to their domestic market and can relatively easily add new banks in new markets. These intermediary services can therefore quickly and easily offer cross borders payments.

The merchant community can play a pivotal role in expressing their needs for Internet payment methods which better match their requirements in terms of usability, security, price and scope. This, coupled with competition by intermediary services, will raise the awareness with banks that the e-commerce sector is a profitable business sector. And that this sector is very open for innovation of payment instruments and other solutions that will increase the overall operational efficiencies (Boer, et al, 2010).

China and the world: Chinese online payment industry has characteristics which are different compared to other countries, as its most preferred online payment instrument is remittance (debit transfer), collection (credit transfer) and collection with acceptance China is a vast market and its development represents a real challenge to e-commerce across the globe. In 2009, the Chinese online payment market has not been affected by the financial crisis, registering rapid growth in terms of both number of users and market scale. The number of users has climbed from 52 million in 2008 to over 90 million in 2009, while the online payment market hit EUR 42.28 billion (CNY 430 billion), up from EUR 20.65 billion (CNY 210 billion) in the previous year. 27. Within China, the largest online payments method is Alipay. Alipay is part of the Alibaba Group, founded in 1999, which also own the Alibaba e-commerce platform. Alipay is an escrow service that lets consumers pay online by credit card or online bank. Alipay keeps the payment until the goods are delivered and then transfers the funds to the merchant. As competition in the online payments industry continues to intensify, Alipay is set to expand its footprint and challenge PayPal by revealing plans to top eBay`s division by transaction value in two years. Alipay has already reached the 270 million user milestone by late 2009, as compared to 200 million users reported in July 2009. Alibaba has already started expanding into the rest of China, but in 2009 also entered the United States and the European markets. It is unlikely that in the short term this entry will impact online payments, but as their base in China continues to grow their foothold in the US and Europe may leave a sizable footprint (Boer, et al, 2010).

Country	% online population using online banking
Netherlands	52.9
France	49.9
Sweden	48.4
UK	46.1
Belgium	39.0
Germany	38.6
Denmark	36.7
Spain	35.2
Norway	34.4
Flanland	33.1
Ireland	28.4
Turkey	28.0
Italy	26.9
Austria	23.4
Portugal	17.2
Switzerland	15.9
Russia	6.0

Banking on Internet and mobile is gaining popularity: However, security threats continue to loom The Pew Internet & American Life Project Tracking survey of December 2010 said that nearly 60% of all Americans who used the Internet did some banking over it. In the United Kingdom, the number of bank accounts registered for Internet banking grew sharply from 28 million in 2006 to 45 million in 2010. With over 100 million, a Chinese bank has the largest number of Internet banking users in the world. Cut to mobile banking. A research firm estimated that about 110 million people worldwide used mobile banking and related services in 2010. It also indicated that the geographies of Asia Pacific, Middle East and Africa would be the most important markets for financial services using the mobile device. Another one forecasts a stupendous 660% growth in mobile banking and payment services between 2009 and 2014. A number of factors, including lower cost of connectivity, greater Internet and mobile Internet penetration, affordability of devices and the arrival of the smartphone have gone into popularizing online (Internet and mobile) banking around the world (Mobilizing Customers: Mobile Banking in the US.,2013).

Mobile Banking in the World wide: Mobile Banking has really caught up in India – according to recently conducted survey by ACI Worldwide, 76% of Indian mobile respondents used their mobiles for banking in last 6 months. This percentage is highest across the world. Comparatively, only 38% respondents from US, and 31% from UK used mobile banking in last 6 months. China came in after India with 70% users using mobile banking followed by South Africa (61%). The global average for Mobile Banking adoption rate stands at 35% Importance of Mobile Payments & Money Movement -According to the survey, the countries with highest levels of mobile payment adoption also display highest importance on mobile payments and money movement. Roughly two-thirds of Indian consumers consider making payments and moving money using their mobile phone in the next three years to be - very important to them -in contrast only one in 10 French and Canadian consumers think mobile payment is -Very Important. Replacing Traditional Payment Cards with Mobile Payments-Over 8 out of 10 Indians responded that they would prefer using a mobile phone to make a payment instead of traditional payment cards. The lack of importance of mobile payments and money movement in a number of countries belies the interest that many consumers across the globe have in using their mobile phone to replace carrying payment cards. In Brazil, for example, although 39% of consumers consider mobile payment and money movement to be -very important, 75% would use their mobile phone to replace cards. Even in France, where just 9% of French consumers place a high importance on mobile payments and money movement, 44% express interest in replacing their payment cards. One surprising fact in all the above findings is that western countries like US, UK, France, Germany etc. are low on mobile banking and payments. One of the reason I see is that they transact more from Desktop PC‘s. Whereas in countries like India & China, majority of consumers only have mobiles on which they can carry out mobile banking / payments (as they don‘t own personal computers) (Mishra , and Sahoo, 2013).

Status quo of internet and online banking users: Over the past decade the share of the German population using the internet has swollen to a total of roughly 56 million (as of 2011). In particular, among the younger age cohorts between 14 and 39 over 90% of the population is more or less routinely familiar with the internet. By contrast, there is still considerable latent growth potential in the 50+ cohort. Many people in this cohort have yet to come into contact with the internet in either their private lives or on the job. However, changes are shaping up on the horizon: the sharpest increase can be observed in the 60-69 cohort. There, the share rose by 6.4 percentage points within two years, to 60.4% (2012). The proportion of online banking users in relation to total internet users has also grown over the past few years. In 2011, one internet user in two utilised online banking offers from financial service providers. The 65+ age cohort posted the fastest growth between 2006 and 2011. On average, the share of the pensioner generation increased by over 15% per year. Given the relatively low starting level this growth rate is set to continue for some time. Some 69% of 25 to 44-year-olds were familiar with online banking services last year, while the figure among 45 to 64-year-olds was only 51%. There were virtually no changes in the cohort of those aged 10-15. This young generation had a share of less than 3% on an annual average.

Challenges of Electronic banking systems

Here we note some challenges of Electronic banking systems:

Challenges before system

1. Lack of outline plans & sufficient study to perform new technology.
2. Lack of choose that how perform technology with the highest efficiency.
3. Lack of culture and knowledge of banks about Electronic banking.
4. Lack of engagement of banks management in the system.
5. Lack of management to use experts in IT section.

6. Traditional attitude toward data reengineering.
7. Lack of economic justification and risk to use Electronic banking systems.

Challenges with performing system

1. Weakness of available facilities
2. Lack of money protection
3. Lack of special enterprises or their support, ca, gateway institutes such as ps ps & VISA
4. Lack of content & customers interest

Challenges after system

1. Lack of legal rights and electronic justification
2. People don't like to reveal their financial policies
3. Lack of motivation and culture training
4. Lack of trust in users
5. Lack of electronically security e.g.: E-sing & PKI

Conclusions and Recommendations

Information technology is considered as the key driver for the changes taking place around the world. Due to a pervasive and steadily growth of information and communication technology, the world banking industry is entering into new phenomena of unprecedented form of competition supported by modern information and communication infrastructure. Low level of infrastructural development, lack of suitable legal and regulatory framework, inadequate banking system, high rates of illiteracy, resistance to changes in technology among customers and staff, frequent power interruption and security issues are the main challenges for developing ebanking in Iran. In order to promote and develop viable e-banking in Iran the following recommendations are forwarded:

- Banks should invest in automating their banking system and it is imperative to devise strategies that involve alliances and collaborations between and amongst private and public banks. Such alliances and collaborations would enhance e-banking initiatives in Iran.
- Current laws don't accommodate e-contracts and e-signatures and hence a comprehensive regulatory and legal framework for e-banking and e-commerce should be developed.
- Public awareness on the use of ICT, e-commerce and e-Payment need to be raised. -Provide incentives for financial institutions to invest rigorously on ICT and use of e-commerce and ePayment.
- Ongoing efforts by ETC to expand ICT infrastructure should be encouraged.

- The government should consider the liberalization of the telecom industry to enhance efficiency and competition within the sector.
- The government should consider the liberalization of the financial sector for foreign bank entry to enhance the introduction of modern technology in the banking sector.
- Frequent connectivity failure in telephone line and electricity should be drastically improved.

REFERENCES

1. Akbari Moghadam, B., 2012. Does Internet Advertising Affect the Internet Banking Effectiveness? A Three Dimensional Model for Iran. J. Int. Bank. Commer., 17 (3), pp1-16.
2. Banking the Unbanked: Going Mobile in Africa., 2009. pp1-8. Avaliableat: http://www.infosys.com.
3. Boer, R., Hensen, C., Screpnic, A., 2010. Online payments Increasingly a global game, pp1-117. Avaliableat: http: //info@innopay.com.
4. Elli, S., 2011. Investigating Factors Customer's Intension For Choosing Electronic Banking SERVICEs (Proposing the hybrid model _UTILISM', an ANP approach), Joint MSc program in Electronic Commerce, Luleå University of Technology Department of Business Administration and Social Sciences Division of Industrial marketing and ecommerce,pp1-130.
5. Jano, Z., Janor, H., Shamsuri, E.R., Saad, M.D., 2011. E-banking adoption strategies among the academicians: the case of Malaysia.pp1-10.
6. Meihami, B., Varmaghani, Z., Meihami, H., 2013. The Effect of Using Electronic Banking on Profitability of Bank. Interdiscipl. J. Contemp. Res. Bus., 4 (12), pp1299-1318.
7. Meyer, T., 2012. Update on online and mobile banking 47% of Germans will use online banking in 2012. E-Banking Snapshot 39. Deutsche Bank Res., pp1-5.
8. Mishra, S.K., Sahoo, D.P., 2013. Mobile Banking Adoption and Benefits Towards Customers Service. Spec. Issue Int. J. Adv. Comput. Theory Eng., (IJACTE), 2 (1), pp78-83.
9. Mobilizing Customers: Mobile Banking in the US., 2013. pp1-6. Available: http://www.infosys.com.
10. Oye, N.D., Shakil, M.A., Iahad, N.A., 2008. E-Banking: A Case Study of Askari Commercial Bank Pakistan. Int. J. Eng. Res. Appl., (IJERA), pp1152-1167.
11. Tapas, K., Gargi, B., Indrajit, R., 2010. E-Banking IN India: A Comparative STUDY.pp1-22. Electronic copy available at: http://ssrn.com.

INDEX

I

M

O

P

Q

R

S

T

U

W